RAFAEL BARRETT (1876–1910) was a Spanish essayist, journalist, and social commentator whose writing, including his powerful work on Paraguay, was praised by the likes of Jorge Luis Borges and Eduardo Galeano. After a period of intense persecution and exile, he died at the age of thirty-four.

WILLIAM COSTA is a British freelance journalist and translator in Asunción, Paraguay. He has written for the Paraguayan and international press on issues relating to the land struggles of Indigenous and campesino communities, the environment, and yerba mate.

Paraguayan Sorrow

WRITINGS OF RAFAEL BARRETT,
A RADICAL VOICE
IN A DISPOSSESSED LAND

translated with an introduction by
WILLIAM COSTA

MONTHLY REVIEW PRESS
New York

Copyright © 2024 by Monthly Review Press
Translation © 2024 by William Costa
All Rights Reserved

Cataloging-in-Publication data available from the publisher.

ISBN Paper 978-1-68590-078-6
ISBN Cloth 978-1-68590-079-3

Typeset in Bulmer Monotype
Cover image by Alberto Barrett Viedma, used with permission.

Monthly Review Press, New York
monthlyreview.org

5 4 3 2 1

Contents

Foreword by Mirna Robles | 7
Introduction by William Costa | 9

PARAGUAYAN SORROW | 47
The Market | 49
Women That Pass By | 50
Corner of the Jungle | 50
On the Ranch | 51
Passing Through | 54
Guarani | 63
The Poetry of Stones | 65
Gathering Herbs | 68
Beast-Oracles | 71
Dreams | 75
Familiar Devilry | 77
Burials | 79
The Pombero | 81
Magdalena | 83
A Ride on the Streetcar | 85
Doctors | 86
Revolver | 87
An Intellectual | 89
Juries | 91
The Veteran | 93
Panta | 95
The Madhouse | 97
What I Have Seen | 99
Hatred of Trees | 101
Primary Education | 103
The Teacher and the Priest | 105
Sad Children | 108

Bitter Truths | 110
Wounded Homes | 112
The Deal | 115
The Crisis | 117
The Loan | 120
Stamped Gold | 122
Workers | 124
Eternal Agony | 127
Land | 128
Strikes | 134
The Sexual Problem | 140
On Politics | 145
The Political Virus | 147
The Authorities | 150
Terrible Meanness | 152
Education and Politics | 154
Torment | 155
Trophies | 157
Torture | 159
The State and the Shadow | 162
Failure of Violence | 165
After the Bloodbath | 166
The Revolution | 167
Under the Reign of Terror | 170
THE TRUTH OF THE YERBA MATE FORESTS | 173
Slavery and the State | 173
The Cattle Drive | 177
The Yoke in the Jungle | 181
Degeneration | 184
Torture and Murder | 188
The Spoils | 191

Notes | 195

Foreword

By Mirna Robles

I was around seventeen or eighteen when one of Rafael Barrett's books first found its way into my hands. His name was familiar to me. I had often heard him spoken about in the Paraguayan leftist circles that I was beginning to become part of, even if his texts were not used in the educational activities they ran. I remember that it was not easy to get hold of his books: my brother had been lent one by a fellow member of the party he had joined, and that is how the book came to me. I treasured that copy for some time.

Barrett's writing appeared as a combination of superb aesthetic style and socially engaged criticism that I admire to this day. I was amazed by the breadth of his knowledge, the sharpness of his readings of social and human issues, and the firmness of his decision to put his work at the service of those who had been dispossessed and left without a voice.

At the start of the twentieth century, in a Paraguay struggling to recover in material and ethical terms from the bloodiest war in Latin American history, Barrett's words and message came as a ray of light. He laid foundations for a critical and committed journalism that continue to be felt in our country.

Barrett's work also stands as a point of reference for our modern literature through its wealth of images, its exuberant descriptions of the landscapes of the forest and rural life. It was satisfying to read—I do not remember when—that Augusto Roa Bastos himself, Paraguay's most celebrated writer, saw Barrett as a forerunner of the nation's prose.

For several years after that first encounter with Barrett, his books were guiding texts for me. I often went back to them to refresh my understanding and spirit, and his work became the great embodiment of two activities that increasingly define me as time goes by: writing and social activism.

I have always been struck by the deep imprints left by some foreigners on aspects of Paraguay's modern history. To name a couple: the Swiss botanist Moisés Bertoni and the Slovenian anthropologist Branislava Sušnik. Rafael Barrett, a Spaniard, was another. In turn, Paraguay also left a profound mark on him. Despite the hardships he faced, including exile, he wanted to live here, to love here, to believe in a hopeful future for his son and for all the country's children.

I have had the good fortune of accompanying, from a distance but with great excitement, William Costa's work on this English translation of *Paraguayan Sorrow*. As well as putting Barrett's texts within the reach of a wider readership, the book's introduction offers a thorough biography of the Spaniard, complete with some new and overlooked details. It is a valuable contribution to the task of spreading Barrett's work, which still has so much to offer to critical thinking and social struggles.

—Mirna Robles
Writer, Social Activist, and Coordinator,
Casa Karaku Cultural Space,
Asunción, November 2023

Introduction

The sound of gunfire echoed through central Asunción, Paraguay's capital, as a lone mule-drawn cart cautiously made its way through the streets. The driver of the small vehicle, normally used to deliver beverages, was a wide-eyed man, visibly fatigued and on edge: the white flag flown from the cart had not prevented it from becoming a target for the guns. It was July 3, 1908, a second day of fighting as the perpetual internal disputes of the political elite plunged Paraguay into the chaos of a military coup.

The driver's voice, often interrupted by a deep cough that shook his whole body, was marked by the tones of distant Spain. While he may have been from afar, the actions of Rafael Barrett had shown him to be deeply entwined in the reality of this nation in the heart of South America. Alongside his friend José Guillermo Bertotto, a young Argentine socialist, he had spent the previous days searching the urban battlefield for the injured who had been left abandoned in the total absence of emergency services.[1]

"Driven by the desire for good, [Barrett] gave himself up to danger, passing underneath the cannons, amid the bullets, on the street corners, everywhere, picking up injured people, who he himself carried in his weak arms," Bertotto recalled of his friend, whose health was fading under the strain of tuberculosis.[2]

Exposure to danger was not new for Barrett, but his struggles had typically been carried out with pen and paper over recent times. The prolific writer had made powerful enemies on his way to becoming one of the fiercest denouncers of the array of injustices suffered by Paraguayans: hunger, official violence, poverty, exploitation, and landlessness. It was a population overwhelmed by the enduring trauma of the hellish War of the Triple Alliance (1864–1870), which had inaugurated an era of national elites at the service of neocolonial foreign interests. "History's most merciless war,"[3] as Barrett described it, had utterly devastated the landlocked nation and shattered its promising nineteenth-century development.

At a time when few intellectuals in Paraguay focused on social issues, Barrett's diverse articles, essays, and short stories—published day by day in the Asunción press—stood out for their compassion, deeply critical stance, and literary quality. Over the weeks preceding the 1908 uprising, he had published *The Truth of the Yerba Mate Forests*, a series of powerful articles that dealt a fearless blow against the international companies and a complicit state that enslaved Paraguayan workers in the depths of the country's forests to extract the prized leaf of the yerba mate tree.

However, when he arrived in Paraguay in 1904, amid the drama of another "revolution," there were few signs that Barrett would soon become a key ally of the labor movement and develop a view of society and the state rooted in anarchism. After stepping off the boat as an individualistic republican liberal, he was quickly and profoundly transformed by his collision with the painful reality that surrounded him in this new home. He wrote almost all his ideologically mature work in a flurry of activity over four short years while facing illness, poverty, persecution, and exile.[4] Beyond his writing on political and social issues, he also covered an enormous array of topics from a variety of disciplines, such as philosophy, music, art, and mathematics.

As he moved through the danger of Asunción's streets in July 1908, he must have already sensed that his days were numbered. Just two and a half years later, at the age of thirty-four, the tuberculosis festering in his lungs would take his life. Published posthumously, *Paraguayan Sorrow* would bring together a compelling selection of texts on Paraguay from his final years, providing one of the most valuable examples of social, cultural, political, and literary writing on the country in the early twentieth century. At the same time, the book exhibits the unfurling of his own nuanced vision for political change based on an ethics of altruism, and an anarchistic rejection of power structures and private property.

The twentieth century would see Barrett's figure embraced by left-wing movements in Paraguay and across Latin America, and he became recognized as a precursor of anti-imperialist writing in the region. He would also be praised by some of the continent's towering literary names, including Argentina's Jorge Luis Borges and Uruguay's José Enrique Rodó. Augusto Roa Bastos, Paraguay's most celebrated twentieth-century writer, would go so far as call him the "discoverer of Paraguay's social reality" and would be strongly influenced by the Spaniard in his own work.[5] Outside activist and literary circles, however, Barrett's striking work has often failed to receive the attention it merits, being omitted altogether or relegated to footnotes.

Today, as neocolonialism continues to contribute to inequality, dispossession, and environmental destruction in Paraguay and across Latin America, Barrett's writing feels more relevant than ever. His message continues to inspire many involved in the struggles against Paraguay's rigid system of elite domination, which has been strengthened by yet another victory for the neoliberal, oppressive right in the 2023 presidential elections. It is not surprising that renewed appreciation and interest in Barrett is sweeping across Paraguay, South America's Southern Cone, and further afield, as he continually reveals himself as a writer ahead of his time.

This edition aims to contribute to the spread of his work by bringing the contents of the book *Paraguayan Sorrow*, which includes the articles of *The Truth of the Yerba Mate Forests*, to readers for the first time in English.

Madrid

For years after his death, information about Rafael Barrett's origins was shrouded in mystery. "No one knew his story,"[6] wrote Bertotto, as far-ranging guesses about Barrett's place of birth accumulated.[7] It is as if Barrett himself had purposely turned his back on his origins, barely alluding to his past in his writing and surviving correspondence. Nevertheless, with the passing of the decades, certain details have slowly emerged.

Rafael Ángel Jorge Julián Barrett y Álvarez de Toledo was born on January 7, 1876, in Torrelavega, northern Spain, just miles from the Bay of Biscay. His mother, María del Carmen Álvarez de Toledo y Toraño, was from the province of León and a distant relative of the Duke of Alba, one of the highest titleholders of the Spanish aristocracy.[8] His father, George Barrett, was an Englishman described on Rafael's birth certificate as a "literary writer"; he had published at least two books on Spanish finance and taxes.[9] Rafael's Paraguayan widow, Francisca López Maíz, writes that George was an accountant involved in British interests in Spain.[10] Rafael, and his only sibling, Fernando, born in 1881, received British citizenship through their father.[11]

While the family's wealth did not compare to that of their titled relatives, they were embedded in the privileged classes of an extremely unequal Spanish society. A few photos of a fair-haired child—all that remain of Barrett's earliest years—appear to show that they made trips to France. By 1888, the family had settled in Madrid, where Barrett was one of the tiny minority of Spaniards to receive secondary education, becoming a prize-winning pupil at prestigious schools, before going on to start a degree in civil engineering.[12]

He was trilingual, and his abilities in Spanish, English, and French gave him privileged access to an array of texts, as would be evidenced by the broad range of topics and citations that he would include in his writing.

However, before his literary and journalistic career began, he showed himself to be a talented mathematician, publishing articles in the field.[13] In 1900, he pushed his way into the highest intellectual circles by becoming a secretary for science at the Ateneo de Madrid, Spain's most important private cultural institution.[14]

During this time, Barrett was also engaged in the fertile artistic and philosophical circles that appeared among Madrid's youth in the aftermath of the country's traumatic defeat in the 1898 Spanish-American War, which saw Spain lose almost all its remaining colonies. Some of his close friends—such as Ramón del Valle-Inclán[15]—would be recognized as leading voices of the age, later being categorized as part of the renowned "Generation of '98" literary movement. The young Barrett drank from the same fountain of values as his contemporaries: renovation, rebellion, vitalism, and liberal individualism.[16]

Ramiro de Maeztu, an intellectual at the center of the Generation of '98, described Barrett as a "youth of unforgettable bearing and beauty" who "lived the life of a young aristocrat for a spell, more inclined toward ostentation and good company than the world of pleasure."[17]

From the heights of his Paraguayan activism, however, Barrett would look back on this period with regret, reportedly telling his sister-in-law: "I was a fool, Angelina, imagine that I imposed myself through my elegance. How useless my life was back then . . . !"[18]

His ascent into the Madrid elite was not to last, and in April 1902 his fall played out in the most public of fashions.

After Barrett was denied membership in an extremely exclusive gentlemen's club, he accused a journalist of slander and challenged him to a duel. A court of honor promptly declared Barrett unfit for the bout. Infuriated, he used a riding whip to beat the head of the court, the Duke of Arión, during a theater performance. The incident made the front pages and cost him twelve days' imprisonment.[19]

Barrett had been purposefully cast out of high society. Following his parents' deaths, he had spent his inheritance, possibly on gambling,[20] and, as Maeztu wrote, "there is no place in the 'high life' for poor lads, except when they are docile and humble."[21] Barrett had shown repeatedly that he did not possess these traits: just months earlier he had been involved in two other duel challenges, one of which had ended in the exchange of four pistol shots without injury.[22] In years to come, this hotheadedness and rash bravado would be put at the service of others.

Months later, a false report of Barrett's suicide circulated in the Spanish press. While this may have been a machination of his adversaries, it did hold some truth: his life as a Madrid "dandy" had ended.

A brief article was published to refute the suicide claims, stating that Barrett had relocated to Paris, having left Spain without concluding his engineering studies.[23] He would soon head farther afield.

Buenos Aires

In November 1903, "indignant at the ignominy and weary of the *rich boy*'s life he had led till then," in the words of López Maíz,[24] Barrett arrived in Buenos Aires, Argentina.[25] Although the twenty-seven-year-old quickly assimilated into the city's established Spanish intellectual elite, immigration also brought him into contact with the working-class Spaniards pouring into what he labeled as an "inextricable tangle of men and ambitions from all nations."[26] Six million Europeans settled in Argentina from 1860 to 1930, as official policy looked to "Europeanize" the nation while brutally subjugating the Indigenous population.[27] The influx of impoverished, working-class immigrants, who were met by economic inequality and repressive policies from the Argentine state, had contributed to the country developing one of the world's most important anarchist movements.[28]

Barrett's first surviving journal articles, many adopting the style of the short opinion essays that would come to characterize much of his work, began to appear in Buenos Aires publications linked to the Spanish Republican movement, which he had joined. He immediately displayed the huge reach of his pen, tackling an array of philosophical, social, and political themes that transcended borders. He showed himself to be intensely anti-monarchical and anti-clerical, and he displayed acute awareness of class conflict. However, there was little sign that he sided with the oppressed, and instead he pointed to individual strength and greatness as the ultimate values.[29]

In late 1904, after over a year in the swelling metropolis, including another frustrated duel, he received an offer that would come to cement his connection to the continent. The editor of the newspaper *El Tiempo* asked him to cover an uprising that had been shaking neighboring—but distant—Paraguay since August.

Barrett would confess that, before setting off upstream into the vast

Paraná-Paraguay river system, he knew nothing
nation, beyond the pictures and descriptions shar
Eliseo Meifrén, which had led him to believe tha'
painters."³⁰ Regardless, and full of the spirit of a
the faraway rebellion "to see if I might find the bulle

The Island Surrounded by Land

Barrett was far from alone in knowing little about Paraguay. The country had been isolated and overlooked for much of its history. Roa Bastos would famously describe his homeland as an "[island] surrounded by land because of the immensity of its jungles, its impassable deserts."[32]

Paraguay had, though, experienced a period of prominence in the early years of the Spanish Empire. Asunción, founded in 1537, had been a key base for the ongoing conquest and colonization of South America. However, as the province of Paraguay was found to have none of the precious metals prized by the European invaders, it was soon relegated to a backwater. The small Spanish population came to be primarily concerned with exploiting the region's Indigenous Guarani peoples and their lands, despite over more than a hundred years of Indigenous uprisings.[33] The economy of the highly impoverished province became tied to the harvesting of leaves from the wild-growing yerba mate tree, used to prepare a stimulating infusion that became popular throughout much of South America.[34]

Jesuit priests arrived to establish evangelizing missions that would house tens of thousands of Guarani people. These priests held much of Paraguay's military, economic, and political power, as the province was continually hit by attacks from unconquered Indigenous peoples and raids from the neighboring Portuguese colony of Brazil.[35] Isolation led to an early consolidation of local identity and contributed to the survival of the Guarani language, which, although highly marginalized, remains Paraguay's most spoken language to this day.[36]

By the time independence was declared without bloodshed in 1811, Paraguay had become a de facto sub-colony of the regional colonial capital of Buenos Aires.[37] As the Spanish Empire disintegrated, distant port city called on Paraguay to fall in line as a province of what would become Argentina. However, Paraguay refused. From that moment on, pressure on Paraguayan independence from giant neighbors Argentina and Brazil would be an ongoing existential threat, playing a major role in shaping the country's fate during the nineteenth century and beyond.

When the stoic Dr. Gaspar Rodríguez de Francia was given powers as supreme dictator in 1814, he effectively sealed the country off from the outside world to ensure its survival. During his long rule, he employed an iron fist to strip the Spanish and Church elites of their power and gave campesinos[38] access to state-owned land.[39] After Francia's death, the authoritarian president Carlos Antonio López (1844–1862) adopted more outward-looking policies that allowed for an expansion of trade and diplomacy, and at the same time carried out militarization to ward off foreign territorial threats. López implemented a state-led development model that included the creation of a railroad system and an iron foundry.[40]

The final ruler of what would be known as Paraguay's "Nationalist Era" came to power in 1862: the flamboyant Francisco Solano López, son of Carlos Antonio. He oversaw the peak of the ongoing tensions with the other young republics of the region and, as the geopolitical balance crumbled, Paraguay was rapidly drawn into—or thrown into by López[41]—a war against the combined forces of Argentina, Brazil, and Uruguay.

The War of the Triple Alliance, a period of immense terror from 1864 to 1870, was perhaps the world's deadliest war per capita in the last two centuries.[42] Around half of Paraguay's prewar population, including López, had died by the time the devastated nation was defeated, having struggled to the last against overwhelming military force and the ravages of disease and starvation.[43] Argentina and Brazil partially fulfilled their territorial ambitions by annexing large parts of the smaller nation's territory, and a six-year Brazilian occupation saw the installation of puppet governments in Asunción. Postwar Paraguay quickly moved in line with the model of imperialist subjugation that had unfolded over much of Latin America: state possessions were privatized, and huge debts were contracted with British bondholders.[44]

Elements of the emerging Paraguayan political elite became extraordinarily wealthy as, in response to the enormous war debt forced on the country, they sold off vast extensions of state-owned land to foreign companies—primarily from Argentina, the United Kingdom, and the United States—that sought to extract yerba mate and tannin-rich quebracho trees for world markets. Around 40 percent of the country's total land area was bought by just thirty-two companies.[45] Paraguay's rural population, already driven into the utmost poverty by the war, was excluded from the use of land it had enjoyed since the days of Dr. Francia and forced to migrate or become indentured laborers.[46] In a few short years, Paraguay had gone from having a largely independent development model to being a semi-colony of Brazil, Argentina, and the international companies that now owned much of its territory.[47]

The political elites consolidated into the two parties that have dominated Paraguayan politics ever since: the National Republican Association—known as the Colorado Party—and the Liberal Party, aligned with Brazil and Argentina respectively. In practice, there were few ideological differences between the groups, with both pursuing laissez-faire policies.[48] In 1904, following twenty-four years of Colorado rule, the Liberals set in motion the military uprising that would bring Rafael Barrett to the country. The rebels declared their intentions to combat rampant corruption and repeated economic crises, and to consolidate Liberal values under the banner of progress and modernization. Behind the scenes, Argentina sought to counter Brazilian influence.[49]

Just downriver, Barrett was drawing nearer to the beleaguered nation's latest political crisis. Perhaps, as Eduardo Galeano writes, as he passed from the Paraná River into the Paraguay River, entering Paraguayan territory, he "felt he had arrived in a place that was waiting for him, because this accursed place was his place in the world."[50]

Paraguayan Reality

In October 1904, Barrett disembarked at the rebel camp at Villeta, just south of Asunción. He had traveled in the company of his friend Joaquín Boceta, a pianist from the elite circles of Madrid who had seconded him in several duels.[51] The Spaniards soon struck up friendships with several young liberal intellectuals in the ranks, and the only dispatch Barrett sent back to Buenos Aires showed that he held a deep faith in the promises of the revolution and its leaders.[52] Indeed, he had made the leap of taking up arms with the rebellion, though he would later pride himself on not having fired a single shot.[53]

The rebels achieved victory in December, and Barrett entered Asunción with the troops.[54] He would stay there, quickly settling into the city's small, nascent bourgeoisie. His revolutionary connections allowed him to get a job in the new government's statistics office and he soon became secretary of the high society Club Español, where he would meet teenager Francisca López Maíz. They would marry in April 1906.[55]

"Within a few days, Barrett became an interesting figure in the Asunción intellectual circle," Argentine writer José Rodríguez Alcalá, then resident in Paraguay, would recall.[56] Barrett's privileged education and talent undoubtedly set him apart and, as he continued to brandish his pen, he became the first writer in the Paraguayan press to be regularly paid.[57] His early Paraguayan texts continued in the vein of the work he had produced in Argentina, exploring a wide-ranging variety of philosophical and political themes, and often flaunting the elitism and individualism characteristic of some of those that would come to be considered part of the Spanish Generation of '98.[58]

In Asunción, another major literary movement was now brewing around him—Paraguay's first.[59] Many of his intellectual friends from the 1904 uprising would form part of the "Generation of the 1900s," a group set on restoring Paraguayan identity and esteem after the devastation of the War of the Triple Alliance. They looked to achieve this by offering reinterpretations of the country's traumatic history. While there were fierce conflicts among these intellectuals over the meaning of the past, the most successful faction promoted the myth of a glorious golden age under the authoritarian rulers of the prewar nineteenth century. They enshrined the war as the epic national saga, fought under the messianic figure of Marshal Francisco Solano López. This highly nationalistic narrative, which was often devoid of historical evidence, would nonetheless have a profound impact on Paraguayan society, for better or worse.[60] The focus on the past by these intellectuals, who were often embedded in the interests of the elites, left little room or desire to examine the horrendous social ills that screamed out around them in a country still largely in ruins.[61]

From the beginning, Barrett distanced himself from these myth-making exercises and, over time, also began to diverge from his friends' disregard for the problems facing Paraguayans outside the bourgeois bubble. By the end of 1906, his elitist perspective had noticeably faded, and his writings suddenly began to take an extremely critical view. While he continued to produce eclectic articles on philosophical, cultural, and political issues from Paraguay and around the globe, he now used many of his texts to defend the oppressed,[62] rally against the greed of capitalists,[63] and expose the hypocrisy and cruelty of the imperialist powers of the day.[64]

This profound transformation was undoubtedly driven by Barrett's contact with the harsh reality of Paraguay—what he would come to label "Paraguayan sorrow." He left a job at the British consortium that had acquired the country's railroad following the war after he witnessed the exploitative treatment of Paraguayan workers.[65] Subsequent work in rural areas as a land surveyor brought him face to face with the extreme deprivation faced by the population.[66]

Through intimate portraits, which avoided the romanticization of poverty seen in other writers of the time, Barrett explored the dreadful circumstances of "those that live in exile on their own soil."[67] The war, followed by the installation of the merciless neocolonial model, had inflicted physical, psychological, and spiritual damage that was being passed on from generation to generation of a neglected population. "What can a mere thirty years do to heal wounds like these?" he would ponder.[68]

Barrett had also become strongly disillusioned with the 1904 revolution, which had initially enthralled him. The uprising had led to a period of intense political instability, driven by the unrelenting infighting of the Liberal Party. During his time at the statistics office, he had witnessed—and even participated in—the inefficiency and corruption of the state,[69] and he had observed how the change of government had allowed foreign powers to further tighten their grip on Paraguay. As the eminent labor historian Francisco Gaona writes: "From total dependence on Brazil, this 'revolution' took us . . . to total dependence on Argentina."[70]

This disappointment had entirely eroded his faith in politics, writing: "A fertile politics exists: not doing politics. An effective way of gaining power: fleeing from power and working at home."[71] The young liberal had withered, and the seeds of his radical stance had sprouted.

Manufacturer of Ideas

Events in Barrett's personal life were also shaping the writer and activist he would become. Shortly after the birth of his only child, Alejandro (known as Alex), in February 1907, he developed the first symptoms of tuberculosis. His friend Herib Campos Cervera would write that the knowledge of his likely death from the then incurable disease was a major driving force behind the intensity that Barrett's production of texts would take over the coming years.[72]

As the quality and quantity of his progressively more critical articles increased, he drew away from the Asunción intellectuals, not without imploring them to open their eyes to the reality around them: "University students with your plans for regeneration, rhetoricians of sacrifice, leave that central hive and spread yourselves over the humble corners of your country, not to suck the nectar from the naïve calyxes, but to distribute the honey of your fraternity."[73] Their reaction would be to expel him from the Instituto Paraguayo, the city's liberal intellectual club.[74]

At the same time, Barrett began to find a place for his thinking in the growing labor movement, which was beginning to exercise important influence in overwhelmingly rural Paraguay for the first time. Paraguay's first central labor organization, the Paraguayan Regional Workers' Federation (FORP), was created in 1906, based on the principles of the strong anarcho-syndicalist organizations of Argentina. Barrett's presence in Paraguay also coincided with a period of intensified strike action as the movement gained vigor.[75]

The Spaniard strengthened his ties with the workers. He began teaching at a mutual aid society, and by 1907 he had started giving speeches at federation meetings. As his continuous publications in the Asunción press became more aligned with the interests of the labor movement, Barrett himself even began to identify as a worker: a "manufacturer of ideas."[76] This shift in his perception of the working class was monumental. Whereas a year earlier he had vehemently demonized striking workers,[77] he now declared himself in favor of "strikes, holy strikes!"[78]

His contribution to the workers' struggle would reach such a point that Francisco Gaona wrote: "Rafael Barrett was the first doctrinaire of our labor movement during its early development, and indisputable innovator of all revolutionary literature of the twentieth century in Paraguay."[79]

The Truth of the Yerba Mate Forests

The year 1908 was definitive in Barrett's life and work. He continued to move closer to the workers, delivering celebrated speeches at events run by the FORP at Asunción's National Theater.[80] His anarchistic condemnation of private property as the root of Paraguayan suffering and appeal for greater women's rights were listened to with "religious silence" and "thunderous applause."[81]

Despite having a young family and modest income, he also gave up his work as a land surveyor, a step in a process of "proletarianization" as his principles drove him to leave the security of bourgeois society to experience financial and social precarity firsthand.[82] Barrett told Bertotto, whom he met that year when the two spoke at a workers' meeting, that he could no longer stand the hypocrisy of surveying:

"What! Speak against property every day, with fierce repetition, and the next moment measure plots of land like oceans and authorize the exact position of their boundaries? No!"[83]

It was during this period of intensifying ideological coherence that Barrett published his most poignant work, *The Truth of the Yerba Mate Forests*, a series of six articles released in the newspaper *El Diario* over the month of June.[84] The texts struck with unprecedented force at the heart of neocolonial power and exploitation in Paraguay, denouncing the terrible abuses suffered by the rural workers that harvested yerba mate in the vast forested enclaves that were in the hands of international capital. Barrett focused his gaze on the Anglo-Argentine Industrial Paraguaya Company, owner of almost 5.3 million acres in eastern Paraguay.[85]

His exposé was part of an emerging tradition of writers who were then using the press to uncover the inhumanity of extractive imperialism around the world, such as the exploitation used to extract rubber in the Congo Free State, which Barrett references.[86] The Spaniard was not the first to expose the horrors of Paraguay's yerba mate forests, although his work is the most celebrated. Around the same time, French writer Julián Bouvier, who lived in the south of the country, was also reporting on the atrocities.[87] Furthermore, whispers of the age-old systems of abuse in the subtropical forests had circulated for centuries.

Yerba mate had been entwined with violence and exploitation since the beginning of the colonial era. As the abundant yerba mate trees became the cornerstone of the province's meager economy, Indigenous Guarani people were forced to harvest and transport the "green gold"—their own sacred leaf—under terrifying conditions to meet booming demand across Spain's South American domain.[88]

"It is a common complaint, and something experience places before our eyes, that dealings in this herb are diminishing the numbers of Indians in the Province," wrote governor Baltasar García Ros in 1707.[89]

The bloody competition for control of the yerba mate market, as well as the Indigenous people exploited to harvest the leaf, would be a major driver of key events in the history of colonial Paraguay. Later, during the oft-glorified Nationalist Era of the nineteenth century,

Carlos Antonio López's enemies would accuse him of acting to wipe out the Indigenous people who were forced to harvest yerba mate on lands that he himself had expropriated from them.[90] Then, in the aftermath of the War of the Triple Alliance, the incoming foreign companies set about perfecting the centuries-old mechanism of debt slavery in the forests.

Barrett describes this system in excruciating detail, showing how the humanity of the *mensú*[91]—the unfortunate men lured into the deep forests through the deceitful advance payment they were given—was eradicated under the giant loads of yerba mate they were forced to carry endlessly. As the companies extracted and destroyed Paraguay's natural wealth, they erased the very souls and identities of the workers.[92] Barrett put the details of this methodical abuse before the eyes of Asunción's elite, who either preferred to look the other way or were fully complicit.

Barrett did not shy from naming the companies and individuals responsible for the heinous exploitation, showing the involvement of those in the very highest circles of power, including President Benigno Ferreira. He fearlessly revealed the details of the state's own central role in the atrocities: laws had been passed that stripped workers of all rights, effectively legalizing slavery in the domains of the yerba mate corporations. In addition, state officials—judges, police, surveyors—were on the payroll of the companies and fully complicit in the brutality.

In this way, Barrett inverts hegemonic notions of civilization, showing that it was not in the jungle, but in the elegant salons of Asunción, Buenos Aires, and Rio de Janeiro that savagery was to be found in its purest form.[93] According to scholar Ana María Vara, *The Truth of the Yerba Mate Forests* thus positions Barrett as an early innovator of the "fundamental elements of neocolonial counter-discourse on natural resources" in Latin America.[94] This current would come to be central to anti-imperialist thinking on the continent and would be exemplified by Eduardo Galeano's 1971 canonical book on dependency theory, *Open Veins of Latin America*.[95]

While the Paraguayan government took no action to investigate Barrett's accusations, the reprisal to his brave affront to the neocolonial model was almost immediate. Former president Juan Bautista Gaona, who had once inspired Barrett's hopes when he took office after the 1904 revolution,[96] promptly moved to block the use of the National Theater for a workers' conference at which Barrett was scheduled to speak.[97] Gaona was a major shareholder in the Industrial Paraguaya Company. As a result, the conference was held on the streets of Asunción; Barrett was applauded by yerba workers as he spoke.[98] The Spaniard would soon also feel obliged to stop working with *El Diario*, one of his key remaining sources of income. The paper refused to publish one of his articles, and, after it publicly accused him of having employed "incredibly personal terms,"[99] he saw it as looking to appease the powerful interests upset by his attack on the yerba mate companies.[100]

Germinal

In July 1908, just days after the publication of the final article in *The Truth of the Yerba Mate Forests*, the perpetual internal disputes of the Liberal Party led to a military uprising under the command of Coronel Albino Jara, an old enemy of Barrett's.[101] The nation was thrown into turmoil.

Despite the worsening symptoms of his tuberculosis, it was now that Barrett would commandeer the mule cart to aid the wounded during the massacre that left one hundred and fifty dead.[102] He would write of the coup with anarchistic frustration and scorn: "The innocent blood that has been spilled is not, however, entirely useless; it will contribute to private citizens averting their eyes from the political leprosy with greater disgust."[103]

Ironically, the successful uprising protected Barrett from becoming a victim of the seething anger of the overthrown government. Police documents uncovered during the violence saw him described him as "the anarchist, socialist, strike-agitating thief Rafael Barrett."[104] The yerba mate companies would try to take advantage of the chaos, however, as men who "reeked of yerba," according to López Maíz, made an unsuccessful attempt on her husband's life.[105]

Barrett was soon dealt a blow by the new regime: by August he had been blocked from writing in almost all Asunción publications. His response was to sell everything to start his own paper, *Germinal*,[106] with the aid of Bertotto, along with some economic support from workers.[107] Over just eleven issues, *Germinal* would give a voice to the workers' movement and the oppressed while working to expose the worsening official violence. Francisco Gaona describes the weekly as Paraguay's first "revolutionary and ideological paper."[108] A manifesto in the first issue set the tone:

> *Germinal* will not be on the side of the old, but of the new; it will oppose dogma with ideas, and authority with scrutiny.
> It will prefer truth to rhetoric.
> It will not defend gold, nor power, but labor.
> It will not accept what is legal, but what is just.
> It will organize the resistance and the advance of those that produce and create. It will not deal in politics; it will deal in humanity.[109]

On October 4, as Barrett's poor health and "supreme poverty"[110] were biting, he became one of hundreds to be detained in a wave of repression. Just hours before his arrest, he had distributed the blistering pamphlet *Under the Reign of Terror*, where he had decried the murderous abuses of the regime and raised an internationalist cry: "Truth and justice, whatever mouth might defend them, are not foreign anywhere in the world."[111]

Bertotto,[112] arrested days earlier, had been tortured, including being forced to eat pages from *Germinal* soaked in salt water.[113]

Following intervention from the British consul, Barrett was deported from Paraguay, spending uncomfortable days in the heart of Brazil's remote yerba mate country before securing passage to Montevideo in November.

He would stay in the Uruguayan capital for three and a half intense months. It was an exile that would give him a taste of the acceptance and success as a writer he had been consistently denied in conservative and repressive Paraguay. He found a place in the Uruguayan press, concentrating on producing the highly philosophical and reflexive texts that had been a constant throughout his career. He soon attracted praise from renowned figures in a city whose air, according to Uruguayan writer Luis Hierro Gambardella, "was full of the deepest and most understanding tolerance for the ideas of men."[114]

Nonetheless, Barrett's spirit was irresistibly drawn back to Paraguay, the country where his wife and son remained, and which he tenderly described as "my only country, which I love dearly, where I became good."[115]

The tuberculosis that ravaged his body left him hospitalized in early January 1909, but did not stop him from writing articles that continued to captivate his Uruguayan readership. The disease even fueled a series of moving texts based on his experiences of being bedridden among other sufferers. By the end of February, he had left Uruguay, nominally on doctor's advice to seek warmer climes, but driven by his underlying longing for Paraguayan soil.

His gaunt frame was smuggled across the Paraná River from Argentina to a ranch near the remote town of Yabebyry, on Paraguay's southern border.[116] He would spend the next year living in an isolated wooden house on the ranch owned by his brother-in-law in the "imposing desert of the Paraná."[117] As he struggled against his disease and looked to maintain contact with the outside world, he was immersed in the sights and voices of rural Paraguay, experiences that would further refine his readings of the country's social reality. Fortunately, his most fervent desire—to be reunited with his family—became reality as López Maíz and Alex joined him on the solitary ranch while he continued to write for the Uruguayan press.

"Writing is undoubtedly bad for me, according to science," he would tell López Maíz, dreaming of books he would not have time to write, "but when I consider that my days are perhaps numbered, I will not resign myself to not producing. I want to leave behind as much work as possible."[118]

What I Have Seen

Improvements in the political situation allowed the family to move to San Bernardino, near Asunción, in February 1910. In the lakeside town, where they had previously lived in 1907, Barrett received visits from labor-movement leaders and reestablished his contact with the Paraguayan press. He was overjoyed to receive the very first copy printed of the only book he would see published in his lifetime, *Present Moralities*, released in Montevideo.[119] The collection of articles—drawn from his press publications—flaunted the breadth of his thinking, consisting of reflections on ethical, philosophical, and political topics from around the world. He was disappointed that the book could not be sold in Buenos Aires, as its title was viewed as "suspicious" by a repressive and paranoid Argentine government.[120] Soon after, true to his internationalist spirit, he would condemn the terrible situation faced by Argentine workers, especially immigrants, in the defiant pamphlet *Argentine Terror*.[121]

Back near the Paraguayan capital, Barrett would have cause for a final confrontation with the intellectual elite of Asunción, leaving no doubt about the chasm that now separated him from many of his former friends and his former self. His article "What I Have Seen," where he denounced the tremendous poverty he had observed over his time in Yabebyry, was met by the response "What Barrett Has Not Seen" from former Vice President Manuel Domínguez. Domínguez, who had been a witness at Barrett's wedding in 1906, accused the Spaniard of pessimism and distorting reality. Barrett, perhaps reflecting on his own process of transformation in Paraguay, passionately responded:

> Until pain embraces your innards, until one day of abandonment—just a single day—makes you once again part of vast humanity, you will not understand it.... You can no longer tell truth from lies, those who love your country from those who suck its blood.[122]

With his final strength failing, Barrett decided to seek experimental treatment for his tuberculosis in France. He secured a position as European correspondent for the Uruguayan paper *La Razón*, allowing him to leave Asunción alone on September 1, 1910. As he set sail downriver toward the ocean, he gazed back on the city, writing: "I know that behind those unmoving walls there is sorrow.... And Asunción, with its feigned calm, fades, perhaps forever, from my retina."[123]

During a brief stopover in Montevideo, he received a hero's welcome—*Present Moralities* had been an enormous success. A photograph of a painfully thin Barrett—which has become the most widely used and recognized image of him—was taken during these short hours in the Uruguayan capital. He never stopped writing, continuing to produce articles for several South American publications, even as he arrived in Barcelona and then Paris to begin treatment.

Tragically, the experimental cure, which consisted of injections of seawater, was unsuccessful, and Barrett's health continued to deteriorate. He was sent for the winter to the town of Arcachon in southern France, nestled on the Bay of Biscay, the body of water that had seen him come into the world: "My sea!" he wrote.[124] He died on December 17, 1910, at thirty-four years of age. His anonymous remains lie in the ossuary of the cemetery of Arcachon.[125]

In his final days, he asked his English aunt, Susan Barrett,[126] who had traveled from her home in Spain to be with him at his bedside, to send the carefully prepared manuscript of *Paraguayan Sorrow* to Montevideo for publication.[127] He had been unable to find a publisher in Asunción due to fears of government reprisals.[128]

His last bloodstained message to López Maíz and Alex displayed strong hopes for them, hopes that surely extended to the entire long-suffering population of Paraguay: "My soul is peaceful and full of confidence in the life that you will have as a reward for your sorrows, if you examine and endure them with loyalty and courage."[129]

Paraguayan Sorrow

As Barrett's life came to an end across the ocean, Paraguay entered a period of further instability. Repeated brutal coups led to a total of seven presidencies from November 1910 to August 1912. Barrett's daring and critical voice was not forgotten during the turmoil, with tributes published in newspapers in Paraguay, Uruguay, and Argentina. In 1912, a group of Paraguayan workers founded the Rafael Barrett Social

Studies Center, an organization that disseminated the Spaniard's ideas and would come to hold strong societal influence.[130]

Nevertheless, the intelligentsia of Asunción continued to turn their backs on his vision, producing little in-depth analysis of his work[131] and still lamenting his lack of "ability to evoke the past," as Domínguez wrote in a short booklet on Barrett.[132] His texts clearly continued to pose a threat to those in positions of power in Paraguay and beyond; in 1911, three workers at an Argentine labor-movement printing press were imprisoned for reproducing his 1910 pamphlet *Argentine Terror*.[133]

Barrett's spirit was felt even more strongly in South America when *Paraguayan Sorrow* was published in Montevideo in April 1911. The diverse articles and speeches that make up the collection span the period of his residence in Paraguay and are united by their focus on the country. They provide an unprecedented examination of Paraguayan social reality in the early twentieth century.

While the six articles of *The Truth of the Yerba Mate Forests* were included as part of Barrett's original manuscript of *Paraguayan Sorrow*, editor Orsini Bertani excluded them from the 1911 first edition. The editor explained in a note that this decision was taken because his publishing house had recently released a separate compilation of Barrett's attack on the yerba mate companies, with an introduction by Bertotto, of which it appears Barrett was not aware.[134] *Paraguayan Sorrow* and *The Truth of the Yerba Mate Forests* would be brought back together in several subsequent editions, but would be considered separate books within a single volume. In this English-language edition, the articles of *The Truth of the Yerba Mate Forests* are reincorporated as an integral part of *Paraguayan Sorrow* to honor Barrett's vision of his book.

Paraguayan Sorrow's evocative descriptions of subtropical urban and rural landscapes are filled with Barrett's careful portraits of the country's marginalized majorities—rural workers of the ranches and yerba mate forests, domestic servants, impoverished children, people with mental illnesses—which, as literary critic Carla Benisz notes, "do not immobilize the subject, but rather give depth—socially, historically, and psychologically—to their degradation."[135] Barrett shows a heightened sensitivity to the extreme levels of oppression suffered by women, such as the "servant of servants" Panta, a domestic worker at the ranch in Yabebyry. He implores male workers to repair family social networks and abandon the heightened *machismo* toward women that had been unleashed by the war. "What is your poverty compared to theirs?" he interrogated them.[136] In time, he would come to staunchly reject the idea of innate differences in intelligence and abilities between the sexes, which is present in some of his earlier writing, and push for the advance of women's rights and opportunities.[137]

While showing strong sympathy for the oppressed, Barrett does maintain elements of the paternalistic stance inherited from his privileged origins. He rejects the ideas of suffrage and juries,[138] viewing the masses as unprepared for collective decision-making. He fears, as he writes elsewhere, that they would hand power to "the scoundrels and the imbeciles" and perpetrate injustices.[139] However, Barrett shows faith that through their struggle they would become morally equipped for power,[140] and is convinced that workers were to be the agents of the inevitable rebirth of the world, unencumbered by the evils of private property, money, laws, and the state. For Barrett, it is "those at the bottom—those that work, dream and suffer—that will make human fraternity a reality."[141]

In his texts, Barrett places figures from the popular classes in the rich milieu of Paraguay's ancestral culture and traditions. His exquisite cultural descriptions were a radical departure at a time when the nation's traditional legends, dress, and knowledge were stigmatized by the elite as backward and were even outlawed.[142] This discrimination was especially prevalent in relation to the autochthonous Guarani language spoken by the vast majority of the population.[143] For example, Domínguez had declared: "Paraguay has a great enemy to its progress in the Guarani language. It is a shame for us Paraguayans that this language is still the only one spoken by certain inferior social classes."[144] In contrast, Barrett shows himself to be a defender of the language— though it is unclear to what extent he spoke Guarani—signaling the importance of its intrinsic relation to the Paraguayan people and land, and the innate benefits of the use of both Guarani and Spanish that characterizes many Paraguayans to this day.

The Spaniard does little to mask his rejection of Paraguay's bourgeois intellectuals, characterizing them as insufferably pretentious and functional to the interests of oppressive power. Equally, he moves away from their predominant "great man" readings of history, turning his back on figures like Napoleon Bonaparte that had once fascinated him. Even when writing about the War of the Triple Alliance, he makes little mention of Marshal Francisco Solano López, whom he refused to accept as national hero. Instead, he prefers to focus on a soldier's testimony of the horrors and to condemn the barbarity of Argentine politicians who defended their nation's actions as bringing "freedom" to Paraguay.[145]

Barrett's reluctance to focus on the past coincides with a fixation on the present and an unshakable faith in the possibilities of the future: a common characteristic in European intellectual circles of the time. However, his vision of the future diverges from dominant contemporary views. For Barrett, human progress is to be achieved, not through science and technological advancement, but through ethical transformation.[146] In line with anarchist thought, he sees the education of youth as vital to this ethical revolution, a concern that is evident throughout *Paraguayan Sorrow*.[147] He shows acute concern for the intergenerational transmission of trauma dating from the war—and far earlier—to young Paraguayans: "These children have been born old. They have inherited the disdain and resigned skepticism of so many defrauded and oppressed generations."[148] The solution is clear. Education must be wrested from the hands of the state so that children's "free curiosity"[149] can be stimulated and they can be taught "to distance [themselves] from politics and to scorn power."[150]

While Barrett is indeed fascinated by science, seeing it as an exciting collective endeavor shared by all of humanity and a potential tool for anarchistic liberation, it causes him grave concerns. In texts not included in *Paraguayan Sorrow* he expresses fears that technological advances might extinguish the presence of mystery in the universe, which, in spite of his fervent rejection of religion, he views as an essential element of human experience and moral progress.[151]

His wariness toward science also stems from a perception of its potentially destructive impact on the intricate relationship between humans and nature; this is a recurring theme in *Paraguayan Sorrow* that has led to Barrett being hailed as an early environmentalist thinker.[152] For Barrett, science has given humans the ability to dominate the immensity of the natural world, but this does not stop them from being an irrevocable part of that world.[153] As such, he is suspicious of contemporary hegemonic ideas of progress built on endless technological advancement and domination of nature. He writes: "It would seem that men are no longer able to feel, to imagine the life within the venerable trunks that tremble under the iron and collapse with a pitiful crash. It would seem that they do not understand that sap is also blood and that their victims were conceived in love and light."[154]

Accordingly, the guardianship and use of the natural world is a key issue for Barrett, especially in relation to the land. He considers land to be an essential element for the creation of wealth, a task that can only be carried out by labor. Consequently, he views Paraguay's large landowners, who illegitimately monopolized resources that were the common heritage of humanity, as the country's ultimate scourge. Foreshadowing the cries of movements such as that of the Mexican revolutionary Emiliano Zapata, he states: "The land is for all men, and the wealth of each man should be in relation to the amount that he works. Natural riches—the water, the sun, the land—belong to everyone."[155]

Barrett's Anarchism

While *Paraguayan Sorrow* provides a vision of numerous aspects of Barrett's political and social thought, his nuanced worldview is also developed in many other texts written over the short years of his intense literary outpouring.

Barrett has often been categorized as an anarchist thinker, part of a wave of anarchism that swept across Latin America during a brief period when the abolition of the state seemed a real possibility.[156] However, this characterization has been disputed at times. His friend Campos Cervera, perhaps influenced by his own standing in the Asunción bourgeoisie, wrote: "[Barrett] didn't love anarchism but rather the poor."[157] More recently, Spanish writer Gregorio Morán has described Barrett as a "radical socialist" marked by an individualistic aversion to all forms of authority.[158]

Barrett certainly engages directly and frequently with anarchism, displaying firm conviction in many of its fundamental tenets: a desire to bring an end to authority, coercive law, and private property.[159] A celebrated passage from his text "My Anarchism" reads: "[Anarchy's] etymological meaning is enough for me: 'absence of government.' The spirit of authority and the prestige of the law must be destroyed. That is all. It will be the task of free examination."[160]

While he rarely goes beyond these underlying principles to dialogue with prominent thinkers and debates of anarchist tradition, he shows immense interest in the ethical aspects of anarchism, emphasizing the possibilities of transforming the world by nurturing an underlying altruistic love. He expresses much more affinity with those he considered ethical radicals who strove to align their actions with their high principles, such as Jesus[161] and Tolstoy—whom he viewed as exemplary anarchists—than with Bakunin and Kropotkin.[162] This has led the historian of anarchism Martín Albornoz to interpret Barrett's anarchism as "a minimal anarchism.... A portable anarchism. It is an anarchism that you can take along with you within your own body. It is not necessarily linked to the big doctrinal debates."[163]

Barrett's vision of achieving societal change through internal ethical renovation—where the collective would facilitate the transformation of each individual—brings him into dialogue with Ernesto "Che" Guevara's later concept of the "New Man," reflected in other towering Latin American figures such as José Carlos Mariátegui and José Martí.[164] As part of this renovation, Barrett believes in the transformative potential of intense action, of using all of one's ethical vigor to contribute to the "universal effort" in which everyone and everything is engaged.[165] He wrote, "Discovering your inner energy and giving it up to renew the world; this is altruism."[166] This certitude that humans must pour their energy out into the world also reconciles him with death. Individual mortality is vital so that humanity can be replenished with the dynamic strength of new, better generations: "We will sense that we must die because we are not yet perfect and our blood is indispensable for new attempts."[167]

Barrett wrote little of the form that society would take after his yearned-for ethical reconstruction, but showed total faith that the coming generations would put this new order in place as a natural progression of liberated humanity: "What does the shape of things in the future matter? Reality will reveal them. We should feel sure that they will be beautiful and noble, like those of a freely growing tree."[168]

The free-flowing nature of Barrett's anarchist thinking allows him to reject the dogmatism often associated with political philosophies. As a result, he is saddened by the divisions within the "emancipatory avalanche"[169] of leftist movements, suggesting:

> The antagonism between anarchists and socialists is the final trick of the bourgeoisie. . . . If the current International succeeded in uniting the two branches over the relatively neutral ground of syndicalism, the minutes that capitalist society has left would be numbered.[170]

Indeed, the malleability of Barrett's views sees him bridge this divide between anarchism and socialism. He frequently collaborated with socialists—in the pages of *Germinal*, for example—and he even places his own political vision under the socialist banner at times.[171] As early as 1918, journalist and writer Alberto Lasplaces would describe his admired friend Barrett as "outside of all classifications."[172]

Underlying Barrett's ideological unorthodoxy is a firm belief in the ultimate importance of independent, critical thinking. He wants his readers and listeners to analyze their own circumstances, whatever the conclusions they draw may be: "I am happy that your intellect might continue in motion after mine, even if it goes against mine. My goal is to provoke a small earthquake in your views and your morals, unbalance a foundation, produce a crack in a wall."[173]

Barrett projects a strongly anti-imperialist and internationalist outlook. He continually denounces the imperialist actions carried out across the globe by the privileged classes of European nations and the

United States, ridiculing their claims to be the representatives of civilization. At the same time, he calls for fraternity between the oppressed classes of the world[174] and comes to deplore the violence of war, which he sees as the sterile fruit of the manipulative concept of patriotism implanted by the elites.[175] However, Barrett is also reluctant to endorse the deadly violence that was being employed by anarchists at the time, especially in Argentina, instead favoring the peaceful methods of struggle that he sees reflected in figures such as Tolstoy. Nonetheless, he is clear in his view that anarchist violence is an understandable response to the enormously greater terrorist violence perpetrated by the state against the masses.[176]

While consistently opposing imperialism throughout his writing, Barrett's work, including *Paraguayan Sorrow*, does contain statements implying the existence of racial hierarchies.[177] He would later come to firmly reject this position, denouncing ideas of racial superiority and confronting racial discrimination; notably that perpetrated against African Americans in the United States.[178]

Memory and Neglect

Over the course of the twentieth century, the figure of Rafael Barrett simultaneously occupied currents of memory and neglect. In the decades after his death, testimonies from those who knew him, both in Europe and the Americas, were slowly released, adding depth to a very limited sketch of his life. He remained respected in anarchist and socialist circles in Uruguay and Argentina, and he was a legendary figure for the perpetually embattled Paraguayan left.[179] Paraguayan radical leader Obdulio Barthe would pen a tribute to Barrett just three years before acting as one of the heads of the ill-fated Taking of Encarnación in 1931, which saw the southern city become an anarchist commune for a few brief hours.[180]

Sadly, however, Barrett's work became less well known than his name. Although collections of his articles, essays, speeches, and short stories were sporadically released over the years—López Maíz made at least one journey to Montevideo, in 1918, to arrange the publication of further compilations of Barrett's texts[181]—it was not until 1943 that the first edition of his complete works was published in Argentina. By the 1970s, his old comrade Bertotto wrote with regret that it was incredibly difficult to obtain Barrett's texts, even in cosmopolitan Buenos Aires.[182] In Barrett's Spanish homeland, both his name and works had been largely forgotten.

In Paraguay, despite the prestige attached to Barrett's name, none of his books were published until 1988, when an edition of his complete works was released, recovering many articles that had lain forgotten in the archives of Asunción.[183] This conspicuous absence can be attributed to his distance from the bourgeoisie during his lifetime and the many years of chaos and repression that awaited Paraguay throughout the twentieth century.[184]

Despite the scarcity of copies of his work in Paraguay, he was a key influence on many eminent writers, such as Julio Correa, Augusto Roa Bastos, and Josefina Plá. In his famous introduction to the 1978 Venezuelan edition of *Paraguayan Sorrow*, Roa Bastos stated: "Barrett taught us Paraguayan writers of today to write; in dizzying fashion, he introduced us to the glimmering, simultaneously nebulous, almost phantasmagorical light of the 'delirious reality' of [Paraguay's] historical, social, and cultural myths and counter-myths."[185]

Roa Bastos's own texts were filled with Barrett's influence. His writing on the exploitation of yerba mate workers in the 1960 novel *Son of Man* takes many references and images from the powerful content of *The Truth of the Yerba Mate Forests*.

Barrett's work would be largely absent from academic circles in the twentieth century, with just a steady trickle of valuable studies on his work released over the decades. Investigations by key researchers such as Vladimiro Muñoz, Miguel Ángel Fernández, and Francisco Corral would provide important insights into the Spaniard's life and work, and the 1967 publication of Barrett's letters to his wife, Francisca López Maíz, complete with her own commentary and notes, stood as an enormous milestone in understanding his trajectory.[186]

Descendants

Beyond his texts, Barrett's name has also been inscribed in the history of Paraguay and Latin America through the lives of his descendants. Numerous members of the Barrett family have followed Rafael's example of dedicating their lives to social struggle and confronting the powers that dominate in the region. All while facing persecution, exile, and even violent death.

Alex, Rafael's son, would be a witness and participant in a large number of the moments of hope and tragedy that would sweep over Paraguay in the twentieth century.[187] With the rise of the influence of communism in the Paraguayan labor movement, he became involved in the nascent Paraguayan Communist Party in the 1920s.[188] He then went on to fight for Paraguay's victory in the tortuous 1932–35 Chaco War against Bolivia, a conflict that, beyond the territorial claims of the two nations, has been linked to U.S., British, and Argentine interests following the discovery of oil in the arid Chaco region.[189]

Under the banner of the Communist Party, Alex then took part in the short-lived February Revolution of 1936, which ended more than thirty years of almost uninterrupted Liberal Party rule. Subsequently, when the Liberals returned to power, he faced persecution, imprisonment, and exile in Argentina. He later returned to Paraguay to fight in the unsuccessful 1947 revolution that looked to displace the Colorado Party, which then backed the dictatorship of General Higinio Morínigo.

After Alfredo Stroessner, another general, violently seized power in 1954, Alex joined the United National Liberation Front opposition guerrilla movement, along with several of his numerous children. He was captured by the regime in Asunción in 1960. Stroessner, adamantly supported by the United States due to his anti-communist stance, would become the longest-ruling dictator in Latin American history, maintaining a sultan-like grip on power until 1989. His rule, centered around a marriage between the Colorado Party and the armed forces, would be characterized by horrendous human rights abuses: torture, extrajudicial executions, disappearances, mass murder of Indigenous people, and the systematic sexual abuse of young girls.[190] He also harbored Nazi fugitives, such as the "Angel of Death" Josef Mengele.[191]

After release from prison, Alex and his family became part of the enormous Paraguayan diaspora forced into exile by Stroessner, whose regime employed omnipresent spy networks and generalized fear as its main tools of repression, effectively crushing almost all opposition.[192] As much as a third of the population was forced to leave the country.[193] Following in his father's footsteps, Alex found refuge in Montevideo, until the rise of a military dictatorship in Uruguay in 1973 forced him to leave for Venezuela, where he died in 1980.

Many of Alex's children also became prominent activists as South America entered an era of fearsome right-wing military dictatorships under the umbrella of the U.S.-backed Operation Condor, which saw the authoritarian regimes collaborate to repress opposition. The Barretts would experience exile upon exile.

"All of us, the grandchildren of Rafael Barrett, have been deeply influenced by his work and life. We were active in every possible Paraguayan leftist organization, including the Communist Party, up until the establishment of 'democracy,' as well as in some organizations in other countries during all our experiences of exile," recalls Rafael Barrett Viedma, one of Alex's sons and an important figure in the history of the Paraguayan Communist Party.[194]

His brother, Alberto Barrett Viedma, was also a resolute political activist and was tortured by the military regime in Argentina.[195] Alberto was a talented artist: his drawing of his grandfather Rafael appears on the front of this book. Their sister, Soledad Barrett Viedma, after being violently kidnapped in Uruguay due her communist activism, received training as a guerrilla fighter in Cuba.[196] She traveled to Brazil to fight against the military regime, where she was killed by the state in 1973. She had been betrayed by the man who was her partner, the notorious "Corporal Anselmo," José Anselmo dos Santos, an infiltrated collaborator of the regime.

A poem in memory of Soledad Barrett by the great Uruguayan

writer and poet Mario Benedetti touches on qualities shared by multiple generations of this internationalist family caught in the whirlpool of serial exile:

> *At least it will not have been easy*
> *to close your big bright eyes*
> *your eyes in which the best violence*
> *was able to make reasonable truces*
> *to become incredible kindness*
>
> *and even if they have finally shut them*
> *you are probably still gazing*
> *Soledad, compatriot of three or four nations*
> *at the pure future for which you lived*
> *and for which you never refused to die.*[197]

Barrett Today

"In the night of Paraguayan misfortune, Barrett's life and work was a meteor that shone, sadly, for only a brief moment. That light, however, projected visions of the future that are fully relevant today,"[198] wrote Roa Bastos in 1978 during his long exile from Stroessner's Paraguay. Even though time has distanced Paraguay in many ways from Roa Bastos's trope of the isolated island "surrounded by land," his affirmation of Barrett's continued relevance holds true: the country continues to suffer under much of the same sorrow that Barrett observed more than a century ago.

A 1989 coup removed Stroessner from power and ushered in a period of nominal democratization in Paraguay, but the Colorado Party elites that were central to the regime have maintained an iron grip on power, doing next to nothing to investigate the horrendous human rights violations of the dictatorship. Seventy-five years of almost uninterrupted Colorado rule has meant that Paraguay's political system continues to be a forum for competing elite interests: the country currently has the second-highest corruption perception ranking in South

America.[199] Since Barrett's day, the blue flags of the Liberal Party have been replaced by the red flags of the Colorado Party, but little has changed.

The nationalist myths of the Generation of the 1900s, in which Barrett refused to engage, were weaponized as the ideological core of the Stroessner regime, with the dictator positioning himself as the successor of Dr. Francia and the Lópezes.[200] This authoritarian nationalism was ironically accompanied by pandering to foreign imperialist interests. Stroessner gave unwavering support to the United States, allowed Brazilian farmers to become the most powerful groups in Paraguay's east, and converted the country into a subsidizer of Brazil's energy consumption through an unequal treaty for the joint-owned Itaipú Hydroelectric Plant.[201] As an enormous part of the population was forced into exile, the labor movement was effectively reduced to a tool of the dictatorship.[202]

This formula has continued since the 1989 coup, with Colorado governments still using the same worn nationalist narratives while granting land and power to Brazilian farmers and transnational capital that have turned the country's east into a "green ocean" of soybean fields for export on international markets.[203] While soy growers enjoy the benefits of extremely low taxes, the environmental destruction has been incalculable. Only 7 percent of the Atlantic Forest, which dominated eastern Paraguay until recent decades, remains.[204] Simultaneously, cattle ranching continues to drive some of the world's fastest deforestation and endangers Indigenous people living in voluntary isolation in the Chaco region of western Paraguay.[205]

With the waning of the fearsome yerba mate companies attacked by Barrett—yerba mate is produced today almost exclusively as a cultivated crop—soy is the latest extractivist industry to bring widespread misery and suffering to rural campesino and Indigenous communities. The use of dangerous agricultural chemicals on genetically modified soy crops poisons nearby settlements, forcing families from their homes and into the exile of urban poverty belts in Paraguay and abroad. As economist Luis Rojas writes: "The yerba became soy, and the campesinos became unnecessary; moreover, a hindrance for 'modernity.'"[206]

Just as Barrett himself observed and experienced, the justice system continues to be used by the powerful to protect themselves while criminalizing all opposition, including those rural people who struggle for land ownership. Despite having special legal protection on paper, the twenty Indigenous peoples that inhabit Paraguay continue to be society's most marginalized groups. They are frequently blocked from accessing their ancestral territories and endure poverty rates far higher than those of the general population.[207]

While Indigenous and campesino communities struggle to access land, post-dictatorship politicians have followed the example of Stroessner and the leaders of the era after the War of the Triple Alliance by continuing to appropriate enormous amounts of state-owned lots for their own ends. During the Stroessner dictatorship, more than seventeen million acres—16.6 percent of Paraguay's total area—were stolen by those close to the regime through fraudulent use of an agrarian reform.[208] These practices have contributed to the country's status as having one of the most unequal distributions of land ownership in the world.[209] As Barrett observed over a hundred years ago, the monopolization of the common resources of nature is still at the heart of Paraguayan woes.

Paraguay has also come under the shadow of another violent, extractivist industry. Drug production and trafficking, which was consolidated by key actors of the Stroessner dictatorship,[210] has reached new heights as notorious Brazilian gangs have pushed fiercely into Paraguay over recent years. The country is the Western Hemisphere's biggest producer of marijuana and has become a major cocaine trafficking route. The gangs have brought terrifying levels of violence to the country's northeast, and their ever-deeper infiltration on the political system—labeled "narcopolitics"—has contributed to Paraguay's recording the fourth-highest level of criminality in the world on the 2023 Global Organized Crime Index.[211]

Amid endemic instability, insecurity, and discrimination, many Paraguayans make enormous efforts to preserve the cultural expressions that Barrett observed, recorded, and valued. Ancestral legends and knowledge of nature remain strong, especially in Indigenous communities, and long-stigmatized Guarani continues to be the country's most spoken language.[212]

Barrett has remained a legendary talisman of resistance for the Paraguayan left. During the only break in Colorado rule, the 2008 electoral victory of progressive former bishop Fernando Lugo, the Spaniard was featured in the president's inaugural speech:

> "We would like Rafael Barret with his 'Paraguayan Sorrow' and Augusto Roa Bastos with his 'island surrounded by land' to rest in the certainty of a legacy that has been redeemed," declared Lugo amid hopes of a new era.[213]

Tragically, Lugo's government, and aspirations for lasting change, would be truncated. A "parliamentary coup," in the form of a rushed impeachment, was unleashed by Colorados and Liberals in 2012 after a massacre took place between police and campesinos struggling for access to land.[214] Subsequently, Horacio Cartes, an enormously wealthy businessman linked to cigarette smuggling and money laundering by official reports, won the 2013 presidential elections for the Colorado Party, inaugurating a period of even sharper neoliberal privatizations and submission to foreign powers.[215] Cartes famously incentivized Brazilian businessmen to "use and abuse Paraguay."[216]

The 2023 elections saw yet another victory by the Colorado elites under Cartes's protégé, Santiago Peña. The new government is already acting to further deepen neocolonial and authoritarian dynamics while holding the three branches of the state in a vise grip: the executive has received greater powers to rule by decree,[217] the legislative has witnessed the arbitrary expulsion of a highly voted opposition senator,[218] and the judicial branch displays an incapacity to investigate numerous serious accusations made against powerful figures, such as Cartes, who is now president of the Colorado Party.

In this context of strong adversity, Rafael Barrett's message feels evermore pressing and relevant. Perhaps it is for this reason that his work has experienced a strong resurgence since the turn of the millennium, with a sharp increase in the number of scholarly publications in Paraguay, Latin America, and farther afield. In addition, Barrett's critical realism continues to be felt in the writing of Paraguayans like Damián Cabrera, who explores the social impact of the capitalist extractivism in the soybean fields of eastern Paraguay.[219]

Efforts are being made in his adopted homeland to bring Barrett into schools, to organize conferences on his work, to provide information on places related to his life, and to produce more editions of his texts.[220] A film about his life is being recorded by students in Yabebyry, where the remote wooden house in which he found shelter still stands. Excellent books, including two novels based on his life, have been published in recent years, and a mural emphasizing his brave attacks on the yerba mate companies now adorns an Asunción bookstore.[221]

His descendants are still to be found around the capital and near Yabebyry, as well as in the other South American countries that marked his existence—Uruguay, Argentina, and Brazil—and other countries in the Western Hemisphere. For around fifteen years, numerous members of the family, both inside and outside Paraguay, have been involved in running the Rafael Barrett Foundation website, where they look to provide information about their forebear.[222]

These extensive reminders of the life and work of Rafael Barrett continue to represent a hope for a long-awaited end to Paraguayan sorrow. His faded portrait, produced as part of the Lugo government's 2011 celebrations of the bicentenary of Paraguayan independence, hangs in the Literaity Cultural Center in Asunción, a community-run space that provides a forum for some of the nation's current generation of critical minds. It was under the gaze of the poster that much of the work on this translation took place.

Translating Barrett

There has been little published in English on Rafael Barrett. Whispers of his work and activism did find their way into English-language workers' papers toward the end of his life,[223] and a book by a British resident in Asunción even recorded Barrett's brave actions during the 1908 uprising.[224] However, with the exception of a moderate rise in academic mentions in recent decades, references have been largely rare. A London-based publishing house named the Rafael Barrett Press briefly appeared in the late seventies and early eighties, but its publications were not directly linked to Barrett's work.[225]

English-language translations of excerpts of Barrett's work are scattered on websites and in compilations of Paraguayan and Latin American texts. However, no English translations of his books have been published. Unfortunately, there appear to have been only two publications of any of his works in languages other than Spanish: a 1979 Italian version[226] and a 2012 Portuguese version[227] of *The Truth of the Yerba Mate Forests*.

The motivation for this project was born of my own work as a freelance journalist in Paraguay. I had referenced *The Truth of the Yerba Mate Forests* in an article for a British newspaper about a campesino association producing agroecological yerba mate in the heart of what was formerly the extractivist enclave of businessman Domingo Barthe—nemesis of Barrett's contemporary, journalist Julián Bouvier—in southern Paraguay. It is a courageous project by the families in an area that is now sadly dominated by soybean planting.[228] After a friend read the article, he asked me to point him in the direction of an English-language version of Barrett's work: no such translations of his valuable texts were to be found.

The translation has represented a challenge. I have tried to transmit the powerful content of Barrett's work while also hoping to preserve some of the enormous literary value that is a constant in his writing. At times I have made the decision to tame some of his rather anarchic use of commas. Terms in Guarani have been updated to reflect current spelling conventions, as these had not been standardized at the time Barrett wrote.[229]

Barrett's use of language and some views that I do not condone—such as the assertion of racial hierarchies—have been translated faithfully to provide a more complete picture of his character and work, and to reflect the historical period in which he lived. Dates of the individual texts—where available—have been taken from the 2011 Germinal-Arandurã edition of Barrett's complete works unless otherwise stated. All notes are mine.

As mentioned, all texts, including those of *The Truth of the Yerba Mate Forests*, appear under the sole title of *Paraguayan Sorrow*, in accordance with Barrett's original plan for his book. As there is no record of where Barrett placed the articles of *The Truth of the Yerba Mate Forests* in his manuscript, they appear here at the end of the collection.

Many thanks to Michael Yates, Martin Paddio, Rebecca Manski, and Erin Clermont at Monthly Review Press for giving this project a home and for all their support, and to the numerous friends and colleagues in Paraguay and elsewhere who have generously shared their knowledge and enthusiasm. My gratitude to Rafael Barrett Viedma, Rafael Barrett's grandson, and Bolívar Garcete Barrett, his great-grandson, for their generous help, and to Cecilia Ibáñez for allowing the use of her late husband Alberto Barrett Viedma's drawing of his grandfather on this book's front cover. Special thanks are due to my parents—always—and to my partner Lis García for her guidance and companionship in exploring her country's past, present, and future.

May Rafael Barrett's work continue to serve as an inspiration for struggles against all forms of oppression in Paraguay, Latin America, and around the world, as his call to action reaches new readers:

> My friend: let us set our sights high, let us not allow our pen to tremble nor waver. May nothing stop us in our march toward supreme justice.[230]

PARAGUAYAN SORROW

I have picked out the articles relating to Paraguay from my literary work of recent years and have brought them together here. The reader must therefore tolerate the shortcomings typical of such compilations.

It is only fair to mention the discrete collaboration of my wife at the front of the book; her subtle spirit brings joy to some of these pages.

—RAFAEL BARRETT, 1909

The Market

Under a sun that evaporates hues and shades from the intensely green grassland, the women, wrapped in sheets that flap in the wind, look like a flock of white birds that never quite land. But their bodies, upright or huddled over, are still. With a noble, prophetic gesture, they keep the light out of their black eyes, rulers of the plain. Next to their dark-skinned feet, which caress the ground when they run, there are modest, necessary things: lukewarm eggs, soft *chipa*[1] that is used as bread and dessert, milk, manioc, maize, golden oranges, and watermelons that are as cool as a fountain in the shade. Barely a word is spoken. No one offers their products, haggles, or argues. A melancholy dignity in the figures and movements. The girls have serious gazes and the reflection of a bygone time on their bare brows. Later, they will give up their swaying waists of barefooted females, their dark breasts, and brown mouths to poncho-wearing men, with the same silent gesture....

---

1. Hispanicization of the Guarani word "chipa." The stress falls on the second syllable in Guarani, whereas the first is emphasized in Paraguayan Spanish. A dense and chewy savory bread that is traditionally made from manioc flour, fresh cheese, eggs, lard, milk, and aniseed.

Women That Pass By

They are barely women yet. . . . The habit of going barefoot, with Rebekah's jug atop their heads, has given them a wild and flexible way of walking that sways their young bodies; springtime branches on which the divine fruits of their breasts tremble. Almost as intelligent as hands, the naked, dexterous feet of the girls caress the hot earth. They make a mockery of our obscene civilized feet, whose toes—weak, diseased, calloused, warped, glued one to the other, the toes of a mummy—flaunt the grotesque ugliness of impotence. Miserable, shiny hooves! The village women carry no contradictions in their flesh nor in their simple, hardy souls.

They pass by with the faint gentleness of a sigh. Their large black eyes gaze upon you wide-open, candidly, and carefully. They are serious, perhaps solemn. They come from the impenetrable past and are permeated by truth. Graceful and passive, they are the terrible sex in which we are born and depleted, sacred like the earth; they are the love to which our thirsty lips and our weary souls bow.

Corner of the Jungle

The immeasurable, contorted foundations emerge from the earth in the disarray of a paralyzed desperation. The trunks, like thick naked roots, multiply their limbs, eager to grab, to snare, to strangle. Life here is a motionless and terrible labyrinth; the infinite vines descend from the vast foliage to envelop and squeeze and choke the gigantic trunks. A mournful vapor rises from the ground drenched with acrid sap, trapped humidity, and all-consuming rot. Under the vault of somber vegetation, glacial, cave-like hollows open, in which the vague horror of twilight allows a glimpse of death lying in ambush. Only the odd flower in the air, suspended in the void like a wondrous insect, smiles frivolously with the innocence of its rosy calyxes.

On the Ranch

This is true nature, the august wilderness.[2] In the places I have been in Paraguay so far, it seemed to me that the terrain and vegetation wanted to draw in, to surround and imitate man, to keep him company among his modest crops, in his small and sedentary life, offering him slender horizons, lazy undulations, views cut short by impenetrable gardens rather than virgin forests, thin and slow-moving waters, homogenous and even tones, narrow landscapes of familial and almost domestic tranquility, of the faint melancholy of an old abandoned orchard. Here, things do not remember us, they do not see us: endless plains of buffalo grass, crisscrossed by treacherous marshes; forests that place a harsh, dark bar on the limits of visibility; masses of weeds complicit with the jaguar and the viper; danger and majesty. Not even fate itself reconciles us with this definitive solitude. There is nothing human around us. Anthropoids, backbone of our strange species, might never have emerged from the mysterious unbeing to which so many other species returned when their time came, and these plains would maintain their infinite rhythm in identical fashion, and these woodlands would exhale the same wild breath in the gloomy intimacy of their depths. Immensity holds us prisoner. "No," says the sky, broadened by the earth; "No," says the tree that raises its eternal limbs over the sinister thickets; "No," repeat the immobile vultures, death's spies. To come to lock yourself away in everlasting confinement, with such imposing witnesses, to face such a grand and fatal spectacle every day, till the last of our meagre days, you must carry another grand negation in your soul: a relentless hate, or a fierce contempt, or an awful calm, or a granite resignation.

How I sympathize with you, coarse servants of my host, sullen cowherds! The skin on your hands is weather-beaten like the leather of your drovers' catapults; you are cast in rough clay, like that which your

---

2. This article was written at the Laguna Porã ranch near the small town of Yabebyry in southern Paraguay. The property belonged to Dr. Alejandro Audibert, Barrett's brother-in-law. Barrett would later spend a year in hiding at the ranch when he was smuggled back into Paraguay after being deported.

untiring feet tread; the lines of your sallow faces contain the impassiveness of these arid fields. Your silhouettes do not disturb the secret harmony of the environment, and your craft is the only one that does not defile it. You return the bulls, captured and driven to madness for senseless amusement by other generations, to their wild homeland, and you allow them to roam over a domain stretching leagues and leagues on their slow, powerful hooves. You watch over the silent herds: riches that distant people weigh up and put a price on. Here, they are figures of truth and beauty. You make the untamed heads, with the robust glory of their horns, rise to attention over high, wild faces, and prompt the watchful, magnificent mirrors of the beasts' eyes to light up. You fill the somber paradise with the only inhabitants that are worthy of it.

The hidden rustic deities accept your numb sorrow. The hope in your hearts has been extinguished, as has the curiosity in your minds, and you adjust to the wasteland, to the desperate bareness of your shacks and your instincts. For mistrust, fear, and inert submission weigh on your flesh. For you carry the weight of the memory of the nameless disaster. For you have been conceived in wombs shaken by horror and you wander stunned through the former theatre of history's most merciless war, the parricidal and extermination-bringing war, the war that did away with the males of an entire race and dragged the females barefoot along trails that were opened by horses, perhaps ignorant of your orphanhood and your grief; you live faded away in the shadow of terror.[3] You are the survivors of the catastrophe, the stray

---

3. Barrett refers to the War of the Triple Alliance (1864–1870) that saw Paraguay fight the combined forces of Brazil, Argentina, and Uruguay. The grueling conflict, which largely took place on Paraguayan soil, saw the country devastated, with best estimates placing the death toll at around half of the prewar population, including an enormous proportion of the male population. The lone nation's defeat was sealed by the death of Marshal Francisco Solano López, Paraguayan president, at Cerro Corá in northern Paraguay on March 1, 1870. After the war, Paraguay was occupied by Brazilian troops for six years and governments that favored the interests of the allied victors took power. An enormous amount of state-owned land was sold off to foreign companies, effectively excluding Paraguay's rural population from land ownership and intensifying poverty.

specters of the night after the battle. What can a mere thirty years do to heal wounds like these? You follow your fate, sullen cowherds. Around you, flowers have covered the graves; no one can endanger the earth's formidable fertility; iron and fire itself fertilize it; there are no acts of murder for the earth. For that reason, in its indestructible vitality, the earth that received the bones of the useless heroes is not to deny its austere peace to the children of the tragedy.

Who will try to heal, to console those that lost everything: faith in work; the serene poetry of the home; the ardent, tender poetry that chooses, dreams, and sings? Who will comfort those that have still not broken down in grief and anger? Who has enough perseverance to combat the ominous ghosts, enough pity and respect when touching the bleeding roots of the disease, enough patience to wake up the dumbfounded minds, enough gentleness to win over the ill creatures? University students with your plans for regeneration, rhetoricians of sacrifice, leave that central hive and spread yourselves over the humble corners of your country, not to suck the nectar from the naïve calyxes, but to distribute the honey of your fraternity. Continue to thrive, generous talented youths; become honest schoolteachers, humble village priests. Attend to simple everyday tasks and, in the transparent evenings, when they are on their way back from the fields, speak into the ears of your brothers that suffer, that suffer so much, that know not that they suffer! But if you have no love within you, stay in the hive and busy yourselves with politics. Your participation would be the last and worst of plagues. Did I mention politics? I had forgotten—apologies!— I had forgotten about politics. I had forgotten about that blessed subject matter, the poultice of *official newspapers*, the oratorical bandage. I had forgotten about the parliamentary pharmacopoeia. We have taken steps forward regarding religion: from many gods, we are down to one, and we are on the way from one to zero. Our earthly power has made progress in the opposite direction: we have gone from the tyrant to the gang. The tyrant, whether bad or good, represented God; we should not imagine that the gang represents some mischievous and carefree Olympus. It represents the people; yes, sullen cowherds, there are a few frivolous men that represent you. Perhaps you do not believe it;

perhaps God has never believed himself to be represented by Juana the Mad[4] or Charles the Fat.[5] God has not yet come down from the heights to explain himself, nor have you, patient people, risen from the depths to explain yourselves. You would like to understand what happens in the chambers of government, but the administrative mechanism is so wonderful, so complicated, that the eloquent speeches reach your backs transformed into the foreman's whip. And you, arduously, shrug your shoulders ...

Enough. This is *too human* for this imperious and solemn panorama. I am not bucolic and naïve: I know that elegant plants steal air and light from one another; that svelte stems twist to strangle each other; that it is not for the sake of aesthetics that the swallow adorns space with the graceful curves of its flight, but to devour invisible prey. I know that beauty and vigorous strength are born of rotten carcasses. And I feel, however, that a sublime certainty arises from the healthy cruelties of nature that is absent from the fanatical and callous cruelties of men.

[*El Diario*, June 1, 1907]

Passing Through

Fleeting visions of the journey. . . .[6] Underneath the piers of the capital, at midday; hammocks fastened to the dark posts, men in ponchos laughing, women with clothes unbuttoned and dark skin, untiring little

---

4. Juana I (1479–1555), known as Juana the Mad, was queen of the Kingdoms of Castile and Aragon on the Iberian Peninsula. She was declared insane during her reign, although the truth of this is debated.
5. Charles III (839–888), known as Charles the Fat, was a Frankish king who oversaw the disintegration of the Carolingian empire. Often considered incompetent as a ruler.
6. The five texts grouped under the title "Passing Through" were written around the time that Barrett traveled to the town of Arroyos y Esteros, approximately forty miles from Asunción, in early 1907. He conducted land surveys while staying at the house of the priest Fidel Maíz, his wife's uncle. Maíz had played an important part in national events in the nineteenth century, including a notorious role in the bloody trials implemented by Marshal López against suspected plotters during the War of the Triple Alliance.

ones, a loud and disparate crowd, eating watermelons, enjoying the cool, wet shade. Over there the sun, making the sand glisten, the violent colors of the hulls and the rigging, of the red earth and the green field, a luminous, hectic mosaic, a far-off fluttering of indistinct flags. Here, the gloomy water that shudders, the roaring laughter, a parrot that lets out its emerald cry, the dozing rowboats . . .

Now the wheels of the steamer rhythmically churn the river. The sky seems to me enormous and freshly washed. The rivers are an immensely pure, lustrous, translucent slate gray. Thoughts do not collide with bedroom walls, nor with the walls of the street, covered in dirty paint. Ideas can go along with one's gaze. The soul does not feel like a prisoner of civilization. I am overcome by a vast pleasure as I reflect that the wide current heads down to the ocean with the same sovereign impassiveness as if man had never existed, and that the forests huddled on the banks were not planted by our hands. The breeze caresses my brow, a balanced, constant breeze; we set off; I hear the tormented breathing of the cylinders. Beneath my feet there is a small hellhole, a group of half-naked wretches, smeared with grease and sweat, working in an atmosphere that would suffocate me. It is them, and not the machine, that propel me without touching me, they that give me this delicious breeze and this landscape that passes by smoothly and this sensation of freedom. On the prow, curled over a chain that he grasps in his bronze fingers, I see one of the slaves. I see his round head, the fleece of his African hair, the biceps that rowed in the galleys of the Catholic kings, the short nape, a true pillar, suitable for the yoke. The slave sings, his gaze finds me, and a look of scorn and sinister happiness rises like a wave of blood to his leathery face.

Evening. We silently tear into the trembling liquid muslin. Twilight falters along the riverbank. A *mbigua*,[7] knife with wings, cleaves the air horizontally. Night descends from the sky until it meets the night that rises from the bottom of the Earth. The stars awaken one by one; their reflections pulsate under the bow wave like pale flames. The mass of

---

7. Guarani, *mbigua*. A bird of the shag/cormorant family. *Phalacrocorax brasilianus*.

the American bushland pours a dismal blackness onto the trembling mirror. Black waters, of a gleaming and oily black, of a lugubrious and concave black, whose mysterious bank is reached by the ripples of our wake, drawing from it a sumptuous and ominous metallic black reflection. Black waters, concealers of snakes and drowned souls with stones around their necks. And that blackness penetrates me, hinting to me at its coldness from beyond the grave. And behold, death once again taps me on the shoulder with its finger, and whispers its familiar, horrible words into my ear. A specter's sigh faintly stirs the air, and it seems to me that the entirety of nature is suffering the anguish of a nameless nightmare.

*

I was on the verge of hunting a jaguar. My hair stands on end when I remember. There were five of us men, armed to the teeth. I thought that my Winchester's nine bullets were far from enough. As afternoon fell, we reached the domains of the beast: the curved, low bank of the Manduvirá.[8] A beach of white, firm sand, where the horses' hooves sank noiselessly. A hundred meters away, the impenetrable forest, a layer of undergrowth and squat trees whose naked roots, polished by flood waters, twisted, intertwining like the bones of a buried army that has been unearthed. The secretive, frozen shadows of those unexplorable hiding places stood out against the paleness of the ground over which we slowly trod. A mournful solitude and silence. Not the buzz of an insect nor the cry of a bird. We marched with our eyes on the ground, combing for possible tracks. Suddenly, F. stops and shows us fresh, deep prints, which seemed enormous; there were the animal's paws, the claws had stabbed out the shape of a fan. We are shaken by a shiver, we fall silent and, at last, L. cries out:

"It's just the dogs!"

Yes: they were our dogs' tracks. We sigh gladly and continue onward.

---

8. The Manduvirá River passes near the town of Arroyos y Esteros—whose name literally means "streams and marshes"—on its way to the Paraguay River, of which it is a tributary.

We delve between clumps of vegetation, skirting the thicket. Nothing. A fieldhand gets off his horse and gestures to us. Stop. Our hearts almost leap out of our mouths. The fieldhand stalks, readies his shotgun, crouches down, slinks like a wildcat. We do not breathe, fingers on triggers. The man of nature sees what we do not see and hears what we do not hear; he steals forward; only he perceives the phosphorescent pupils of the feline; only he *knows*. But what? The man of nature returns to his saddle, uttering words I do not understand.

"What is it?" I ask L.

"Not much. A duck that idiot wanted to shoot."

The journey back. A cloudscape imagined by fairies. The magnificent night, gilding the edge of its cape in the sun's dying flame. The endless marshland. Palm trees rise straight and cylindrical across the landscape, distant from one another, spreading out their still hands in the air. The pale reeds form an immense sea in which we immerse ourselves up to the waist; the horses almost disappear. They beat their legs against the invisible bottom, flooded by the recent rains. One would not believe that they are walking, but rather swimming, and that the menacing abyss lies below us. There is no moon. The towering stars ignite their thousand damp lights, and around us, the smitten insects ignite theirs. A great untiring voice, a great prayer, a great vague moan goes up to the sky: all the voices and groans and sighs of life. The toad lets loose its mysterious whistle, a warning that I do not understand, perhaps beckoning me into the darkness where horrible things are conceived. The whistle is falling behind, and then suddenly it rings out at my side. The world becomes liquid, all outlines meld together. I can no longer make out my companions. I am completely alone in infinity; I feel myself being absorbed by the forces and instincts of impenetrable reality. I want to lean back in the soft sea of reeds, touch the cool mud where the toads whistle and, like a centaur overwhelmed by fatigue, fall into the longest and stillest of slumbers.

*

The sun. The air burns like an invisible flame. Between the scorched earth and the dry, thirsty brambles, insects swarm. All is white: an unrelenting white of molten metal. The temperature is so excessive that it can hardly be felt. Bewilderment, the feeling that we are twice as heavy, that we are sinking into a bonfire that does not consume us because we are perhaps no more than ashes. Impossible to think. The intangible breath of the furnace pushes us along as we walk. The sun: we are inside the sun.

We reach a wide well, flooded with a liquid the color of spoiled milk. Water! We will live. An old woman washes her rags by the well. Her face is black, her hands too. Coal. She does not even look at us; but we cry to her, and she gives us a can from which we drink with closed eyes, deliciously. On one of the can's rounds, it appears with an agile green and red ribbon that twists and swims and forms bright rings that hug the brim. It is the most venomous of vipers, the smallest and most graceful: the *ñandurie*,[9] for whose bite there is no cure. Its elegant little head rises and freezes for a moment, like an agate with gold enamel. Its forked tongue, as fine as a butterfly's antennae, quickly jolts out. A lightweight gem of creation, made doubly beautiful by its power for death. We contemplate the reptile without daring to breathe . . .

And suddenly, Celé—the most sullen and ugly of our fieldhands, the one with the rough, stiff face, the one with the deep eye-sockets cast in shadow by wild eyebrows, the one with the glaucous, unequal gaze—draws near with his stride of a numb servant and, stretching out his callused fingers, grabs the viper with an indifferent, confident gesture. Our shudder of horror before the suicidal man who squeezes the trigger. . . . And the delicate snake coils around the callused fingers, and the elegant, deadly little head reclines lovingly on the servant's flesh . . . and Celé, in a dull, slow, even voice, murmurs:

"It doesn't bite. . . . When I can't see it, I'm afraid. . . . When I can see it, I'm not afraid. . . ."

Celé has stowed his *ñandurie* under his wide-brimmed hat and we continue on with the white-hot march under the beating sun.

---

9. Guarani, more commonly "*ñandurire*." A small snake that is widely believed to be highly venomous. However, the fear surrounding the reptile is unjustified; the *ñandurie* is not venomous and poses no threat to humans. *Dipsus turgida*.

*

Evening dance, on a ranch. A smoking lantern has been hung from one of the thick posts that hold up the straw roof. On the grass, women seated with bottles of rum in front of them and the burning stub of a candle. I enter the barely lit room, where couples appear and whirl around like ghosts; outside, under the trees, raucous, uncouth music that pierces the ear and the heart. Naked feet rub against the earth, and two heads pressed together, two breasts embedded in one other, parade for instants under the glow of the meagre light, and then submerge themselves once more in the shadows. The female, flattened against the male's chest, seems to be asleep; the man shows his bronze face, covered with a gloomy severity; the sweat flows down his metallic hair in large drops. Face of executed Christ. A beardless youth passes, lock of hair behind his ear, slouch hat cocked, and fan in his closed fist. His glassy pupils gleam, and his lips curl into a vile smile. He has taken a gaunt, monkey-featured harpy prisoner; her sparse hair, greased with oil, sticks to her scalp. And then a colossal old man comes forward, head-on. His poncho stops me from seeing the person hidden among its long, frayed edges. Later I can make her out, leaning into the pirate's broad arms. Her narrow, pure brow shines in the shadows; gentle brightness, rocked by the human swell. At times, the swell turns her toward me, and I admire her innocent eyes, her immaculate mouth amid the nauseating stench of the bodies in heat. And she later reappears and reappears like a celestial vision, and I lose her, and I find her, and she departs forever into the unforeseeable wave of the dance. The light-colored hair goes, the white blouse goes, clasped halfway down by a hairy paw.

Half an hour more and it will be night. The countryside in front of me rises slightly; a distant undulation draws out a long blue brushstroke under the dark belt of the sky. All is fading into darkness. The green of the flat, succulent vegetation displays its thousand immobile, shadowed silhouettes. Now the wall of dense cloud cracks, and a winding line of fire—radiance of the hidden sunset—crosses the broad horizon. The hard-working, meek little settlement of Carobení[10] lies underneath the vague darkness. But above, high above in the fantastic sky, silver flashes suddenly shine. The *moiré* of white luminous silk pulsates in space. The air carries the sweetness of milk. It is the moon, the smooth, pale aurora of the moon, the reverie that rises over the humble fatigue of the concluded workday. I hear a guitar being shakily tuned near me. In the nocturnal calm, poetry visits the hearts of men.

A male voice, free of Italian vanity, of loud, theatrical complacency. That voice cannot hear itself. It is a pantheistic voice. A twang that gets lost among the scraped strings, a rhythmic sigh. Two monotonous keys. The unchanging cycle of wave and undertow. The sound of tired wind, of poor water. The garbled sounds of miserable, rustic life.

And the murmur speaks, it explains, it laughs in slow, mournful guffaws. Jokes that a lament transforms into solemn chants. One folksong is soldered onto the next; love and death and mockery let loose their endless litany to the unchanging strumming of the guitar. Stubborn sadness is the solution launched into the impassive sky, where the same old stars reign.

The aridity and obstinance of the groan seem inescapable: destiny? How much resignation there is in that drowsy muttering! The words shudder through comic episodes with a spasm of harsh irony. Women: quick and fierce desire, another spasm. And the continual backdrop of all this is the threat of the knife, the glory of the knife. Souls are the color of blood.

The chaste light that transfigures the atmosphere is of no use, nor is the warm rest in which the animals slumber, in which the inexhaustible earth prepares the fertility of a new day. The peace in which our thoughts are reconciled with necessity, in which we accept pain and strengthen our embattled hopes, is of no use: the moan of the guitar repeats the eternal poem of blood...

*

---

10. Carobení is a village near the city of Villarrica. It is said to be named after its first settler, Carlos Benítez.

I have wasted no time in Villarrica.[11] I have met Bernardo. He cannot bring himself to say his last name "because it's too ugly." Does he himself know what it is? He works in the quebracho forests, on ranches, if he wants to and how he wants to, when he needs money, which is something that almost never happens to him. He is twenty years old. He spent three years, when he was very young, in the yerba mate forests.[12] His employer gave him rotten donkey and mare meat to eat for the price of gold. The unfortunate youth withstood the rheumatism and the fevers. He did not smoke, he did not drink; by virtue of sobriety and orderliness, he was able to settle his account and flee. Bernardo is one of the few slaves that have not left their bones in the Paraná. Since then, he has crossed Paraguay in all directions, guitar on his back and a song in his mouth. They call him crazy. He takes happiness and freedom with him everywhere he goes.

He has small, black, luminous eyes; they must call him crazy because he looks at you face-to-face with intense exuberance. Strong teeth, packed together like a barricade; long and mobile lips; lean cheeks; wild hair. A gorilla's thorax and long legs. Vest and bandanna around his neck (nothing political), baggy pants. Constant movement. One might say that he is continually ready to take off into the air.

He speaks in a loud voice, with incredible roaring laughter. His larynx, with its extensive register, contains a world of howls, of melodies, of muffled murmurs, the music of the virgin forest. He is incapable

---

11. Villarrica, city in the center of Paraguay's eastern region, eighty miles from Asunción.
12. The Paraguayan government sold off vast extensions of land to foreign companies in the decades after the War of the Triple Alliance. In Paraguay's east, these companies were mainly interested in the *yerbales*, native forests containing yerba mate trees. The prized yerba mate leaf, which is used to make a popular infusion, was harvested through horrendous exploitation of workers. Barrett provides a resounding exploration of the debt slavery perpetrated in the yerba mate forests in his series of articles *The Truth of the Yerba Mate Forests*, which is included in *Paraguayan Sorrow*. In the country's western Chaco region, the companies sought the wood of the native quebracho tree. The extremely hard tree, whose name is derived from the Spanish *"quiebrahacha"* (axe-breaker), was valued for its high tannin content.

of distinguishing between masters and servants, between those that flaunt suit jackets and those that wear sagging ponchos. To him—an extraordinary thing—everyone looks alike. He treats everyone the same. He speaks to us with his hat on and plants his noble mitt on our shoulders, plastered in the red earth of Guairá.

He goes into houses and ranches; he calmly takes a seat. He laughs at the indignant faces, he disarms with his naïve jokes, he plays music and sings and charms with his primitive, penetrating art. Children adore him. Women . . . ? They too are children. As soon as he arrives in a town, Bernardo is the love letter of the girls in courtship, and the lover or boyfriend of the unattached ones. Whether his own or someone else's. He parades love, a tolerant and calm love, without concerns or jealousy, a love that plays and escapes like a bird, and a poetry that is changeable and exhilarating like the wind travels in his guitar. Bernardo is a Lohengrin[13] without tragedy, a good omen crossing the sky. And languid young women go to chat with him in the semi-darkness of kitchens and patios.

Bernardo knows nothing of his parents. Overflowing with boisterous fraternity, he does not yet plan to have children. The image of an abandoned rural girl in rags, among her little ones, dirty and wan, horrifies him.

He will make his nest later, when he is no longer so "crazy." At present, he still feels "new." Bernardo does not suspect that he will always be "new," that he will never grow old!

This uncouth man is ahead of his time. He practices no notion of property. He eats and dresses without thinking. He takes what is necessary for his simple existence, and he takes it without concealing it, smiling just like Robinson on his island. A rancher was shamefully exploiting Bernardo. Bernardo, fed up, got on the establishment's best

---

13. *Lohengrin* is an 1848 opera by German composer Richard Wagner. It tells the story of a knight who appears mysteriously to defend a noblewoman. The knight then marries her on the condition that she promises never to ask him his name nor where he is from. When she breaks her promise, he leaves, and she dies broken hearted.

horse, and *shot off*. It was the only way to save himself. When he thought he was safe, he threw the saddle into some scrubland and set the animal loose. Months later, he bumps into the owner, who threatens him with jail. Bernardo immediately accepts because "he'd never been there." They send him to the police, where he becomes an intimate friend of the chief, of the sergeant, of the officers, due to his unshakable cheerfulness, due to the deep humanity that radiates from his head held high. And he leaves them, inconsolable at his absence, after a few weeks.

Bernardo's soul has not been stained by anger, nor by greed, nor by lust, nor by fear. The stars and the fleeting goodness of men are reflected purely in it. Soul of a *madman* . . . soul of a poet.

Bernardo has told me of his plan to visit Asunción.

[*Los Sucesos*, December 27, 1906,
and January 2, 15, 21, 1907]

Guarani

For some, Guarani is backwardness.[14] They blame it for hindering the functioning of the mind and for the difficulty that the masses seem to find in adapting to European ways of working. The commonly used argument is that every language has a corresponding mentality, that is, a mentality that is defined and rendered by that language. And, as Guarani is radically different from Spanish and other Aryan languages—not only regarding its lexicon, which would not be of such grave importance, but in the very structure of its words and sentences—the work of civilization must necessarily come up against serious obstacles in Paraguay. The obvious remedy follows: wipe out Guarani. They hope that by attacking speech, the mind will be modified. They hope that by teaching the population a European grammar, it will be Europeanized.

---

14. Paraguayan Guarani is a language descended from the languages of the Indigenous Guarani peoples of the region. To this day, it is Paraguay's most spoken language and the only native language in the Americas to be spoken by the majority of a national population, including by non-Indigenous sectors. At the time that Barrett wrote, Guarani was even more widely used, and, in contrast, Spanish was far less used than it is today.

It is indisputable that Guarani is different from Spanish in its essence. It is a primitive language, in which abstract concepts are scarce, in which the logical structure reached by cultured tongues does not yet reveal itself. Guarani shows its primordial nature through its confusion, its lavish richness, its diversity of expressions and meanings, the complicated disorder in which terms—almost always born from a naïve imitation of natural phenomena—are bound together. "Far from beginning with simplicity," says Renan, "the human spirit, in reality, begins with complexity and obscurity."[15] Closely related to the mysterious inextricability of nature, Guarani varies from one place to another, forming dialects within a dialect, which in turn is one of the innumerable dialects of central South America. Undoubtedly, nothing could be more different from Spanish, a full-grown adult child of universal Latin.

This is all fact, but it is not an argument. In Europe itself we see that it is not bilingual districts that are the most backward ones. And it should not be believed that the second language used in such districts, the one that is common and domestic, is always a variant of the other national, official language. Vizcaya, a region where they speak a language as distant from Spanish as Guarani, is a prosperous and happy province. Something similar occurs in the French Pyrenees, in Brittany, in the Celtic regions of England. And if we look at regions where a dialect of the new national language is in common use, we learn a lesson about the tenacity with which language endures in the face of outside influences, however easy it may seem for it to be absorbed into the bosom of another more powerful and related language. Catalonia is a good example of this, as is Provence, whose luminous tongue has been regenerated and effectively reseeded by the great Mistral.[16]

History shows us that bilingualism is not the exception, but rather the rule. There tends to be a common, textured, irregular language, apt

---

15. Ernest Renan (1823–1892), French philosopher and theologian.
16. The mistral is a strong north-westerly wind that blows along the Rhône Valley into the Mediterranean. *Mistral* means "masterly" in the Provençal dialect of the Occitan language.

for the emotional outpourings of a people, and another language that is reasoned, refined, artificial, apt for diplomatic, scientific, and literary expressions. Two tongues, whether related or not; one plebeian, the other enlightened; one specific, the other extensive; one disordered and free, the other ordered and rhetorical. There has been almost no age or country in which this has not been the case.

It is poor understanding of the human brain to assert that it can find two languages incompatible. Contrary to what the enemies of Guarani assume, I deem the simultaneous use of both languages gives the mind additional strength and flexibility. They view two things as opposites that perhaps complement one another. Who could doubt that Spanish is more applicable to the relations of modern culture, which, by its nature, is impersonal, general, dialectical? But is Guarani not more applicable to the individual aesthetic and religious relations of *this race* and *this land*? Undoubtedly so, too. Lovers, children who babble to their mothers for the first time, will continue to use Guarani and will do so just fine.

The economy and the division of labor are invoked. Well, through these things Guarani will be preserved and Spanish will be adopted: each for what it is useful. Necessity itself, desire, and the greater or lesser benefit to contemporary life, will determine the future law of transformation and redistribution of Guarani. As for directing this process through the *Official Gazette*: this is a dream of politicians who have never been concerned with philology. It is as feasible to use a decree to modify a language as it is to use one to transform the very faces of the population.

[*Rojo y Azul*, November 3, 1907]

The Poetry of Stones

Is there anything further from a spirit than a stone? Everything in this world is spirit, as all peoples that have appeared on the face of the Earth have recognized through the prophetic power of their being. Therefore, we must ask ourselves what indescribable pain turned light into dullness, weightlessness into heaviness, and subtle movement into dismal immobility. What accursed criminal lies in the pebble that rolls beneath our indifferent foot? What doomed race plasters its despair onto the vast rocks that break up the mountain like badly buried bones? Victor Hugo dared to name certain dark ridges after individuals who have dishonored history. Novalis,[17] who is more tender-hearted, sees statues in the crags. "Only in these sculptures, which we have left from bygone times of human beauty," he says, "are the deep spirit and unique understanding of the mineral world revealed. And in their presence, the thoughtful beholder feels himself enveloped in a rocky crust that seems to form inwardly. The sublime turns things to stone, which is why we are not permitted to be surprised at the sublimity of Nature nor at its effects, nor to be ignorant of where sublimity is to be found. Might Nature not have turned to stone at the sight of the face of God, or because of the terror that it felt on the arrival of men?"

Paraguayan campesinos,[18] heirs to many Guarani beliefs, understand the sadness of stones. They rarely associate them with good omens. Perhaps because they are unfamiliar with transparent gems, which are less captive to doom, since the variable and nuanced light of day can visit their solid breasts. Practically no pebble represents a joyful secret. Metals, glasses and crystals and mirrors gleam because of human ingenuity; the dark designs of their earliest origins are wiped from them. Dull minerals, as they are in their raw state, barely offer up a smile to Paraguayan innocence.

However, just as the inorganic substance that forms in the entrails of some fish, and floats in the sea when they expel it,[19] represents a wel-

---

17. Georg Philipp Friedrich Freiherr von Hardenberg (1772–1801), whose pen name was Novalis, was a German poet and writer. He was an early member of the German Romantic movement.

18. The closest English translation of the Spanish *campesino* is probably "peasant," in the sense of a small-scale, subsistence farmer. However, *campesino* is largely free of the strong negative and disparaging connotation of the English word "peasant."

19. Barrett may be referring to ambergris, a waxy substance that accumulates in the digestive tract of sperm whales before being expelled. Ambergris has been highly valued by many cultures for uses such as in the production of perfumes.

come sign for certain European populations, here legend foretells great fortune for those who seize the tiny stone watched over by the magical *kavure'i*,[20] the small bird of the night and of destiny. Some claim that the little stone is inside the bird's head, just as the famous diamond of tradition is found in the head of the boreal toad. Others claim that it is at the bottom of its nest. The *kavure'i* holds other mysterious powers, to which I will turn my attention when I address the poetry of wings. In general, however, the enigmas of stones are melancholy. "Do not gather stones: they bring misery," is the counsel of popular wisdom. "Do not sit on stones, or you will become lazy." I perceive in this sighing phrase a confession of tropical indolence, of the dense snares that tie man to the ground and paralyze his energy. Stones belong to dreams devoid of fantasy and to death. Around the anonymous little crosses that are dotted here and there in the solitude of the fields, you will find piles of small stones; they are offerings to the deity of the graves. Instead of the broad tombstones on which the wealthy etch a vain inscription, rustic piety constructs a rough burial mound in which the scattered humility of stones plays a role. Stones, roaming corpses, meditate endlessly in a funereal manner and are the faithful companions of oblivion.

A strange myth exists in the heart of Tasmania. Beyond the grave, souls wander an infinite and desolate grassland in search of eternal peace or eternal grief. Salvation depends not on a god that judges the actions of earthly lives, but rather on the most undecipherable of all gods: chance. There are two stones on the fateful plain, one white and the other black. He who comes across the first reaches paradise, and he who comes across the second falls into inescapable hell. Tiny white stone, hidden in the *kavure'i*'s nest, take pity on the naïve nostalgia of a stricken people and clothe their desolation in visions of the impossible!

[*Rojo y Azul*, February 23, 1908]

---

20. Guarani, *kavure'i*. A small owl widespread over the American continent. *Glaucidium brasilianum*.

Gathering Herbs

By living in the company of plants, campesinos have been able to uproot some of their secrets. The plant world seems so different from the animal world that, to explain the presence of such strange beings on our planet, the curious hypothesis of stellar germs brought by meteorites or rocks from the heavens was invented. However, the ingenuousness of nations has allowed for the discovery of some relations, both practical and symbolic, between man and Earth's most humble organisms.

All our illnesses have their remedies in the herbs of the countryside. This truth that is not accepted by medicine, set as it is on resorting to chemistry and bacteriology, is known by Paraguayans who have not been contaminated by civilization. The simple heart of shamans, healers, and madmen is needed to recognize the natural medicines that grow in open meadows or in the mystery of jungles. They see what we do not, that which our intelligence hides from us, according to Anatole France's remarkable phrase.[21] Both purity and faith are required for the remedy to work. He who is saved is not he who wants to be saved, but he who deserves to be; nothing is as venerable as this harmony between justice and science. Let he who has no faith go to the doctors.

There are innumerable species that are suitable for primitive and complete therapeutics. I have neither the knowledge nor the time to mention or classify them. I will gather herbs in this herbarium, I will glean their poetry. It moves us to discover that white carnations cure the heart, jasmine the eyes, and that the Paraguayan rose heals wounds. Flowers that cure us, on top of captivating us and prompting us to dream, are the holiest of flowers; they resemble those pretty sisters of charity, whose pure white wings are rustled by the wind. It is delightful to think that there are petals that protect us.

Even the dew itself, when it settles on certain privileged leaves,

---

21. Jacques Anatole Thibault (1844–1924), whose pseudonym was Anatole France, was a French poet, novelist, and journalist. He won the 1921 Nobel Prize in Literature. Barrett displayed his great admiration for France in many of his texts.

soothes and beautifies us. Accordingly, girls are well aware that to avoid freckles and to bring tenderness to their faces, they must get up while it is still night and gather the chaste dew that trembles on the *kapi'ipe*.[22]

And what to say of morality, which is much more important and real than the physical realm? There are poisonous and medicinal plants; there are those that are dire omens and those that are joyful signs. There are those that revive the flesh; there are those that encourage passions and gladden the spirit. Rue in your home will give rise to good fortune, but you must pick the small flowers on St. John's Eve, and this is not possible for everyone. Condemned souls will do all they can to hinder you from the nocturnal shadows; they may groan at you and scare you, they will pull at your clothes and put out the lights. In contrast, chinaberry brings misery and grief, weeping willow death and ruin, and as for basil, it will undoubtedly bring pretentious folk to your home who will give rise to compromising situations. Fear the coconut palm: it attracts lightning. Young women should not harbor its aroma, or they will never marry.

Ka'avo tory[23] favors love and is much sought after. Girls carry it at their breast without saying a word. If you are not to the liking of nature's malicious temperament, this little herb will become invisible in the countryside. Even as you yearn to find it, you will step on it without realizing. *Toro ka'a*[24] will win over your desired man: you must—oh, sweet virgins!—kneel before the plant, clean it and caress it. It does not hurt to pray an Our Father to it, as long as you do not make the sign of the cross. If you wish to free yourselves from the poison of jealousy, braid the *toro ka'a*, and if the following day you find the herb unbraided by the ardent horn of a bull, you can be at ease.

---

22. Guarani, *kapi'ipe*. Name given to several species of grass, including Bermuda grass.
23. Guarani, *ka'avo tory*. The name means "plant of happiness": "*ka'avo*" (plant) and "*tory*" (happiness). Flowering plant with medicinal properties. *Hypericum Connatum*.
24. Guarani, *toro ka'a* literally means "bull plant": from Spanish "*toro*" (bull) and Guarani "*ka'a*" (plant). This medicinal, aromatic plant is also used to treat heatstroke and is sought after by cattle. *Pterocaulon polystachyum*.

Mate[25] reigns as the sovereign of most ancient lineage over this subtle trade between plants and the human population. Almost all wild medicines are absorbed through mate. People fall in love, kill, and bewitch through mate. A gesture, dust, a strand of hair, are enough for things beyond repair. And from the depths of the Chaco, where a tentacle of humanity sinks into the Sphinx's breast, come fateful concoctions.[26] If your brain suddenly boils and maggots erupt from your nose, or if you are overcome by another equally monstrous illness, remember which white hand, trembling with hatred, offered you mate. All the evil and good of history is in mate: communion of lips and fantasies, fetish of a race, dark husk, hollow geode in which the ages sleep, unextinguishable radiance, heat of blood passed between generations from one palm to the next. Mate has heard everything, it has foretold everything: terrible secrets, hopes forever dashed, dark oaths. Put your ear up against it and you will perceive the thousand hazy voices of the immense past, like the murmurs of the sea in an old shell.

[*Rojo y Azul*, March 1, 1908]

---

25. Mate is a drink prepared from the leaf of the yerba mate tree, which is native to Paraguay. A quantity of the toasted and milled leaf is placed in a gourd or other suitable recipient called the *guampa*. Hot water is gradually poured over the leaf and drunk through a metal straw that has an attached filter (*bombilla*). The drink is highly social, with a single *guampa* and *bombilla* passed between drinkers. In Paraguay, an extremely broad array of plants and herbs valued for their flavor and medicinal properties are added to the infusion. Mate is drunk in other countries of South America's Southern Cone. An ice-cold version of the drink, *tereré*, is very popular in present-day Paraguay.
26. The Paraguayan Chaco forms part of the Gran Chaco ecoregion, which stretches across parts of Brazil, Bolivia, and Argentina. The ecoregion is divided into subregions with conditions varying from humid to extremely arid. Today, the Paraguayan Chaco accounts for 61 percent of the country's territory; however, it is inhabited by less than 2 percent of the population. In Barrett's day, it was predominantly populated by the Indigenous Peoples who have inhabited the region for thousands of years. Paraguay's border with Bolivia in the Chaco was firmly set only after the bloody Chaco War (1932–35) between the two nations.

Beast-Oracles

Small, strange beings; small monsters that trot, buzz, flee, claw, fly, look, or scratch. They hold symbolic meaning connected to grand designs. They effectively preside over fortune, and pensive gazes follow them to their hiding places.

Butterflies, flying petals, bode no ill. They are joyful messengers, like dragonflies, whose marvelous glosses shine in the sun. Oh, divine dragonflies that make love in the air! "No gesture of higher amorous beauty can be imagined," says Gourmont,[27] "than that of the female slowly curving her blue body halfway toward her lover, which, upright on his back legs, bears the entire weight of the movement with tensed muscles. One might say that, in this fashion, the spectacle is immaterial and pure, two ideas that come together in the clarity of a necessary thought." The butterflies made of impalpable silk and dragonflies adorned with subtle diamonds are fleeting smiles of nature. As they pass by, they promise us good fortune.

But wasps hide a venomous sting, and even if the black ones limit themselves to announcing the mysterious arrival of a forgotten, distant traveler, the yellow ones signify death. The beetle, sacred in other places, does not have the slightest influence in Paraguay; no one pays attention to it. If you find a cicada at home, laugh and sing along with it; it is the bearer of happy news.

The ant is as wise as the cicada is carefree. The ant is alchemist, architect, warrior, and necromancer. The ant understands Guarani. I do not dare claim this is true of all species of ants, but there is no doubt

---

27. Remy de Gourmont (1858–1915), French poet and novelist. Author of *Physique de l'Amour* (1903; *The Natural Philosophy of Love*), an essay on the sexual instincts of animals.

about *guaikuru* ants:[28] those that are fierce par excellence, those that devour their companions. If, on crossing the forest, you find a cordon of *guaikuru* ants and you have the hapless idea of saying to them, "Adio, áğa pyhare tapejumi che visitávo," or rather, "Hello, come pay me a little visit tonight," do not threat, they will make you jump from your bed and will leave your home devastated by a great invasion. So, if you speak to them in Guarani, be careful.

Irritating, innumerable, and funereal cockroaches may not understand human languages, but if you make use of some interesting subterfuge, you can succeed in convincing them that they should go away. Write the word *cockroach* on a piece of paper and throw it out onto the street. As soon as a passerby picks it up, the cockroaches will emigrate en masse from your dwelling to the fool's.

Who would suspect that the viper intuits pregnancy and even shows respect for it? A woman who is met by a snake in the countryside is pregnant with a boy. The reptile will be very careful not to attack her.

It gives me great satisfaction to find out that the agile lizard foretells happiness, just as frogs and toads do when they are very young. This restoration of the reputation of little toads, which are so amusing with their rears pinned to the ground and their small heads raised and motionless, is incredibly just. Little frogs are even more childlike and shy. And when toads and frogs, in the wet shadows of rainy twilights, play their sonorous guitars with desperate lyricism, is when we appreciate the treasure of their aching, romantic souls. The *jakare*,[29] despite its infernally cheerless appearance, has no legend. How might this be explained? South America, according to the beliefs of geologists, is one of the oldest of the land masses that today rise from the

---

28. *Guaikuru ant*, a very aggressive ant that tends to attack other species of ants. *Ecyton crassicorne*. "Guaikuru" was also used as a derogatory term to describe a group of Indigenous Peoples from the Chaco region, such as the Toba-Qom, who remained unsubmitted by the Spanish Empire. They carried out raids on colonial Paraguay and were feared by the Europeans and the Guarani Peoples. They were known as incredibly strong warriors.

29. Guarani, *jakare*. A species of caiman endemic to Paraguay, Argentina, Brazil, and Bolivia. *Caiman yacare*.

sea and during the Jurassic Age represented one-third of the colossal Antarctic continent. Our *jakares* are the grandparents of the crocodiles that came to dominate the fantasies of roaming tribes in Africa. In Madagascar today, native morality and civilization are still impregnated with the sinister spirit of the great saurians. "In the case of the crocodile," narrate the Leblond brothers,[30] "indigenous people submit to the strength, and basically the tyranny, of ugliness. Its ugliness has wounded them, and they copy it in their gestures of terror, and they sing of it in semi-comical ritornellos composed to be shouted out when crossing infested rivers. They admire this ugliness in the same way that the Annamese[31] worship the tiger; some families feel great honor in being descended from the crocodile. Male and female shamans boast of living alongside it in the reed beds, having managed to patiently tame it, perhaps making it eat a certain root that tightens its jaws...."

The only thing whispered about the *jakare* is that it corrects its own fecundity by slaughtering a portion of its offspring. The father *jakare* condemns those of its young that do not know how to swim. To do this, he throws a small stick into the water and forces them to play with it. He watches them for a while and gulps down the clumsy ones. Through this trait, we get a glimpse of the sinister ingenuity that was born of the abyss.

There is nothing more suitable than wings for bearing omens. Where could good or bad news come from with greater speed and mystery than through the air? A bird crossing the sky resembles a thought. It is a swift symbol of the present that passes by infused with the future. Nocturnal birds, of cruel and velvety flight, of demented eyes ringed by somber dark circles, are an awful portent on the other side of the Atlantic. Here, owls are free from bad repute. However, the *guyra*

---

30. Marius and Ary Leblond were the respective pen names of Georges Athénas (1877–1953) and Aimé Merlo (1880–1958). The two historians, art critics, and journalists were cousins from the French colony of Réunion.
31. *Annamese* is a term that was formerly widely used in the West to refer to people from Vietnam. Offensive.

jagua[32] does have that reputation, and a funereal reputation it is. Its short and strange cry—*kua!*—means "pit," "grave." It foretells death. The *karāu*[33] is a sign of strife. Its appearance is sorrowful. Its story noteworthy. It was once a good-looking young man. One day when the young man was parading himself at a dance, he was told that his mother was near death. "There's time to laugh, but not to cry," he replied, and continued enjoying himself. When he returned home, his mother had died, and since then the *karāu* is the image of melancholy and cries endlessly. Pigeons bring misery. The *chahā*[34] stands as a faithful sentinel, like classical geese. The hen makes its hatred known when it fights with one of its companions, and, if it forgets its own sex to the point of imitating the crow of the rooster, announces misfortune. The peacock produces dislike and upset; girls that keep the magnificent feathers of Juno's friend as decorations in their bedrooms do not marry easily. Such a belief is a sign of Paraguayan discretion, contrary to all false pomposity. The *pitogue*[35] has three different ways of singing: one foretells a visitor, another a wedding, and the third reveals that the woman that hears it is pregnant. The hummingbird, prodigious and tiny, is a bearer of happiness; children themselves show mercy to this aerial concentration of frenetic life and pulsating grace. To kill a hummingbird, to attack the bird on whose vivid description Michelet[36] exhausted his talent, is to risk a tempest destroying the home of the guilty party. The place where the hummingbird hangs its nest is blessed by the Virgin.

---

32. Guarani, *guyra jagua*. Literally "dog bird": "*guyra*" (bird) and "*jagua*" (dog). A mythical, monstrous bird. See León Cadogan, *Mil apellidos guaraníes: Aporte para el estudio de la onomástica paraguaya* (Asunción: Toledo, 1960), 38, 48.
33. Guarani, *karāu*. Limpkin, a large wading bird broadly distributed across the American continent. Mainly feeds on aquatic snails. *Aramus guarauna*.
34. Guarani, *chahā*. Southern screamer, a waterfowl species that is one of the largest birds in southern South America. *Chauna torquata*.
35. Guarani, *pitogue*. Literally means "muffled whistle": from Spanish "*pito*" (whistle) and Guarani "*gue*" (muffled). Great kiskadee, a bird of the tyrant flycatcher family that is widespread across the American continent. *Pitangus sulphuratus*.
36. Jules Michelet (1798–1874), French historian and writer. His 1856 book *The Bird* includes descriptions of hummingbirds.

Just as swallows drew the barbs of the tragic crown from the temples of the crucified one, hummingbirds drew sharper and longer thorns from the heart of the mother of Jesus. But the *kavure'i* is the jewel in the collection. It brings health, abundance and, above all, love. Even old women of dubious conduct guarantee themselves generous gallants if they stuff the bird's head and keep hold of it. The *kavure'i* has its *paje*:[37] it is a black fly that comes to see it every Friday at three o'clock in the afternoon. If the fly perishes, its master goes along with it.

Hunting a fox is a serious undertaking. The fox is wise, and its power extensive. Be afraid of its dirty tricks. It may be the one hunting you. It has struck up alliances with malevolent spirits in the forest. Its yowl prophesies disasters, like the pitiful howl of the dog that sniffs its own death. They say that the devil appears to the dog, and that if you smear your forehead with the canine's drool and look through its legs, you will discover the demon himself in the distance. There is a shaved, dark-colored little dog with ridiculous gray hairs on the back of its head and tail; they call it *peloncho*.[38] People suffering from bad moods are cured by sleeping with it. The poor animal absorbs the illness with resignation. The billy goat is terrible. The hairs of its beard, mixed with tobacco, produce endless flatulence when smoked. The nanny goat is a creature of Satan, who is almost always mounted on a white horse when he reveals himself to mortals.

This is the only detail I do not quite understand.

[*Rojo y Azul*, April 5, 1908]

Dreams

If life is a dream, dreaming is also life and a hidden spring from which sad, superstitious souls drink. Dreams, the children of weariness and the night, images of death, may hold secrets similar to those that death

---

37. Guarani, *paje*. Enchantment used to benefit or harm the person targeted.
38. "*Peloncho*" is a moniker derived from the Spanish "*pelo*" (hair). An approximate translation is "baldy."

conceals. When the bitter lyre of the disagreeable Quevedo[39] touches on this matter, it finally gives out sweet, deep tones. The common view is that dreams speak to us of what most worried us during the day. However, what worries us is not always what is most important to us, and if we believe certain refined minds, dreaming resurrects neglected thoughts. Thus, Dechartre,[40] France's impassioned character, says: "At night we see the unfortunate remains of things we have overlooked in waking hours. Dreams tend to be the revenge of disregarded things, the reproach of abandoned beings. Hence their unpredictability and their occasional melancholy." Whether or not we accept theories on the nervous system from the likes of Räbl-Rückard[41] and Cajal[42] to explain this, we cannot deny—with no need for sleepwalking or *mediums*—that dreams put us in contact with new realities. It is enough to look at the example of diseased organs whose pains *are dreamed before* they are experienced in regular consciousness. This phenomenon is the first symptom of some injuries to the organism's internal, non-sensitive parts. Porphyry[43] observes that, to a degree, we use notions from dreams to reason while awake, but we only gain awareness and perception of these notions through dreams themselves. He draws a notable conclusion: "Through intelligence we can say something about the principle that is higher than intelligence. However, our intuition of this principle is much better through the absence of thought than through

---

39. Francisco Gómez de Quevedo y Villegas (1580–1645) was a celebrated baroque writer and poet of the Spanish Golden Age, a period of phenomenal activity in the Spanish arts from 1492 to around 1659.
40. Philippe Dechartre is a character in Anatole France's 1894 novel *The Red Lily*.
41. Hermann Rabl-Rückhard (1839–1905) was a Prussian neuroanatomist who theorized that the nervous system is changeable, positing that neurons could develop new connections within the brain.
42. Santiago Ramón y Cajal (1852–1934) was a Spanish doctor and scientist credited with starting modern neurobiology. He developed the "neuron doctrine," positing that each of the brain's neurons are physically separate and communicate with each other across synapses. He was joint recipient of the Nobel Prize in Physiology or Medicine in 1906.
43. Porphyry (234?–305?) was a Neoplatonic philosopher born in Roman-ruled Tyre (modern-day Lebanon).

thought." Here is the metaphysical justification for religious ecstasy, which is also a dream.

Let us not ask high mysticism of primitive peoples; let us look sympathetically at the interpretations that Paraguayan campesinos have of their dreams. It is not surprising that dreaming of flowers represents good luck; going up stairs, honors; cats, betrayal; horned animals, unhappiness; blood, crime. An oft-used analogy has it that dreaming about blond people heralds money. If white ghosts appear, death; if bulls, a lover; if pretty children, friendliness; if watermelons, pregnancy. The analogy is poetic in the case of broken eggs, which symbolize misfortune, and deliciously sweet in the case of contemplation of the moon, because it is a sign that a lover remembers their loves affectionately. A violent contrast means that lice and garbage represent prosperity. A woman who dreams of any green fruit can soon expect a pregnancy. An odd illustration of the races: dreaming about black people indicates illness; about mulattos, silver; about Indians, happiness. Carts warn of unwelcome news. Why must we fear dying if our teeth fall out in dreams? And why, if snakes appear to a girl, will she have suitors? And why does meat bring mourning, and the female sex a lucky star? A mystery! But the following, in this long-suffering country, is self-evident: dreaming about parrots means legal disputes, and about jaguars or pumas means a visit from the authorities.

[*Rojo y Azul*, April 12, 1908]

Familiar Devilry

If you do not want to remember what you dreamed about, run your hand across your forehead when you wake up. Afterward, you get dressed and leave the house. Do you trip on the doorstep? Your wife or your girlfriend is cheating on you. Do you tangle up your words when you speak? Someone is thinking of you.

Thinking of you for a good reason or for a bad one? That all depends on your ears. If it is your left ear that buzzes or turns red, they are thinking of you for a good reason. It works the other way around for the upper eyelids: if your left one trembles, misfortune will ensue; if your right one does, good luck will.

The devil tends to play dirty tricks on us. For example, we unexpectedly bump our heads on the furniture, or our spoon warps and we spill our soup. It is the devil that has *swindled* us. He is in the habit of arriving on those vertical whirlwinds that suck up dry leaves and at the sight of which women take fright and shut the windows. The *kusuvi*[44] sometimes snatches up clothing, thick branches, and even children.

Does the middle of your hand itch? Money! Turn your palm in the direction of where there might be some, and you will do wonderfully.

Common illnesses lend themselves to a thousand interpretations. The evil eye—or *ojeharu*—is well known. Hair can fall out if hostile fingers touch it. Do not let a pregnant woman comb your hair: it is a dangerous business. And, speaking of pregnant women: if they ask you for something to eat, go without eating yourself to satisfy their hunger. A likely miscarriage would be the transcendental punishment for your lack of compassion.

When an ulcer appears on the tip of someone's tongue—*kũpía*—the sufferer should try to get another person to say the word; that way they will pass on their ailment and be free of it. Styes are a *widow's disease*. Someone who frequently suffers from styes will marry a widower. There is only one way of curing them: put your arm behind the back of your head and rub your eye with your middle finger while saying the names of seven widows. Sneezing is a fabled complaint that was originally cured by exclaiming: *Jesús!*[45] Today, a discreet *Jesús!* still goes along with every sneeze. A needle suddenly breaks without us knowing why. It is a cold draft that was destined to make us ill. A benevolent spirit saved us.

Home remedies generally consist of three plant species; seven seeds are taken from each one. The numbers three and seven are indestructible residues of an old magic formula.

If the house is swept at night, mother will soon die.

---

44. Guarani, *kusuvi*. Whirlwind.
45. In Spain—though not in present-day Paraguay—the word *Jesús* is exclaimed in response to a sneeze. It is the equivalent of "Bless you!" in English.

On Good Friday there is no killing and no hitting. Even animals are shown respect. But unfinished business is paid for on Easter Sunday, with compound interest.

[*Rojo y Azul*, April 19, 1908]

Burials

Here, the word *burial* does not mean the action of burying but rather the thing that is buried. It refers to things that would be worth digging up. It is a matter of provisional graves, destined to be violated. They are corpses that must be brought back to the light and to life.

Resurrecting the dead of the flesh would not be practical. Heirs would be very sure not to revive the remains of their lamented relatives. But to say "Arise Lazarus!" to ounces of gold, to broad old silver coins, and to solidly crafted cutlery, and to chiseled jewels is a tempting dream. Riches do not die, they do not pass on, even if they are given a grave, as so many terrified Paraguayans did at the time of the bloody dictatorships and the war. Those lordly families, condemned to leave their homes in haste to follow behind the army in a pitiful procession, hid their treasures under their bedroom floors, or at the foot of the trees out there in the middle of the countryside. And the treasures wait, buried and more alive than ever. They are the obsession of indolent, gambling souls, eager for free opulence, for prosperity snatched from destiny in one fell swoop. To discover a burial! Aspiration, hope of many spirits, scrutinizers of mysteries. A national lottery in which everyone takes part to a greater or lesser extent: some in all seriousness, others with a smile on their face.[46] And grass grows on top of the

---

46. To this day in Paraguay there is a strong belief in the existence of *plata yvyguy*, a term meaning "buried treasure" that comes from the Spanish "*plata*" (wealth) and Guarani "*yvyguy*" (below the ground). As Barrett mentions, the treasures are largely believed to have been buried by Paraguayan families fleeing their homes amid the devastation of the War of the Triple Alliance.

fortunes, and the aged walls are lids of chests.[47] The ground is a trunk whose keyhole has been lost. Why sow it, plough it, and work on it if the harvests already lie reaped and solid in its breast? And men search and listen, and probe in the mud, and keep watch in the night.

Because the souls of the old owners return to the place where they hid their worldly goods. Whether dead or not, we are irresistibly attracted to money. The ghosts want to put their gold, which sleeps underground, into circulation; when the riches have been unearthed, a small part tends to be set aside for masses in honor of the proprietor. Oh, souls striving to leave purgatory! Oh, metal striving to leave the grave! All their strength draws upward, demanding freedom. It you are not asleep at the hour when the stars shine at their highest and purest, you will hear a strange and extremely subtle murmur. It is not the insect gnawing, it is not the palm's stiff leaves rustling, jostled by the breeze. It is something else. Human sigh, groan plucked from the silence. The door gently swings in the darkness. Someone has come in; it is the one who lived here half a century back. See how confidently he crosses the rooms. He does not trip; he does not misstep. Silent and resolved, the invisible ghost reaches the garden. Then the sad clanking of the well's chain is heard. Is the mournful ghost thirsty? Or is his lost possession at the bottom of the well, and the shadowy hands, clasped around the damp iron, still want to feel, to caress the immortal gold, symbol of earthly delights? Do not get out of bed now. No matter how quickly you move, you will not see anything, you will not notice anything. Ghosts leave no trace. You will find the doors closed, the well in order. The ghost may have had a drink, but not even a drop of water glistens on the parapet in the moonlight. Lie down and rest. If you have the instincts of a merchant and are perseverant in your desires, if you are used to drawing the final conclusions from a line of thought, if, in short, you are shrewd, dry out the well, dig . . .

Who knows! Perhaps you will be the gold's liberator!

---

47. This phrase appears as *"tapas de cobre"* (copper lids) in Spanish editions of *Paraguayan Sorrow*. However, this may be a misprint of *"tapas de cofre"* (chest lids), an interpretation I have opted to use here.

Paraguay has many scattered mines, in which the metal is already refined and even minted. The ghosts are in on the secret. They point out the exact spot at which the vein begins. Pay attention to them; if you do not listen to them, they will persevere. If you do not free them from their anguish, they will set up shop in your life, they will tap you on the shoulder, they will haunt you in your nightmares, you will feel eyeless gazes go through your skull and, if you continue to be insensitive to their pain, they will take bodily form and will visit you by day. So do not abandon your home in terror, do not be needlessly skeptical, and allow yourself to become rich, like so many others whose names we will not mention and who are known to everyone.

The Pombero

Pombero,[48] in other words, spy. He is the child of the night, the untiring prowler, consumed by a terrible curiosity. What is he looking for? What does he lay claim to? Some treasure lost by his grandparents? Some fantastical vision, distorted in his murky mind?

Prudish souls imagine that he uses *paje* to make himself invisible, to go through keyholes and caress sleeping virgins with impunity. But this is a mistake: the Pombero's power does not go that far. He flees through the brambles at the speed of a hare; dogs cannot catch him, and when he reaches the thickets of the forest, no one can track him. The nocturnal shadows and the strength of his legs allow him to live in hiding. He is not invisible: several people have seen him.

He is small, robust, coppery. He walks on two legs and runs on four. His feet are hairy, and he treads silently. His rough and messy mop of hair falls over his sparkling eyes, full of shyness and malice. He is naked. Were it not for his intelligent gaze, he would be believed an animal, the animal most like man.

When the sun goes down, he leaves the hideaways of the forest and

---

48. The *Pombero* is an imp-like figure from Guarani mythology that continues to be widely referenced in present-day Paraguay, especially in rural areas. He is also known in Guarani as "*Karai pyhare*" (Lord of the Night).

crawls, dreamy and hideous, friend of the toads and the stars, toward the lights of the white people, toward the dangerous windows by which he slowly rises onto his tiptoes to look at the marvelous, hostile spectacle of our civilization. Hidden there, he is suddenly struck by the diabolical idea of frightening, unsettling the powerful invaders that obsess him and among whom, protected by the fraternal trees, he survives by means of desperate cunning. He twists his dark lips and, at the risk of being caught, lets out a vague whistle, whisper, groan, gurgle. He imitates the birds, insects, and reptiles with unprecedented perfection. If he is not heard, he repeats his murmur, louder and louder, until he sees through the glass that the women go quiet and listen scared and stutter out his name. Then, shaken by fear and joy, he opens his large mouth in a long, silent cackle ...

If you irritate him, and make an enemy of him, he will devastate your garden and your vegetable patch, he will steal your chickens, he will unbar your corral so that your cattle scatter, and he will untie your horses so that they go astray. But you will succeed in attracting the Pombero's kindness if you place in his path that Brazilian chewing tobacco that so delights him. He also likes eggs. Make sure not to offend him. He will reciprocate by giving you gifts of fruits, strange flowers, and pelts of beautiful beasts. If you travel by night and dismount, do not worry about your horse. The Pombero will take care of it faithfully.

His constant thought, the true motive for his mysterious expeditions, is to tread in the footsteps of pregnant women, to lie in wait for births.... The Pombero's ever-present dream, his supreme project, is to steal a newborn white child and make of him an invincible king for his tribe, a king that might take back the fecund plains and the magnificent rivers that fell into the hands of the irresistible pallid race. The white child raised among the wild undergrowth will grow up, will save the dispossessed meek; he will do justice, messiah of the blacks. But what the Pombero does not know, little wandering monster, ghost of his own ruins, is that the whites, deprived of their piece of nature, suffer as he does and, like him, await the promised messiah.

[*Rojo y Azul*, February 1908]

Magdalena

Ten or twelve years back, no song was as popular as "Magdalena." It was born in the slums of Asunción and quickly spread. It is a lovers' quarrel:

> *Oh! Magdalena*
> *Anive che quebranta*[49]

That "Oh!", small interrogative cry, resolves into a teasing cadence reminiscent of the ancient

> *Oh, oh, oh, Don José!*
> *How very early you rise!*[50]

of Castilian children.

A great number of *Magdalenas* were played at all musical occasions. The droll refrain spread rampantly by word of mouth, and a light breeze caressed the sorrowful garden of Indigenous souls. One night, as the musicians were leaving a party where they had repeated the famous folk tune a hundred times, they came across a tall woman in the middle of the road; she was dressed in mourning clothes, with her mantle covering her face. "What is it you want from me for you to call to me so much?" she asked them. "Leave me in peace."

And suddenly she disappeared.

Another evening, on passing the gully on Piribebuy Street, dangerous at that time because of the masked man who hid there to throw himself upon passersby and beat them to a pulp, some Magdalena-playing guitarists were stopped by the same woman.

"Magdalena! *¡Che ko! ¡Che ko! Mba'épa peikotevẽ cherehe*. (That's me! What do you need from me?)

The poor men backed away in fright. One of them, who was armed

---

49. Guarani, *"Anive che quebranta"* (Cause me no more dismay).
50. Spanish, *¡Ay, ay, ay, Don José! / ¡Cuánto madruga usté!*

and more daring, tried to confront the ghost, which immediately disappeared.

Fearful rumors started to go around, but the song was so lovely! It continued to be sung and danced to.

A short time later, as a group of cheerful youths were returning under the moon's glow from an enjoyable visit to the countryside, they found the way blocked by one of those coffins known here as *slabs*. They are simple planks on which the deceased lie covered with a cloth. The wind moved the cloth; the solitude and abandonment were deathly. The youths, who had many *Magdalenas* weighing on their consciences, took another path. After walking for barely half an hour, they once again made out the *slab* before them, and that night they did not sleep in their homes.

Finally, as several musicians were returning from the traditional festivities in Caacupé,[51] a striking young woman appeared to them.

"Play me 'Magdalena.' I do so like it," she said to them.

"We're tired of playing it all day."

"Don't refuse what I ask; I beg you!"

Her tempting lips pleaded with such guile that the youths agreed.

She began to dance. Her skirt fluttered voluptuously, and, in the swift twirl of the dance, a flounce fell to the ground. She took no notice; she danced with more haste, and her frenetic movements tore her clothes. Delirium seemed to take control of her. Her convulsive movements undressed her, and soon, before the eyes of the stunned musicians, a horrific skeleton remained.

That was too much. The number of visions were multiplying. From the pulpit, priests banned the sinister song inside and outside the capital. Few dare whisper it today. Why disturb the rest of the redeemed sinner? Let us show respect for her sleeping remorse. And let us heed the warnings sent from the mysterious place that awaits us all.

And so, the playful "Magdalena" disappeared from the errant and melancholy Paraguayan songbook.

---

51. A town approximately thirty miles to the east of Asunción.

A Ride on the Streetcar

It is the streetcar to Tacumbú,[52] the half-eleven one. Loaded with passengers, always the same ones, who scramble on to it from block to block. It has to go uphill for twenty blocks and can be heard from four blocks away. Its arrival is announced by multiple strange noises, the origin of which one later makes sense of. On reaching 25 de Diciembre Street,[53] it is moving so slowly that there is time, without hurrying, to get off, pay a brief visit to one of the surrounding houses, and catch up with it again.

There are more than thirty of us taking up seats, platforms, and steps. A formidable bulk pulled by three mules. But are those animals really mules? They are so small that the coachman must double over and lower his head to strike them. They cannot be seen from the tram. They look like rats. Scrawny, hairless rats that strain with meek desperation under the shouts and the blows.

The strange thing is that it is the shouts and not the blows that spur them on. They are indifferent to the beatings, so many have they taken in their miserable lives. Thus, the coachman, instead of unleashing his whip on their skinny backs, which produces no more than a muffled sound, prefers to discharge it on the roof of the vehicle and on the resonant tinplate of the platform. He uses these objects like drums, adding special rhythmic howls and somber whistles. The sum of all this is an atrocious music that must be heard to be understood. Without this continual flurry, the mules would halt definitively. However, they continually stop, exhausted, at death's door. The wretched coachman then pauses the orchestra and squeezes the break so as to not go back downhill to the port. Two or three minutes of puffing go by and, suddenly, the bellowing, screeches, thumps, stumbling, and clanking restart, and we move forward a few more meters.

---

52. A neighborhood in the west of Asunción.
53. Today, 25 de Diciembre (December 25) Street—presumably named in reference to Christmas Day—is called Chile Street. Barrett himself lived on this street for a time.

The coachman works as hard as the mules. When he feels faint, the overseer comes to stand in for him. Obliging children join us along the way, adding to the commotion. But it is all useless. We always get stuck on the bend in Amambay Street. It is the insurmountable *pons asinorum*[54]—everything at once: bend, hill, fatigue, and dejection! The fattest passengers get off. Others push the streetcar. Most continue their journey on foot. And, in the face of the dreadful spectacle, the same expressions reach my ears every day:

"They don't feed them . . ."

"And *they* don't get paid . . ."

And the mules and the coachmen and all of us resign ourselves to it, month after month and year after year.

Doctors

Several of the young men of our society have been knighted; the uniform title of doctor incorporates them into the country's aristocracy. This rank in the democratic nobility means that the bearer has authority to teach and the merit of knowledge. These things are more in keeping with the present age than military power, dominion over the land, and the trust of the prince, which are the respective origins of the duke, the marquis, and the count.

It is not enough to be the son—or to consider oneself the son—of a doctor to be a doctor. This is a great step forward of our times. Noble lineage must be relentlessly refreshed and improved, and each generation must renew its exploits. We have broken one of the chains of inheritance: we have made people a little bit freer, disentangling them from the past. The crown obtained by virtue of being born is humiliating. By earning honor through our own efforts, we bring logic into our lives, coherence that is indispensable for beautiful destinies. It is worth owing as little as possible, even if it is to your parents. To inherit is to

---

54. Latin, *pons asinorum*. A stumbling block. Literally "donkeys' bridge," as it is a test that separates out the "donkeys" from those that are capable of overcoming the challenge.

repeat, and what is strong is that which is new. It will be a joyful day when neither fortune nor poverty is inherited.

The brand-new doctors will notice that they have more credit at the market. They will immediately measure their social progress by the patience of their creditors—if they have them—or by the ease they have in acquiring them. Their increased economic power will allow them to weigh up precisely the practical importance of their profession. They will also observe that they have become more handsome since signing their theses. They will find themselves languidly contemplated by female eyes. Veiled declarations of love will reach them. They will feel a delicate hand tremble between theirs more often than a year earlier. And it is true love, not feigned love, that they will find in their path. For women are romantic and fall in love with diplomas in the same way that the chaste Desdemona fell in love with the adventures of Othello.

But promises must be kept; what is written on paper must be lived out; the interest aroused must be sustained and justified. Behind the doctor, the man must be built. They must, as of now, start studying.

[*Los Sucesos*, November 29, 1906]

Revolver

Seeing that everyone carries a revolver—or modified pistols with a range of a thousand meters, just in case—one cannot help but infer that we are under the constant threat of an extreme danger.

In the city center, in the middle of the day, elegant and chivalrous youths, mature men engaged in harmless professions, display the distinguished bulge of their Smith, their Mauser, or their Colt. These blameless individuals approach others with precautions befitting conspirators or bandits. Since it is hard to believe we are on the verge of a colossal conspiracy, it must be assumed that there is another reason for so much weaponry.

What do they fear? A sudden invasion? A quick and ferocious attack, demanding the heroism of every citizen? The countryside appears calm. I see only a remote possibility of risk from the Chaco.[55] I have tried to inquire discreetly about what is going on and have been met with vague responses. Something is being hidden from me.

I cannot accept the confusing justifications given by those that took the decision to explain themselves. They spoke to me of possible attacks by thieves or murderers, of the consequences that come from arguments, of unexpected incidents. Evasive explanations! The temperament of Asunción's well-mannered inhabitants is one of great calm and great straightforwardness. Have a look through the press of recent times. You will soon realize that revolvers do not tend to do their job unless they do it against the will of their owner. It would upset me to discover that residents of Asunción are thoughtless enough to use an old revolver—Buenos Aires-style—for fear of an unknown attack, without realizing that they are shattering this illusory safety, and even their real safety, through the continual probability of accidentally killing themselves or killing their neighbor. A new classification: reckless cowardice. Do we live in the wilderness? Is there not a surplus of lawyers and judges? Are the police not making their presence sufficiently felt?

No, it is something else. For a moment I considered an aesthetic explanation. I suspected that the *amateurs* of the revolver imagine themselves to be more attractive, braver, by going about better prepared and safer. Might they have a touch of the illustrious Tartarin of Tarascon about them?[56] He went to the clubhouse with an arsenal on him, even poisoned arrows, and heard footsteps of redskins and roars of jaguars in the tranquil evenings of Provence.

Oh! God forbid me from making fools of those who, sooner or later, must reveal the key to the enigma.

The key . . . ? We are back where we started. A public disaster that will suddenly occur when we least expect it and that obliges us to be armed, right? As a foreigner, they do not want to confide anything in

---

55. Asunción looks across the Paraguay River to the Chaco, which stretches out from the opposite bank.
56. The Tartarin of Tarascon is the protagonist of an 1872 novel of the same name by French author Alphonse Daudet.

me. They do well; but two years have gone by since I arrived here, and I am beginning to feel calmer, to see that they are exaggerating. What unsettles me more is the revolver, the stupid revolver that is aimed at Juan and hits Pedro, and sometimes, unfortunately, hits without being aimed at all.

[*Los Sucesos*, December 13, 1906]

An Intellectual

Doctor X is an intellectual. Twenty years ago, he suffered a decisive case of neurasthenia. Since being on the verge of being left an imbecile due to poorly disinfected abscesses, X discovered that he had talent and spread the word. Today he looks robust and ruddy. His big, round eyes gleam with contented health. Being a doctor, he has earned a lot of money and is terribly busy resting. He claims that the neurasthenia has left sinister traces within him and that it must be fully defeated. Thus, he busies himself with a hygienic and prolonged idleness. When one thinks of the works he could have written, one marvels: what a mind!

He has published three booklets in his lifetime, the longest one has as many as sixty-three pages, without counting the index of subject matters. They all have additional titles, dedications, prefaces and warnings, exhaustive, neat notes, and half-yard margins. The first is political, the second juridical, and the third historical. Each one is worth as much as the others. X is encyclopedic and, furthermore, a corresponding member of some foreign academies. X's wife sighs: "I adore the doctor. He's so scientific!"

Doctor X has himself sent all important books that appear in Europe. The language is irrelevant to him. Each week, Mihanovich's[57] wide steamboats carefully deposit heavy boxes full of printed materials on the dock. X shakes with excitement. He touches, checks, binds, and

---

57. Nicolás Mihanovich (1848–1929) was a Croatian shipowner whose fleet was of great importance for transport and shipping along the Paraná and Paraguay Rivers. These rivers link landlocked Paraguay to the River Plate, which flows into the Atlantic Ocean between Argentina and Uruguay.

catalogs. The library has already reached fifteen thousand volumes. Shame that no one reads them!

Go into Doctor X's office and you will feel yourself overwhelmed by the respect imposed by oratories of knowledge. Tall and gloomy shelves, up against the wall and draped with red curtains, keep the treasures of modern erudition intact. Luxurious objects quietly and disdainfully shine in the dimly lit room. Sitting at the wide, august table, which is conveniently covered in volumes and papers, Doctor X meditates. He has heard you; he generously pulls himself away from his reflections, he deigns to smile, he triggers your shyness with noble kindness. He seems to truly be someone.

Many people visit him because, in addition to the treatises on metaphysics and sociology, he gets sent an exquisite tea and an authentic cognac from *over there*. He has learned very well how he must receive a first-class intellectual, especially one who has two ranches and sumptuous furniture. He does not put a foot wrong for a second. It would seem that he has never done anything else.

Several things are surprising about him: his military figure with athletic shoulders and solid mustache. An excellent body for a laborer or a cavalry sergeant. The doctor stretches out his hand to you and you tremble, foreseeing the formidable squeeze. But there is none; the block of flesh sits inertly between your fingers; a piece of raw loin meat. Then, the slow, ceremonious gestures that pay deferential respect to one another. Then, the measured, well-mannered, even voice. He speaks slowly, keeping his sentences in balance over the ambiance. He understands that posterity is listening to him, and he does not want to go down in history with misprints.

One then wishes to pay attention to what he is saying. This is difficult, and it is more difficult to remember what he says. Does he say anything? Perhaps not. X's talk is a kind of solemn pantomime, with a muted accompaniment of pure luxury.

However, by digging through my memory, I manage to unearth certain examples of X's topics of conversation. I admire the conviction with which the Doctor resolves the most obscure matters. For him, the nineteenth century discovered the key to all enigmas. Büchner's materialism explains in one fell swoop the mysteries that tormented humanity for thousands of years.[58] X pities priests, spiritualists, those that still dream of an afterlife. Poor devils! Weakness of spirit. The Doctor also tends to recount, over long, impeccable, empty periods, the diverse works that he plans to write. At other times, he alludes to the important people who went to see him during the week. He never mentions their names explicitly; he surrounds them with shadows. Thus, he murmurs: "The day before yesterday, the secretary of the Directorate-General for Statistics was where you are now."[59] Or, if not, with even greater secrecy: "A person who played a transcendental role in the political events at the end of '89 came to consult me." As for what these gentlemen said ... absolute discretion.

On one occasion, on just one it is true, I saw Doctor X throw off that Goethean serenity so befitting of a superior soul. We were drinking the renowned tea. A dark-skinned, modest girl came toward us carrying the renowned cognac on a tray, flanked by diamond glasses. The little maid tripped, and the bottle and the glasses shattered. The Doctor, suddenly forgetting who he was, stood up and swung his boor's hand at the frightened girl's dark little face. I contemplated the five blood-stained nails of his mitt and understood that X has not only intelligence within him, but also natural emotions. He is a well-rounded intellectual.

[*EL DIARIO*, OCTOBER 22, 1907]

JURIES

Is there anything more contrary to reason than juries and universal suffrage? Fortunately, suffrage is a farce. Put into practice to the letter, it would have taken us back to a state of barbarity in very little time.

---

58. Ludwig Büchner (1824–1899) was a German philosopher who was one of the leading figures of scientific materialism. His influential 1855 book *Force and Matter* presented a purely physical view of the universe that rejected God and religion.

59. Barrett himself worked in the state Statistics Office for a short period in 1905. At that time, his friend Modesto Guggiari, a liberal intellectual who had also participated in the 1904 revolution, was secretary.

Blessed electoral corruption! It keeps the ignorant from governing the state and stops us from being crushed by strength in numbers, which is the most beastly strength of all. The people deserve our pity and our greatest sacrifices because their pains are enormous and are not the result of the harshness of nature, but of the evil of men. As such, rather than put a dunce cap on their sweaty brow—as was done to Jesus—it is worth respecting their authentic needs and bringing them relief for what is urgent. It would be stupid adulation to believe that they have aptitudes that they have not been able to acquire. Let us free them from hunger and desperation, and then they will be initiated into the sordid mysteries of politics.

In this fashion, product of a ruse, people who are rather inept and undoubtedly rather immoral continue to hold power. But they are capable, due to their greed itself, of keeping order until other more honest and skilled hands have, through their struggle, gained sufficient strength for a definitive victory. Juries are less benign than suffrage; there is less trickery about them. Ignorant, anonymous individuals *really do* sit down every day to judge others. They unleash the anarchy of chance upon serious matters where the action of a pettifogger is preferable. A generally venal judge who is familiar with his profession is not as dangerous as an all-powerful and bewildered courtroom, which has neither the opportunity nor the sense to understand a case file and is at the mercy of the gaudy oratory of the mouthy defense lawyer.

For years, we have seen a multitude of murderers and villains acquitted with unshakable calm. The woefully unprepared jurors do not hesitate to send such a quantity of ferocious scoundrels back into the heart of society with clean records. This thoughtless, passive pardon—true cowardice of the jury—is the opposite of the universal and active pardon that would regenerate the world. It becomes the biggest injustice when we consider that there is no compassion for small crimes. While a father who steals bread so that his children can eat goes to jail, gunshots to the bowels and stab wounds to the back are excused and almost applauded. This is absurdity: an institution that aims to bring justice through popular participation and that irredeemably corroborates—at the expense of the dignity of the people—the cruelest injustice, the punishment of meek sinners. The democracy of the courts has created the aristocracy of crime.

There is nothing to give us hope of progress in the workings of juries. Sensible, educated people have themselves taken off the lists with ever-increasing obstinacy, disqualifying themselves with a thousand excuses that their friends accept. And in a country of personal, abrasive politics, mother of shadowy vengeance, we are moving quickly toward the public sanctioning of murder.

[*Rojo y Azul*, March 29, 1908]

The Veteran

An old man, seventy years old; but a strong old man, of the beautiful and almost vanished Paraguayan race of half a century ago. An old man with a powerful chest, an upright head like a venerable summit in which the marks of lightning bolts are still to be seen. His red face is a broad landscape, crisscrossed by harmonious furrows and crowned by a thick forest of gray hair. His hands, which defended the fatherland and now plant manioc, are the color of the earth. The hero now walks heavily and is a bit deaf; this certainly does not detract from his majesty. He is rustic and large. He interests me more than many doctors. He took part in the entire campaign, from Corrientes to Cerro Corá;[60] he has six wounds. He speaks little and quietly. Interrogating him is the worst way to get brief confidences from him about the war. One must let him be, and not interrupt him when he finally decides to speak. He is full of vague mistrust and regrets. It would seem that ghosts are

---

60. Paraguay captured the city of Corrientes, capital of the Argentine province of the same name, in the early stages of the War of the Triple Alliance. The war's final battle was fought at Cerro Corá in northern Paraguay, today a national park. Marshal López was killed by Brazilian troops, bringing the six-year conflict to an end.

listening to him. Obedience to López[61] has not gone unpunished, and the shadow of that sinister man, who can be abhorred but not belittled, darkens the consciousness of the old and has perhaps impregnated the blood of children. And yet, on a warm fall afternoon, under the fruiting orange trees, at the time for drinking the traditional mate, I heard the following from the veteran:

"I, sir, did not stay with López to the end. I had to escape from the camp before then. I was in the General Staff with the rank of captain, and it was my turn to dole out the meat on one of the rare occasions when there was meat. We wore rags; for months we had been using the leather of our belts and backpacks to add substance to the stew. It was said that they were digging up corpses to make use of them: that I did not see. We had the fortune of finding a tired ox, skin and bones; we had to get seven hundred rations out of it. I did not steal for myself, but for a poor captain who took a bullet from one temple to the other and was left blind. Though he fought, blind and all, he was weak. Believing myself to be acting in secret, I sent a boy to him with a piece of tripe. Unfortunately, they found out and informed the Marshal. The following morning, they took me prisoner. Several officers awaited sentencing alongside me. The weeks went by, and we were not told a thing. One day, at dusk, one of López's aids came with a sheet of paper and joyfully inspected us, saying that soon López would free us. But I, sir, being familiar with certain practices, looked out of the corner of my eye at what the aide was writing at a distance from us. I noticed that he was marking some names with crosses, including mine. My companions were happy; I, on the other hand, realized that I only

---

61. Marshal Francisco Solano López (1827–1870) was president of Paraguay during the War of the Triple Alliance. He was vilified in Paraguay in the decades after the war, presented as a warmongering, incredibly cruel megalomaniac who had caused the conflict. However, his figure was later heavily revised by intellectuals—especially those of the generation of the 1900s—eventually enshrining him as the nation's maximum hero. His figure continues to be used as a symbol by organizations and political parties from across the Paraguayan political and ideological spectrum. At the same time, he remains surrounded by debate and controversy. Barrett never embraced the figure of López, instead viewing him as a tyrant.

had one night left to live. Then, a major arrived for whom I had done favors. He brought me a cup of broth. 'Friend,' he said to me, 'forgive me for not coming to you in all this time; it hasn't been possible,' and as he passed me the cup, he scratched my fingers. I understood, and at midnight when the guards fell asleep, I fled. I got lost in the forest and after three days I came out again in the camp. Fortunately, they did not spot me and, moving away in another direction, I found the path to the border. I lived on bitter oranges. One afternoon, at this very hour, I made out horses by a lagoon. 'If they're Paraguayan,' I said to myself, 'I'm finished.' But I was running out of strength, and I went forward. The saddles, sir, had straps for the horses' tails, which are only used in Brazil. I could breathe again. They captured me, they treated me well, and López fell soon after and the war ended."

"And, how could you not warn your companions on the night of the escape?"

"Ah! Sir. . . . I wouldn't have said a word to my own mother . . ."

A silence.

"Cerro Corá!" he added slowly. "In the camp there were dead women with children on top of them, still suckling from that rot...! And the Marshal ...!"

"The Marshal?"

A futile question. The old man goes silent definitively. The ghosts are listening....

[*La Razón*, May 4, 1909]

Panta

I have a slave—calm down, I do not treat her like one—but she is one.[62] She is convinced that she is one; or rather, she can conceive of no other

---

62. Panta was a domestic worker at the Laguna Porã ranch in southern Paraguay. This article was written during the year that Barrett spent in hiding at the property, owned by his brother-in-law, after he was smuggled back into Paraguay in early 1909 following deportation. The small timber house where Barrett lived still stands and is in use by the current owners of the ranch.

state for herself. If I tied her to a post and tortured her, she would suffer without indignation. She was born this way; neither her soul nor her eyes have changed in tone. Her life has been that of a pulsating object passed from one hand to the next. Perhaps, when she was still a child, they raped her by the side of the road. She has neither last name nor home. Panta... might it be short for Pantaleona? She is old or seems to be. Fifty, sixty, seventy years old? Enigma. She speaks confusingly of the war... months in the forest chewing herbs; the terror of a hunted animal. Now, servant of servants, she cooks the fieldhands' *locro*.[63] Her face is a bundle of wrinkles in constant motion, with two shy, wild irises that gleam in the shadows. There is no thought there, but all instincts are present: gluttony, lust, a dog's loyalty, and a faun's imagination, anger that dissolves in laughter, and fear with its slanting movements, ready for escape. She is dirty: she has never washed; she has reached the definitive equilibrium in which friction and sweat remove as much filth as they leave behind. She is sordid: her shirt, always the same one, slides up her belly, revealing flesh of wrought copper, flesh that no longer feels the bite of the sun nor that of the cold. A torn skirt... and her feet! Poor, cracked, deformed, dark feet. How much they have walked, how much the ground's thorns and pebbles have wounded them! Feet of mud; blood flows beneath that mud. They are the feet that Jesus caressed.

Panta is naïve; she constantly groans, grumbles, or lets out a cackle; she speaks, sings, or shouts everything. She has a raw spirit. No one understands her; no one takes notice of her if it is not to mock her. She is mad, for she cannot keep quiet. I imagine the magnitude that the mishaps of her miserable work take on in her mind. Perhaps Panta lives surrounded by monsters that I cannot see. I compare her to the beasts that tremble at dangers of which man has no knowledge. Every being has knowledge of an aspect of the world. Who could reproach Panta for her peculiarities? When she serves me a plate of food, she never leaves it where she should. She puts it underneath my chin, like

---

63. *Locro*, a thick traditional stew of pre-Hispanic origin containing meat, corn, and squash, among other ingredients.

a wash basin.

"It's for eating!" the poor devil explains to me.

Eat . . . an enormous word! Especially for a mouth that gathers up the leftovers of other people's food.

Panta is often a victim of flirtatiousness. If she gathers ten pesos together, and they are not stolen from her, she buys a yellow, red, green cloth that she hangs from any part of her body. And Panta—let us admit it—is lewd. In the middle of the corral, in broad daylight, she lifts her skirts to entertain the drovers.

I do not want to think here of when she humiliates herself, but rather of when she is brought back to a state of innocence by pain, when there has been a catastrophe in her smoke-filled kitchen, when they hit her, or when she burns her fingers with boiling water. Then she comes to me so I can heal her, whether with oil, whether with arnica, whether with just my idle pity. And she cries by my side, the tears gushing out, with all her sorry wrinkles that rise and fall. I then understand to what extent she is a sister of mine, to what extent her naked, unsteady being holds the weak spark that we hide under useless masks.

[*La Evolución*, June 7, 1909]

The Madhouse

The poorhouse is surrounded by magnificent grounds covering forty-two blocks. You can find everything there: vegetables, fruits, flowers. The beautiful building of the poorhouse is a vast factory where people work; they cook, sew, knit, embroider *ñanduti*.[64] They earn money there—by God!—and everything runs like a barracks. Add to this the twelve thousand pesos from the government each month, and you will understand the response that another charitable association, the Charity Hospital, gave the state when it wanted to take on the hospital: "I'll sell it to you." You do not hand over a business for free.

But near the poorhouse stands the gloomy prison of the mad. Oh!

---

64. Guarani, *ñanduti*, a traditional Paraguayan lace consisting of intricate, circular patterns. Literally means "spiderweb."

Mad people are not good workers; they are useless. Imagine a filthy jail where misery has made the wretches abandoned inside lose their minds. In the mud of a somber courtyard, curled up against the walls, twenty or thirty specters wrapped in sordid rags groan, sing, howl. A series of black dungeons, with bars and enormous locks, overwhelms the eye. A prisoner's face suddenly appears through the bars. Dark, bare, humid cells. Cracks are appearing in the ceiling. The beds are dirty burlap sacks. A foul stench of urine, of the den of ferocious beasts, knocks us back.

With no medical care for them, the lunatics are idle. A heap of rags rustles on the floor. It is an epileptic woman, who will perhaps crack her skull against the wall. Shoeless, with swollen feet, the female idiots, unable to shoo away the flies, are covered in sores. They scrape the earth in which they wallow all day and are left without fingernails. The spectacle is similar on the men's side. Joyful, facing into the sun, an adolescent covered in bruises masturbates.

There is no salvation for the sick people thrown in there. Many of them could be cured elsewhere. There, in that nameless hell, their minds are shipwrecked forever.

For the orphanage and industrious old women, everything; for the madhouse, nothing. The lunatics are unexploitable. The madhouse is a dismal pit where people toss their garbage while looking in another direction. Relatives rid themselves there of those that are a burden. There, they dump the blind person, the cancer sufferer, the accursed flesh. You do not need to be mad to fall into the hellhole. It is enough *not to be needed.* An Englishman, William Owen, who was locked up as a sane man, hanged himself in his cell. During our visit, we discovered a poor woman in her right mind who has been among the lunatics for *five months.* The Little Sister[65] did not know who she was.

"My name is Ursula Céspedes. My daughter brought me here. She doesn't want me. She says that I'm a leper."

And she shows us her pallid feet, the pustules on her legs . . .

---

65. The Little Sisters of the Poor are a congregation of Catholic nuns that care for the elderly poor.

Ah, the admissions register without dates, without names! N.N., N.N. . . . ! Who are they? Who threw them into the pit? The police, a stranger, whoever. Why commit murder? Take your victims to the madhouse.

And when the pit overflows, when there are too many monsters, they are chucked out. Accordingly, the madwoman Francisca Martínez de Loizaga—now cared for in her rural shack—was released from the madhouse *three times* in a year and a half.

We could not conceive of anything like this even in the Middle Ages. Why protest? Why demand justice from the state? That state that, amid so many horrors and so much infamy, does not take responsibility for anything other than changing the uniforms of its soldier boys. There are fifty thousand gold pesos available to quarter a battalion. To ease the lot of the dispossessed, whether mad or not, there will never be anything.

What I Have Seen

In one year in the Paraguayan countryside, I have seen many sad things . . . [66]

I have seen the earth, with its incoercible, wild fertility, suffocate man. He tosses out one seed and obtains a hundred different plants and does not know which one is his. I have seen the old paths, opened during the age of tyranny, devoured by vegetation, dissolved by floods, erased by neglect. Every Paraguayan, free on a piece of constitutional paper, is today the miserable prisoner of a few inches of land. There is no way for him to transport the harvests that he might, in a desperate effort, pull from the ground. He makes do with rows of manioc, gnawed by weeds. Further on, under the squalid orange grove left by

---

66. Barrett wrote "What I Have Seen" after his year in hiding at the Laguna Porã ranch near the town of Yabebyry in southern Paraguay. Political changes allowed him to travel with his family to live in the town of San Bernardino, near Asunción, and to reestablish links with the Paraguayan press.

the Jesuits,[67] stands the small mud and cane shack: a hole in which to die in the shade. Go in: you will not find a glass or a chair. You will sit on a piece of wood, drink muddy water from a gourd, eat corn cooked in a dirty pot, sleep on straps tied to four poles. And just think, this is the rural bourgeoisie.

I have seen that people do not work, that people cannot work, because their bodies are sick, because their souls are dead. I have seen that "hardy" fieldhands cannot go two weeks without a day of diarrhea or fever! Poor flesh, wounded even in the genitals; poor, dark, withered flesh, stripped of all hygiene, with no outside help except the healer's poison, the local official's whip, the saber that drives them to the government barracks or to the revolutionary ones! Poor souls with the "shakes" of terror, for whom, in the night, the knife of the living continually gleams or the ghosts of the deceased turn pale!

I have seen the women, the eternal widows, those that still hold a remnant of energy in their maternal entrails, walk with their children on their backs. I have seen the mothers' humble feet, feet that are cracked and black and so heroic, search for food all along the paths of exhaustion and anguish. And I have seen that those saintly feet were the only things that really existed in Paraguay. And I have seen children, children that die by the thousands amid the world's healthiest climate, child skeletons, with monstrous bellies, wrinkled children that do not laugh or cry, larvae of silence!

And the men, and the women and the children have looked at me. And their human eyes, in which there was an empty space left by hope, have told me that we must return hope to them, because this is the Earth's most unfortunate country. Let us not punish, let us not make accusations. If our brothers have no solidarity, if they do not manage to respect their female companions nor love their children, if they knock on the doors of

---

67. Jesuit priests ran missions in the south of the province of Paraguay during the colonial era. Thousands of Guarani Indigenous families lived in these missions and the Jesuits came to hold enormous economic, political, and military power. The Jesuits were expelled from the Spanish Empire in 1767, leaving their missions abandoned.

lust, alcohol, or gambling to evade their dark pain, let us not be outraged. We must not judge their illness; we must cure it. And how much fraternal patience, how much gentleness must we have in our consoling hands, to cure, across the whole country, the race's sick roots!

And I have seen the saddest thing in the capital. I have not found doctors of the nation's soul and body; I have seen politicians and businessmen. I have seen manipulators of flotations and loans; pharmacists that ready themselves to sell the dying man his final injections of morphine . . .

[*El Nacional*, February 21, 1910]

Hatred of Trees

It is fine for a parvenu to build a house with money earned quickly in honest and secret business transactions. It is less fine for him to build one of those gloomy and offensive and tasteless piles of bricks, with latticed holes and tiled roof. But what makes you shudder is when he declares: "Now I'm going to pull up all the trees around the property so that it *looks nice*."

Yes, the gleaming, stupid façade must look clean, bare, with its brazen colors that profane the softness of the rural tones. People must say: "This is the new house of so-and-so, that man who is now so rich." It must be possible to contemplate the monument to so-and-so's endeavors without obstruction. Trees are surplus to requirement: "They block the view." And there is not only vanity in this eagerness to strip the ground: there is hatred, hatred of trees.

Is this possible? Hatred of beings that, unmoving, with their noble limbs always open, offer us the caress of their shade without ever tiring; the silent fertility of their fruits; the multifarious, exquisite poetry that they raise up to the sky? They claim that there are harmful plants. Perhaps there are, but that should not be a reason to hate them. Our hatred condemns them. Our love would perhaps transform them and redeem them. Listen to one of Victor Hugo's characters: "He saw the country's people very busy pulling up nettles; he looked at the heap of uprooted plants that had already dried out and said: 'This is dead.

However, it would have been something good if they had known how to make use of it. When nettles are young, their leaves are an excellent vegetable; when they age, they have filaments and fibers like hemp and flax. Nettle cloth is as valuable as hemp cloth. Nettles are also an excellent fodder that can be harvested twice. And what do nettles need? Not much soil, no care, no cultivation. . . . With a little bit of work, nettles would be useful; they are neglected, and they become harmful. So they are killed. How many men resemble nettles!' And after a pause he added: 'Friends, know this: there are neither bad plants nor bad men. There are only bad cultivators.'"

Oh! This is not about cultivating, but rather forgiving trees. How to placate the murderers? There is no part of the republic, of those that I have visited, in which I have not seen the property owner's stupid axe at work. Even those people who have nothing destroy plants. Arid wasteland spreads out around shacks, getting bigger each year and causing fear and sadness. According to the Arab adage, one of the three missions of every man in this world is to plant a tree. Here, the son uproots what the father planted. And it is not about making money; I am not talking about those who harvest timber. That would be an explanation, a merit; we have come to consider greed a virtue. I am talking about those that spend money on razing the country to the ground. They are driven by a *selfless hatred*. And concern grows when you see that the only works done in the plazas of the capital consist of uprooting, uprooting, and uprooting trees.

This hatred is doubly cruel in a region where summer lasts eight months. The scorching sun is preferred to the sweet presence of trees. It would seem that men are no longer able to feel, to imagine the life within the venerable trunks that tremble under the iron and collapse with a pitiful crash. It would seem that they do not understand that sap is also blood and that their victims were conceived in love and light. It seems that people are enslaved by a vague terror and that they fear that the forest might harbor villains and engender ghosts. They foresee death behind the trees. Or, obsessed by a formless grief, they wish to reproduce around themselves the barren desert of their souls.

And so, in our own souls, irritation turns to pity. Their illness must be very hopeless and run very deep. In resigned mutism, they have lost the original love, the fundamental love that even beasts feel: the sacred love of earth and trees.

[*Rojo y Azul*, September 27, 1907]

Primary Education

Whether or not teachers teach grammar, geography, and arithmetic is of the least importance.

Firstly, no matter how competent the teacher may be, children do not learn anything before the age of fifteen. A child's brain cannot think abstractly, just as a newborn's stomach cannot digest meat. Until puberty has gone by, the brain cannot generalize, it cannot understand. Why turn children into bad phonographs? Why profane their tender intelligence? It is enough to stimulate their free curiosity, to maintain the elasticity of their innate inventiveness, which is so easily suffocated under idiotic text-based lessons. It is enough to keep their mental health in motion. The opposite is done: children are stupefied using their own memory, their minds are castrated through fear, they are imprisoned and tortured, they are made to hate art and science for life, they are made definitive enemies of books and nature. When they have completed their baneful studies, it is difficult to save them.

A teacher who is not endearing, who does not limit his pedagogy to telling beautiful stories in class, who does not reject the simple task of the Latin teacher in favor of the serious task of inspiring love for truth and justice—even if it is not yet time to become acquainted with the one or practice the other—is a bad teacher.

At school, children must acquire the habit of not lying and of tending to the troubles and suffering of others. They must leave school truthful, compassionate, and polite. That is what is of importance.

And that is what no one takes responsibility for.

Instead of tempering children's moral springs—the only ones within reach—they are earnestly assured that the Earth they walk on is a ball dancing around the sun. There are few social situations that are more horribly comical.

I heard news of a teacher who reminded his pupils of the shape of the planet by telling them to look at his waistcoat pocket, where his watch made a circular bulge. Unfortunately, he forgot to bring the watch on examination day; in its place there was a box of matches. All his pupils answered that the Earth was square.

When, as a boy, they explained to me what was represented by those plaster globes with the continents and the seas painted on their curved surfaces, I believed that the towns and cities were *inside* the sphere. I took the earthly convexity to be the celestial concavity. A very natural mistake, which took me a long time to correct. The only enormous, round body that reality put before my eyes was the sky.

"I remember a schoolgirl," narrates Henry George, "who was very ahead of her age in geography and astronomy, and who was very surprised to find out that the ground of her home's yard was really the surface of the Earth. And if you speak with children, you will find that most of the knowledge they are taught is like the knowledge of that girl. *They seldom reason any better—and often do so much more poorly—than those who have never gone to school.*"[68]

But even if scientific notions were imparted at that age—something that is impossible—what good would they do? How would they themselves improve the human spirit? It is not roughly lucid reasoning that makes the world go round, but the will. Developing brains is not urgent, but developing character is. Teach an evil man, and you will have given him weapons to attack you. Teach an idiot, and you will have bestowed importance and volume upon his idiocy.

People gradually emancipate themselves from the poverty in which

---

68. Henry George (1839–1897) was a U.S. political economist known for proposing a tax on land value. Barrett's Spanish rendering has important differences from George's original text, which reads: "I remember a little girl, pretty well along in her school geography and astronomy, who was much astonished to find that the ground in her mother's backyard was really the surface of the earth, and, if you talk with them, you will find that a good deal of the knowledge of many college graduates is much like that of the little girl. They seldom think any better, and sometimes not so well as men who have never been to college." Henry George, *Progress and Poverty* (New York: Robert Schalkenbach Foundation, 1935), 307.

they live, not through education, but through the strength of their sacred anger. In China, the entire population knows how to read and write; nowhere else are the masses dogged by such a sorry existence.

If education were effective in itself, would teachers themselves not have used it to their advantage? Would they have not succeeded in instilling in the generations that they have educated consideration and respect for the humble class of primary school teachers, who are cruelly treated in every country? Would they not have managed to get better pay for themselves?

Governments have discovered that mandatory education does not put them in danger, as would be the case if the moral vitality of taxpayers were increased in schools. Governments put their academic machinery together with total confidence; they sometimes use it, as occurs in France, as a political bureau. It allows them to always reward their friends with jobs and to spread the bureaucratic epidemic ever further.

It would be a source of incalculable regeneration—especially here, where poorly constituted households do very little for children—to send a heroic regiment of a hundred teachers into the countryside. One hundred men of heart, capable of endearing themselves to children, and determined to sow the seed of sincerity and freedom of thought in dawning souls. But do those men exist in Paraguay? Do they exist in America? Do they exist in this vale of tears . . . ?

[*Rojo y Azul*, December 22, 1907]

The Teacher and the Priest

When I arrived in the town, I asked about the schoolteacher and then about the priest; nothing could be more natural: they represent the eternal dualism of philosophy, the two poles of human spirituality, the relative and the absolute, senses and intuition, the visible and the invisible, science and faith. In that society of two or three thousand souls, the representative of what is relative and ephemeral was worse fed than the representative of what is absolute and lasting. Perhaps this shows that, even for campesinos, heaven is more important than earth and that, above all, it is in their interest to guarantee their harvests in the next world. The teacher is pallid, hesitant, melancholy; the priest plump, healthy, jovial. You only need look at them to understand the difference between the deceitful temptations of this vale of tears and the shining reality that good Catholics will find beyond the grave.

The teacher earns one hundred and fifty pesos a month. It is true that he works no more than eight or nine hours a day and that he has just one hundred pupils. Furthermore, in the classroom, which is a dilapidated shed, there are no benches, no tables, no teaching aids of any kind. Arithmetic is learned there without a blackboard, geometry without shapes or solids, botany without plants, zoology without animals, geography without maps. Everything is ethereal, fantastical. It must also be noted that the one hundred and fifty pesos are not precisely one hundred and fifty pesos. Firstly, he receives them one month in arrears. Governments, undoubtedly for reasons of high politics, have decreed for schoolteachers to be paid last. That is, after the butlers, doormen, and lackeys, after the spies. Moreover, schoolteachers from the countryside are paid *in Asunción*. The poor unfortunates need a middleman to collect their wages in the capital and send them to them. This is a transaction that always sees a few pesos evaporate, if not all of them. There are so few people who can be trusted! In any case, the teacher gets by. What more could he want?

For the priest, and with good reason, getting by is not enough. The glory of the Almighty must triumph in him. The simple people of the small town call the priest *son of God*. As such, he becomes flesh, sometimes to the point of exaggeration. The priest of my story has ten children. It must be the climate! Not one of the ten will end up in poverty; the double father is practically rich. It must be noted that he does not even live in his parish. He makes an appearance there each month; he sings a mass here, a few prayers for the dead there; he baptizes a couple of babies, marries a few scandalous couples, and leaves. Total: five hundred, seven hundred pesos. I scrutinized the church tariff; it amazed me to discover that "a wedding at an appropriate time, with nuptial mass without application," costs five pesos, "with application" eight pesos; "the burial procession of an adult, without pauses for prayer, with singing and a lap of the church," four pesos, "if there are pauses for prayer, an additional 0.50 will be charged per pause"; "for the burial procession of an adult or infant from their home to the church or cemetery, no more than four will be charged for the first block and two for each subsequent block."

The trinkets of worship—parish crosses, candle holders, chandeliers, candelabras, dalmatics, cloths—are rented out for no more than three pesos apiece; but these stipends are for church stewardship and not for the priest. This includes costs related to the bell. The public should be aware that a passing bell costs thirty cents, and the death knell fifty.

So what do the hundreds and thousands of pesos that the priest in question pockets demonstrate?

Ah! The thing is, the teacher is provided for by the men, while the priest is provided for by the women. The miserable fees of the one are paid reluctantly; there are no fees for the other, and the bishop's efforts will come up against inexhaustible female piety. Those heroic slaves have placed all their hopes in heavenly mercy—where else were they going to put them?—and they will deem no sacrifice too great if it means preserving their friendship with the Virgin, the saints, and *the son of God*. Even when man feels love, he is practical and determined; he plans and calculates. Rightly unconvinced of the benefits of education, he is not much moved by the teacher's pallidness and melancholy. In contrast, woman, as soon as she begins to feel love, loves like a mother, and that is all there is to it. She closes her eyes to the priest's mischief; she opens them, full of trust, when he recovers his sacred nature and, in the name of Christ, repeats the immortal, the only words of solace. And woman takes maternal pleasure—Oh, Madonna!—in the priest's round cheeks, in his joviality, and she laughs along with him; the candid, light, quickly restrained laughter of an earnest girl. And the priest will get the fattest hen, the tastiest glass of milk, and the little pile of pesos gathered over long months of cold and sun while walking barefoot along endless paths.

[*Rojo y Azul*, September 20, 1907]

Sad Children

It happened in a town square—a rural town like any other. It was a beautiful day; a radiant sun, a light breeze that refreshed the skin as it caressed it. The clock struck eleven and the school doors opened and out came the children. There were children of a variety of ages; some had only known how to walk for a short time, others looked like little men. There were lots of them. They were in small groups; most of them in pairs; a few stray ones. They had spent three hours sitting, motionless, mortifying themselves with the harsh stupidities of textbooks. They came out of the school in silence, their heads bowed. They did not run, they did not jump, they did not play, they did not get up to any mischief. The soft, wide lawn did not draw a single skip from them, no joyful race of young animals. The rope of the church bell reached down to the ground. Not one of them rung the bell. They were serious. They were sad.

Sad ... And sad every day. Since that morning, I have paid attention to Paraguayan children, grave children that do not laugh or cry. Have you seen happy children cry? Boisterous sobbing, powerful trumpeting, half-faked, deliciously despotic sobbing that foresees mother's exaggerated cuddles, and demands them, and knows that it is getting its way. It is half sobbing and half guffaw, a healthy scream that delights. It would comfort me to hear that sobbing in the countryside instead of mournful silence.

Here, the children do not cry: they groan or they grumble. They do not laugh, they smile. And with what wise expressions! The bitterness of life has already passed over those faces that have not started to live. These children have been born old. They have inherited the disdain and resigned skepticism of so many defrauded and oppressed generations. They begin their lives with the fatigued gesture of those that end theirs in vain.

We can measure the dejection of the campesino masses, the immemorial burden of tears and blood that weighs on their souls, through this formidable fact: the children are sad. The pressure of the national misfortune has destroyed the mysterious mechanism that renews beings; it has tarnished and adulterated love. The ghosts of the disaster of the war, and of the disaster of peace—tyranny—have haunted solitary lovers and tarnished their kisses with their mournful shadow. Spouses have shared intimacy amid distrust and ruin; they have not only trembled with passion. Voluptuousness has been left impregnated with indestructible and tragic suspicion. The torch of immortal desire holds reflections of the funeral pyre and at times seems to be a symbol of destruction and death. The parricidal work of those that enslaved the country has injured the flesh of the fatherland in its most intimate, vital, and sacred site: its sex. They have committed an outrage against mothers, they have condemned children who are yet to be born. How can we be surprised that children, the flowers of the race, do not open their petals to light and happiness! The tree has been torn up by its very roots.

Poor lifeless children! To look into their candid eyes, where there is no curiosity, provokes pity. They do not care about the world. Taciturn and passive like their parents, they let things happen that are usually cruel. Why care about anything? They possess melancholy wisdom ahead of their time. Through their innocent veins run a few drops of that acrid juice that we, whatever our philosophy, eventually extract from unjust reality. They have not yet tried anything, and it would seem they already hope for nothing.

Every time I think about the children of the common people, a memory assails me. Just before I arrived in the small town where I spend summers, a year ago perhaps, a train hit a boy. The wheels broke his weak legs and tore his head from his trunk. The workers gathered up the body and left it on the platform of the station. The victim had laid down on the rails to sleep and had not heard the train. He had been tired, and his sleep was so deep, so like the sleep of death, that it merged with death itself. Or was it perhaps because, on hearing death approach, he felt too tired, too sad to wake up?

I believe that I still see, on the hot sand, the stiff little body, and the pale little broken leg bare from the knee down, and the humble shoeless feet that would walk no more, that would soon sleep beneath the fraternal earth. And beside it, the bloodied little head, placed in an extremely old, shapeless hat, through the holes of which protruded two or three dark, bright, still-shining locks. A compassionate woman—the eternal Veronica—covered that wretchedness with a piece of linen that was white and pure like snow. The local official had been informed and, on his orders, the withered remains were loaded onto any old cart. A farmhand carried the boy's head in the threadbare hat. I then noticed in horror that the official found it funny.

Oh, innumerable sad children! Let us devote ourselves to making sacred, mad laughter flow from your red lips, and we shall be saved. Let us lose all hope as long as the children can shine. Let us prevent some of them feeling so very surrendered to the weight of doom that they fall asleep abandoned in the middle of death's path and do not hear it coming.

[*Rojo y Azul*, November 12, 1907]

Bitter Truths

Wars generally do not have the disastrous effect on the economic development of the defeated nation that one might imagine. North American prosperity after the Civil War, France's admirable upsurge following the disasters of 1870,[69] are classic examples of how little a sudden disappearance of capital hinders the normal functioning of collective production. A warmongering historian would even dare argue that a brief series of battles is a hygienic pruning of the social tree, which puts out more shoots and is more robust the day after the fight. "One night in Paris," said Napoleon, facing a battlefield soaked in blood and covered in victims, "will fix all of this." Just like wounded flesh, mutilated wealth heals itself. Elastic life bounces back after a collision and rises up with fury.

A curious fact proves the above. It has been observed that the period from one commercial crisis or general *krach* to the next lasts nine years. A fortuitous coincidence, perhaps. Here are some dates:

---

69. Barrett refers to France's defeat in the 1870–71 Franco-Prussian War.

1864—Cotton crisis, United States.
1873—Bonds issued by Austria.
1882—*Krach* of the French banks.
1891—Baring *Krach*, Argentine Republic.
1900—Universal Exposition fiasco.

Waves have propagated around the globe from the places mentioned next to the dates, bringing about collapse and revealing a morbid state of universal financial relations. The symptoms of the disease, which are unfortunately reappearing today, are an increase in bank investments and a decrease in reserves. But what matters to us here is the following remark by Jacques Siegfried:[70] "Wars have little influence on the cycle of periods of prosperity and crisis ... war is almost always a sign of new growth in commercial transactions across the entire planet."

Thus, external adversities—wars, earthquakes, hurricanes, floods, locusts, fires, coups d'état, etc.—cannot exhaust the sources of production. This is proof that money is not essential, but that labor is. It shows that nothing can transform and corrupt the moral conditions that make labor fruitful, other than a slow, hereditary, and hence uncurable degeneration.

As a fatal exception, Paraguay's war not only devastated and bloodied the country, but set it back by a long time. It castrated it by destroying the seeds of that beautiful race that still shines in the noble figures of the surviving elderly people. Subsequent generations were cut from a different cloth. They were born to institutions whose words were freer, but they themselves were less free in their inner depths. They were weaker, more poorly armed, more indolent, more flawed, more incapable of emancipating themselves through individual effort. They were a different, inferior caste: another nation that was improvised and welded onto the old one by any means possible. Progress is difficult for the current population. We must not be surprised that the nation's depression has lasted so long. The characteristics of the people have changed; the physiognomy of the fatherland has been erased. It must be restored; the lost riverbeds must be found, and the currents of new life made to flow along them.

---

70. Jacques Siegfried (1840–1909) was a French economist and writer.

The campesino's misery, the deep impoverishment of all activities, the ruin of businesses, in short, are not the consequences of chance accidents, but of a way of being. It is not unexpected things that kill us, but habit. And as the disease comes from within, the medicine must come from within also. People do not work, they are not made for work; they lack joy, confidence, love of the home; they lack a home itself. Consciences must be rebuilt, human dignity returned to men. A bitter truth, but not so bitter, because it is true. It is good for us to laugh at loans, banks, decrees, political machinations, third-rate bores. The task is not so simple; it is not a matter of months, but rather of long years of patient work to educate and console. It is not a matter of searching for capital in the pockets of others so as to pile ever more debt on this society that has been bankrupted by its uselessness. Rather, it is a matter of searching for love. It is not a matter of teaching people to maraud, intrigue, the art of acquiring false credit, but rather teaching them not to lie, not to promise what they will not deliver, to deliver what they promise. It is a matter of teaching them to work and to understand that he who does not provide for his children and feeds himself at the expense of his wife is unforgiveable and does not deserve to be saved.

[*Rojo y Azul*, December 1, 1907]

Wounded Homes

The state of a body depends on the state of its molecules, and a living organism cannot be healthy if the cells it is composed of are not healthy. It is impossible for a country to prosper when the family, which is the social molecule and cell, is not constituted in strength and dignity. The fatherland, the shared home, is wretched and weak because individual homes are weak. And just as in medicine there is an inclination toward the sole method of healing, which is to regenerate tissues through their elements, the work of saving the fatherland comes down to the task of regenerating homes.

Slow, laborious work that is hardly magnificent but is, however, the only fruitful work. Work that is not within the reach of a minister, no matter how skilled and boisterous he might be, nor within that of any politician. In relation to this issue, as in all issues related to the core problems of nations, politics is perhaps capable of doing wrong, but is powerless to do good. It is either a calamity, or it is nothing at all. Politics is never more generous and useful than when it forgoes action. No; the great work of regenerating homes requires several generations of intelligent and selfless men, humble enough to go and bury themselves in the corners of the countryside, heroic enough to stay there to combat the damage at its roots and to dedicate themselves to consoling and healing ill souls. Paraguay is a vast hospital of the deluded and the melancholy. We are not in need of orators or capitalists or sergeants, but rather of doctors, loving doctors whose hands might both cure and caress at the same time.

And these men: where are they? I do not know, but they are needed. They are like strong cells, multiplied through the action of immunizing serums, and whose destiny it is to battle against pathogenic microbes and devour them. We must defeat the enemy on its own turf and with its own weapons or resign ourselves to succumb. In the months that followed the disasters of the Spanish-American War,[71] when not a word was spoken on the peninsula, just as today in Paraguay, Mr. José Echegaray[72] proposed a solution that, more than being about regeneration and new directions, was theoretical and childish: a mathematician's solution. "We must regenerate ourselves one by one," he exclaimed. "As soon as each Spaniard has regenerated himself, Spain will have been regenerated." Very simple and very absurd, because this is precisely what degeneration consists of: of no one managing to regenerate himself without the help of others. An individual who has enough energy to recoup his moral health on his own is already

---

71. The 1898 Spanish-American War saw Spain defeated by the United States of America, producing the loss of almost all its remaining colonies: Puerto Rico, Cuba, Guam, and the Philippines. The defeat prompted a crisis of identity in Spain, feeding the fertile work of the youths of the renowned Generation of '98 literary movement.

72. José Echegaray (1832–1916) was a Spanish mathematician, playwright, engineer, and politician. He won the 1904 Nobel Prize for Literature and was a founder of the Royal Spanish Mathematical Society.

clean and strong. By improving himself he does not generate strength: he displays it. Unfortunately, our situation is different. To say that homes are wounded is an understatement: they are mutilated, and so are consciences. One lifetime will not be enough to get the missing organs to reappear; a series of lifetimes will be needed, as the Indian philosophers claim, a series of reincarnations to reach supreme purification. The undertaking is long and arduous because it is essential. The human bread of the coming ages, leavened by the yeast of educators and secular preachers, will perhaps take centuries to whiten into a redeeming wafer.

The Paraguayan home is a bleeding ruin: it is a home without a father. The war took away the fathers and has not yet returned them.[73] Following the catastrophe, the stray males remain, those that formerly stole from the rubble with a knife between their teeth. Previously, they would rob, kill, rape, wander. Now, their vile horde of a race has somewhat changed; they have been somewhat touched by the silent desperation of the noble women that López dragged barefoot behind the carts. Women that, upon surviving, gave themselves over to the disgusting marauders to repopulate the desolate desert of the fatherland. Somewhat moved by the peaceful beauty of the soil, they take possession of women, engender sorrow alongside life, and move on. Behind them, in the miserable rural shacks, are concubines or widows, but ultimately mothers, who work the land with their orphan children clinging to them in a mournful bunch. Never a voluntary abortion, never an infanticide that other mothers would even commit out of charity. Always abandoned, patient, ignorant, and silent; they feel in the depths of their souls, as they did after the fateful years, the need to raise men—good or bad—the need to launch the possibility of triumph into the world. Grieving mothers, mothers stripped of all vanity and honor, of all happiness, of all adornment! Mothers of sullen children, gloomy planters of the

---

73. The role of women was immeasurably important for postwar Paraguay, especially given that a vast proportion of the country's males had been killed during the conflict.

future: hope is to be found only in you! Only you, on your bent and aching shoulders, hold up your country!

But a mother is not a home. There is no respectable or safe nation without the home:[74] comforting, warm nest; small and sacred theatre of the regular altruisms of our species; source of all lofty beginnings; requirement for all steady and continual work; foundation of all happiness. The progress of English-speakers is exclusively due to them being incomparable fathers. Oh, naïve legislators, concerned with teaching your compatriots to read! Dedicate your efforts to a more important and obscure task: make them respect their wives and love their children.

[*Rojo y Azul*, November 24, 1907]

The Deal

Testimony of an office worker:

"If I say that I'm not rich, people will likely believe me. The worst thing is that, from time to time, it's necessary to spend more money than you have because patience is lacking and temptations abound, as it must say somewhere in the Bible.

On one of those sinful occasions, a friend said to me:

'You don't need to bother anyone. Since it's just a small amount, and since we're at the end of the month, nothing will be easier for you than to pawn your salary. There's a bank here, a true providence, that will indulge your whim by means of very reasonable interest.'

I apologize for revealing these intimate details to the public. I am perfectly aware that no one cares. But be patient, here comes *the interest*:

'And... how much do they take?'

'Two percent monthly.'

A done deal, I thought. Twenty-four percent a year is nothing in countries where money is made by the bucketload. Let's go.

---

74. Barrett uses the English term "home" in this sentence, presumably to accompany the reference to English-speaking fathers that he makes in this paragraph. Barrett's own father was English.

X Bank . . . that's the name that was recommended, keep it in mind. The blessings of those who hunger and thirst for a little gold must rain down on this establishment. Oh, the benefits of credit, foundation of commerce, source of the prosperity of nations!

I go in and approach one of the desks as a penitent approaches the grille of the confessional booth. And with the pleading eyes and the trembling voice of one who is going to receive the immense favor of being lent money, with absolute collateral, at 24 percent interest, I state my case.

'Are you a shareholder?' the father confessor asks me.

'No, sir, forgive me.'

'You have to buy thirty stocks.'

'Thirty stocks!'

'But you will only pay for three stocks this month. On top of the 2 percent, there is an 8 percent deposit. On top of it.'

'Excuse me. Would you be so kind as to tell me how much you will charge me for the three hundred pesos that the cashier at my office will hand to you in a week's time?'

'Yes, sir. *(Quick calculations)* Sixty-nine pesos.' (!!!)

Me. '*(Dizzy)* And I still owe money for . . . twenty-seven shares?'

Him. 'Indeed.'

Me. 'Please, allow me to take my leave . . . I do not feel well.' *(Indignant gaze of the financier)*.

Stunned, I drag myself to the colleague that sent me into the ambush. He looks at me and laughs.

'Result: they get sixty-nine pesos out of me, and I owe them for twenty-seven shares,' I pitifully articulate.

'And what more could you want than to be a shareholder? You can't have ever seen juicier stocks.'

'It really is true that I've never seen anything like them! But where are those blasted shares traded?'

'Nowhere.'

'Who wants them?'

'No one.'

'But does the Bank pay dividends?'

'Never.'

'So . . .'

'So?'

'Nothing. That's how they achieve the American dream: by ruining Americans.'"

The Crisis

A commercial sector that has lost its credit, both inside and outside the country; an ill-fated agricultural sector with everything weighing on it and nothing in its favor; an incipient industrial sector that, for the moment, is incapable of containing the disaster. A state of deterioration that limits liberal activities to being eaten up in legal feuds. A politics of deputies, condemned to go round in circles between a crippled government and a chamber of shadows. This is the picture.

Let us be fair: providence was distracted, and bad luck played its part. If it rained, it rained too much; if it did not rain, it was for long scorching months. Floods or thirst. The locusts moved in; while Buenos Aires prepared itself to reject Paraguayan timber, cutting off the nation's gold provisions, the Argentine Chaco sent its devastating winged armies.[75] The earth and the sky and foreign finance seemed to have been conjured up from the revolution here.[76]

But the vitality of a people is precisely what is measured by the obstacles it overcomes. An attack from the outside should have been met by a clear-headed, firm defense. In the midst of the storm is when the helm should be secured.

It is in the midst of the hostile incoherence of things when we need to have the clearest idea of what we want, how we want it, and how

---

75. There were reports of a plague of locusts across several South American countries in 1907.

76. Barrett seems to refer to the Revolution of 1904, which had put the Liberal Party in power in Paraguay. Barrett himself had joined the revolutionary forces after traveling to their camp in mid-campaign as a journalist for a Buenos Aires newspaper.

badly we want it. "What a force is composed of," says Barrès,[77] "is not only its intensity, but also its direction." We can feel weak; sometimes it is not our fault. All the more reason to stubbornly get our bearings. The horizon is blocked from view; we must keep to the compass of our conscience if we are not to resign ourselves to being shipwrecked.

And what do we see everywhere? Resignation.

This morbid resignation disproportionately prolongs the periods of depression. It is laziness born of sorrow that prevents us from understanding and limiting that sorrow. It is the same laziness that is born of pleasure, which neither understands nor restricts the requirements for prosperity, and makes people embark on ridiculous adventures, turning the periods of happiest development into the prelude of ruin. People who had ten pesos asked for one hundred to invest in businesses whose risks they did not calculate correctly, and now they crash into the closed doors of the banks.

The crisis will not be a punishment so long as it turns out to be a lesson. The year 1907 was a terrible year for the United States. Over there, the railroads were to blame, just as our humble businessmen are to blame here due to their delusions of grandeur: economic megalomania. A time came when railway shares were rejected; the construction works begun under the auspices of the last colossal dividend were halted; thousands of workers and employees were thrown out on the street; factories saw their orders abruptly drop; the price of metals went down; the legions of hungry workers grew; immigrants returned to Europe; the banking establishments hesitated, and a maddened crowd rushed to withdraw their deposits.[78] This blow was not a punishment, it was a lesson. "A great number of men and organizations," says Lévy, "had real need of this test in order to get back on their feet, to shake off

---

77. Maurice Barrès (1862–1923) was a French writer and politician. He was greatly concerned with French recovery of Alsace-Lorraine following the loss of the region in the 1870 Franco-Prussian War.
78. The Panic of 1907 was a large financial crisis in the United States, seeing giant falls in the New York Stock Exchange and runs on banks. It produced increases in unemployment, falls in immigration, and led to the development of the U.S. Federal Reserve System.

the kind of vertigo that this powerful community was allowing itself to be dragged along by."[79]

And it was a lesson that was immediately learned. The leak was heroically stemmed. The public had to be calmed; millions of dollars were needed, and they were found. The formidable pirates of Fifth Avenue fell in line with the sense of national solidarity. Under the leadership of Pierpont Morgan,[80] they opened their treasure chests, and Roosevelt, the epic enemy of the trust, had to thank them for their efforts and join them in the name of the nation. The storm passed. The Yankees live on.

I am not comparing the resources of North America with those of Paraguay. That would be absurd. But keeping proportions in mind, the method for withstanding is the same. Always go to the main sources of wealth and work them relentlessly. Bravely study the dimensions of the disease and sacrifice yourselves all as one when the decisive hour strikes. Make the most of the lesson in order to be less distracted and to make the creations of the future viable.

Read the newspapers: read those weak and conventional articles in which the authorship of a drowsy reporter can be discerned, and in which clichés are piled up with the same indifference as if it were a story from another planet or another century.

But nature is stronger than us, and it will cure us even if we insist on succumbing. The slow and powerful reaction will come. We will convalesce. When I look at Asunción's vacant homes—many families can take no more and are fleeing to the countryside—I think of the earth. Blessed decentralizing crisis! Elegant and useless gentlemen, go scrape the fertile earth! Powdered ladies, spend no more time contemplating the fashions of Buenos Aires; go raise chickens! The earth will save us, the earth from which races send out new shoots.

---

79. It was not possible to confirm the origin of this quote; however, it could be that Barrett is quoting Lucien Lévy-Bruhl (1857–1939), a French philosopher who made important contributions to anthropology. Barrett refers to Lévy-Bruhl elsewhere in his work.

80. John Pierpont Morgan (1837–1913) was a Wall Street banker of enormous importance and influence during the rapid economic growth of the United States at the end of the nineteenth century.

The Loan

Many people are happy that money is coming into the country.[81] They imagine that money is wealth. No; there is no wealth but labor. Is the aim, by chance, to use the loan for the sole purpose of multiplying the amount of labor? Has that been considered? Was there anyone capable of considering it?

For the moment, the loan represents a debt: that really is an indisputable fact. A burden to be added to those that already overwhelm the nation.

The problem is that the burden is unequally distributed. When a person poorly administers their assets and solicits a loan to delay bankruptcy, they receive much less than nominal value. The rest stays in the mitts of the usurer and the middlemen. Currency will be introduced into the market; mathematically, there will be a rise in the price of goods; the poor will suffer, which will not matter much to those who became rich through the deal.

The immoral part of the matter is this: what will perhaps turn out to be a disastrous deal for the community turns out to be a superb deal for a few individuals. Nothing good can come from an immoral origin. The most backward and miserable peoples on both continents are those that have taken out the most loans.

And what is immoral in its origin continues to be immoral as it develops. New credit will be given to those who offer guarantees and to the friends of those in power, that is, to those who neither need nor deserve assistance. As for the hope that even a cent of the money poured out to merchants and politicians will reach the underprivileged: this is a sad mistake. Put a tax on property: at the end of the day, it will be paid entirely by the dispossessed, those who, according to Voltaire's fearfully bourgeois definition, "have nothing but their limbs to live off." Wages will be lowered; poverty and hunger will spread. Instead, give money away to those who already have it. This will not improve the

---

81. It was not possible to find records of the loan in question, but it appears to be the same loan that Barrett refers to in the following article, "Stamped Gold."

situation of the masses. You will have increased the idleness and lack of foresight of the fortunate. It is not money that needs to be handed out nor what is needed, but rather love for the land and work, a bit of peace and trust.

Fortunes that rain down from the heavens corrupt and ruin. There is a common misconception that agriculture and industry require strong capital to function properly. The opposite is true. Things that last and prosper and prevail are born of humble origins and nourished by their own substance. The most powerful organisms begin as microscopic cells. In a region like ours, where almost everything is still to be done, where there are no roads to flee from the authorities, and where the limited population is still unfamiliar with the primary trades and farming practices, wealth must accumulate in small centers—lovingly conceived and nurtured—if we want there to one day be wealth. Capital will not come, nor is it advisable for it to come. Here the main infrastructure consists of madness, disappointment, failure. It is a matter of practical sense; George will explain it to you better than I can: "A small boat is better than a steamship for carrying two or three passengers from time to time; a few sacks of flour can be transported for a lower cost on a fit mule than on a railway train; to put a large stockpile of goods in a warehouse on a cross-country road in the depths of a forest would only be a waste of capital. . . . In the *same* way that a bucket will only ever contain one bucketful of water, no matter how much is poured into it, an amount of wealth cannot be used as capital if it is greater than the quantity required by the production and exchange mechanism *under the existing conditions of intelligence, customs, security, population density, etc.* unique to each nation."

And here we come back to the main point. The duty of the intelligent men of Paraguay is not to bring in money to provide deceptive relief and to honor injustice. Their duty is not to humiliate the nation by begging for things from others when there is strength and health at home. Their duty is to sow the true foundational energies, those that ultimately come down to love: love of the home, of the land, of work. Their duty is to achieve solidarity, peace, trust. And for this task that is long but beautiful, painful but useful—the only useful task—damned be the need for the loan.

[*Rojo y Azul*, October 10, 1907]

Stamped Gold

It has been announced that one million gold pesos, stamped gold pesos, will soon be coming into the country.[82] One and a bit pesos per inhabitant. Opulence.

What to do with a peso? Drink a few glasses of rum and get up the next day with a sticky mouth and no desire to work.

The worst thing is that, sooner or later, due to the renowned generosity of usurers, it will be necessary to pay for this gold. It will be necessary to pay quite a bit more than the amount received, and, as always, some will receive, and some will pay. The rich will receive, and the poor will pay.

This is because the idea of one peso per inhabitant is an equitable fiction. We all know that the adulated pesos will go no further than a small number of pockets. What is truly depressing is the joy with which some victims of the patriotic profiteering view the coming of the stamped gold. They worship the gold even if it is inaccessible. They worship it—oh!—selflessly, platonically.

They believe in its nutritive value, as the drunk believes in that of deadly alcohol. They believe that gold is wealth. Not even the land is wealth. Harvests are not enclosed within the succulent soil, but rather in strong and faithful arms. Laugh, spirited workers, at the aridity of the

---

82. Barrett refers to the *peso oro sellado* (stamped gold peso), one of two monetary units used in Paraguay at the time. The *peso oro sellado* was not generally produced as physical currency and was principally used for accountancy and contracts, while the other unit, the *peso fuerte* (strong peso) or *peso papel* (paper peso), circulated among the general population in the form of notes. The more stable *peso oro sellado* was designed to give creditors protection from the severe devaluations experienced by the *peso papel*. The *peso oro sellado* was also created in response to the widespread circulation in Paraguay of the Argentine peso, which was also legal tender.

soil where you were born. Laugh at the sand and rock, at the snow and sun. Scrape and tear at the world's ungrateful crust; strip it of its terrible virginity. Dig deeper, and at a depth of ten or one hundred meters you will find the immortal seam. Laugh at the gold: soft, dense metal for chains on the puffy waistcoats of the bourgeoisie, gambler's chip, empty symbol of human energy. Laugh at gold and love steel. There is but one wealth: that which is in our muscles, in our faith, in our skulls. Labor is the only wealth, that is the measure of our vitality.

And here the brave ones, those that work, are above all the women.

They are the ones that defenselessly face the harsh reality. They are the heroic ones that awaken the fertility of the fields, that produce what is indispensable for life: the piece of bread, the jug of milk, the vegetable and the fruit. They are the ones that spin threads and weave and sew, that make the clean bed for the master of their soul, and do not dare wake him, and shoo away the flies from him. Hunger, sorrow, uncertainty, solitude: they keep the bad things for themselves. Pleasure, pride, a secure table and roof and clothes, and a little money for pleasure: they reserve all good things for the males: sons, brothers, husbands. But the truth is that they are all just sons of theirs, up until the moment they die. The truth is that these women nurse their fatherland from their breasts.

And for the men—melancholy with sick spirits, still disturbed by visions of the catastrophe, condemned to the traditional slavery of politics—no medicine is invented other than stamped gold. Who could believe that, as soon as the new office is set up and new little lottery tickets are in circulation, skepticism, structural weakness, and social vice will disappear? Who could believe that, through this unexpected loan, the prodigal son will feverishly get down to work? They plan to remedy bankruptcy with more debts and to put out the blaze with firewood. Who could have any doubt as to the outcome?

If it were in our power to evoke scorn for gold, stamped with the greed of merchants, and to ignite the zeal for work, zeal for freedom and peace; if we could keep useful citizens away from the fantasy of politics, even if we managed to bring a little trust, a little healthy joy to the hearts of the silent children, and to lighten the enormous burden that overwhelms the mothers: what an immense revolution it would be! But we can do nothing but blindly cry out our stubborn desire for better fortune; perhaps destiny hears us.

The million pesos—that is what the renowned initial twenty million comes down to after bursting the bubble of financial jargon—would have done us a lot of good if imported in a different fashion. Imagine if it were brought in by ten thousand families of honest agricultural or industrial workers: ten thousand seeds, fallen from heaven, each with its small provision of starch for immediate nourishment, ten thousand homes, guiding nuclei of future customs. An unfeasible dream: between us and the sea are the Argentine steppes, capable of swallowing up half of Europe. Just a few profiteers are the bearers of the million pesos, and that is the problem. There are those who complain about it being such a small amount of money. I am happy about it: if only it were a quarter as much!

[*El Diario*, December 18, 1907]

Workers

A remarkable fact, which is celebrated by some, is the endurance of Paraguayan workers, demonstrated in the timber and yerba mate forests, where it is fully exploited. Meanwhile, the labor force turns out to be of inferior quality and more expensive for less crude tasks. This is not the time to describe the slavery in the yerba mate forests, implemented by extremely wealthy companies that have invented a system of enforced and unpayable debt to increase their criminal profits. The miserable workers succumb to this system, prisoners year after year. An analogous system is adopted in houses of low prostitution; the desperate woman that enters one does not leave again, unless it is to go into another brothel. The initial debt always weighs on her, just like the shackles of a prisoner transported from one prison to another. The prostitutes are forced to buy clothes and food from their mistress. The same thing is done in the yerba mate forests; once imprisoned, it can be guaranteed that the worker will not get another cent for his work. He must allow himself to be robbed in the stores, where the slaver generously supplies rotten meat and comforting rum.

Now, what is extraordinary is that campesinos do not show the maximum productivity of their strength unless under such dreadful conditions. It would appear that this is the only way they live at ease. We never read in the newspapers about one of those good homicides that refresh the soul; one of those cases in which the victim becomes executioner, and the executioner victim. Campesinos kill each other when they have been drinking, but only other campesinos. Drunk and all, they do not lose the respect they have traditionally shown for the Jesuit father, then for the dictator's representative, then for the Marshal's sergeant, and now for the boss and the local official: always for the tyrant or ruffian, grotesque feudal lord on whose coat of arms there are no arms other than the whip. Silent and docile, their great acts of protest amount to fleeing. From time to time, they seem like those domesticated creatures that torture drives back to a savage state; they flee into the hospitable forest or emigrate to the Mato,[83] where, fortunately, there are no beasts other than the jaguar.

Allow them some relief. Raise their wages, or even just pay them their wages. Tolerate them having a few hours of idleness. Then—and what better proof that they are wretches?—you will see them lying face up, looking at the clouds, dreaming. If they have a fistful of pesos, they will immediately throw them away on alcohol or gambling. They are assailed by lust and forget the pain of their bondage before the submissive body of woman. And if there is neither cash nor love, they will prefer to sleep, sleep, to not think of anything! There is no people in the world that is more superstitious and deluded; none that is more indifferent to death and prosperity.

---

83. Barrett refers to the Brazilian state of Mato Grosso, which is today divided into two states: Mato Grosso and Mato Grosso do Sul. "Mato Grosso" literally means "thick forest." Mato Grosso do Sul (Thick Forest of the South) has a long border with northeastern Paraguay. At the time that Barrett wrote, the area was dominated by said forest; today, soybean farming has produced enormous deforestation in the region.

They are intelligent in that respect, ingenious and tactful like all oppressed people. But their intelligence itself advises them to employ passivity, scorn, stoic silence. They have been taught by three centuries of history.

The lamentations of the industrialist *gringo*—the former proletarian who comes to *achieve the American dream*—are comical. "These people!" says one of them. "Paying them more is useless. They don't care about money. I don't understand them, I swear to you. I've decided to pay them as little as possible. It's the only way to get something out of them. I've calculated the amount they strictly need to not die of hunger: three pesos. With that daily wage, they have no choice but to go to the factory every day. I used to pay them six pesos, and they worked no more than one of every two days. On the other day, they slept and infuriated me. What's more, the whip is required. I have an agreement with the local official. He immediately takes anyone who annoys me to jail, and they have their skin tickled. I'm getting by with the store that I've set up next to the factory. It's closed on Sundays. What I mean is that no one drinks on the premises. The rum is sold in bottles; let them get drunk at home. Anyone who misses work on Monday knows what awaits him: locked up and beaten."

Another aspect of their lamentations:

"The problem is that the women do everything; they feed and take care of those slackers. Do you think you have them under your control? Well, you don't. Maybe they'll walk out and leave you high and dry. Of course! Their girl is waiting for them with their grub on the table. Oh! They don't look after their boss's interests; they don't care about you."

If for a moment the gloomy workhand paused his silent disdain for the chieftains, political pirates, and small businessmen that suck his blood and decided to unfurl his lips, he would say:

"I don't care about money because, as soon as I have it, they'll take it from me. I don't plant a tree or grow crops because, as soon as my crops are of value, they'll steal them from me. I don't care about the country's prosperity because, if the country prospers, it will be at my expense, and the walls of my prison will become even thicker. I don't work because there is no hope. Nothing seduces me more than escaping from this world through any old door: alcohol, gambling, lust, contemplation, sleep, death."

[*Rojo y Azul*, November 17, 1907]

Eternal Agony

It is not uncommon for people to try to defend all-powerful usurers, saying that it is not them who are to blame for gold having gone up to 1,400, but rather the imbalance between exports and imports.

They want to bewilder us with empty formalisms and blind us with smoke and mirrors. Let us overlook the fact that we do not know what is imported and what is exported. This is a country without statistics. Besides, most of the big importers usually practice smuggling. Let us assume that one number is greater than the other. Is that detail enough for us?

All doctors quickly discover through experience that there are no illnesses, but rather ill people. There are no imports and exports, but rather importers and exporters. Who are they and how do they behave?

In large regions, where organizations abound and there is regular, established competition between them, the laws of large numbers and the results of political economics can be applied. Not in Paraguay.

The figures on imports and exports, even in the illusory case that they were real, do not mean a thing. They are neither essential nor revealing figures. What is essential and revealing is that exports are monopolized by a few profiteers—very few—who are the same ones that have the two banks where metal is sold at their disposal.

How can the general rules of supply and demand be applied under such conditions? When a highwayman jumps out at you, dagger in hand, it is not a matter of supply and demand; it is a matter of something much more troublesome. When studying the current state of Paraguayan finances, we must leave behind the words "credit" and "trade" and employ "usury" and "theft." We must speak accurately.

Those who produce, the campesinos that hand over the fruits of their labor to exporters via an army of moneylenders, the workers of the timber and yerba mate forests, in short, those that work: What do they import? What do they receive in exchange for the riches they carve out? Some dreadful cotton rag, paid for at a scandalous price, and nothing more. They live on roots and wild fruits, they go about half naked, and yet everything comes from them! How would they respond if you dared tell them that the cause of their poverty is that they import more than they export? They would respond that you are mocking them like villains or talking nonsense like imbeciles. Well, these workers in ruins are Paraguay.

Here there were loans for speculation, but not for labor. The small trust of pirates has lined its pockets with millions, and bankruptcy is the punishment for those that played the unfortunate role of unpaid accomplices in the national swindle. As for those at the bottom, their fate is not taken into account. The whole social machine bears down on them, and broken or not, it weighs just the same.

Land

First speech to the Paraguayan workers[84]

I apologize for how disorganized and rough these sentences are. They do not even have the merit of being very brief. They were written on the fly, just hours before they were to be delivered. The Workers' Union invited me to speak, and I immediately accepted, because I too am a worker, and I do not wish to be anything else.

Worker! The centuries have not gone by in vain, given that I can pronounce that name with pride. Before, a worker that was not a slave or a lackey was an almost unbelievable exception and was criminal to a certain extent. Today we now clearly see that it is an injustice and an absurdity for most workers to still be slaves and lackeys. Worker does not mean slave; it means creator. Those of our race have made

---

84. The following three texts are speeches given by Barrett at events organized by the Paraguayan Regional Workers' Federation at Asunción's National Theater in March 1908. See Francisco Gaona, *Introducción a la historia gremial y social del Paraguay*, vol. 1 (Asunción: Arandú, 1967), 226–45.

everything, created everything. Those that lived their lives with a tool in their fist: hoe, chisel, or pen. Those that were always miserable, always fatigued by the rough path, always burdened by the indifference of the heavens and the cruelty of others, always driven by the hidden greatness of what they made. Those that soaked the mud with sweat and blood; those that, under the whip, scraped and bit and dug out of the bowels of the earth, not a dark den to hide their nudity, but the magnificent future home of humanity. We are finally aware that everything is unmoving and dead except us, that we alone carry the world on our backs.

And worker does not just mean he who builds from dead matter, he who battles to push back the physical limits of what is possible and to pursue, trap, and tame the unseeing energies of nature. It means, above all, he who builds from living matter; he who kneads clay as well as the flesh and the spirit; he who builds the city of the future from hard rock as well as from his own body, from his own reason. He who casts the seed of the invisible harvest at random into the fertile night and casts ideas to the unknown, remote souls that gaze at us in silence from the shadows. This is why I cast to you the vitality and faith of my words.

Socialists, anarchists, neo-mystics, neo-Christians, spiritualists, theosophists... What does it all mean? What is the meaning of this universal movement toward religiousness; this philosophy that becomes sentimental and prophetic; this literature concerned with the afterlife; these poets, historians, and critics that become social reformers; these propagandists of beauties that had been declared useless? What is the meaning of this revival of curiosity, of mystery, of the sacred saving anguish of origins?

That we are wretched! Not through the fault of nature, which we further subjugate to our will and genius each day, but through our own fault. This thirst for profound changes is a thirst for perfection. A vague regret saddens us. We feel inferior to our ideals. We drag along, locked up in the depths of our beings, the radiant reality of tomorrow and, intoxicated by it, we are humiliated, dirtied, and exasperated by the reality of today. We are wretched because we will stop being wretched. We suffer because we will be cured. Our pain is the pain of healthy, strong nerves; it is the pain of life in motion. Wretched, yes, we are all wretched, fortunately for us. Wretched are those that work, and even more wretched are those that do not work. Wretched are those that dream of intangible beauty, and even more wretched are those that do not dream. Poor and rich? No: all are poor! Wealth, true wealth, is being created; true treasures are being unearthed. And we, those bent over the plow, those whose hands are covered in earth, we will be the first to touch the new gold, the inexhaustible, just gold. Ah! We will make it shine in the sun! But not so that undeserving mitts can snatch it from us. Not that: that will have come to an end. We will all have our share of peace and happiness; we will all be in paradise.

And that symbolic gold, that generous lymph that will flow for all, that will not distance itself from misfortune to follow behind those that are falsely fortunate, nor flee from hunger to flatter abundance, nor abandon desperation and agony to satisfy tedium and idleness: where will we get it from? Where does its secret current flow? What crag must be broken? To what sky must we clamor?

Shall we call on the hearts of our brothers? Some hearts are misers' coffers and hold tainted gold. Do not bother knocking on the doors of greed, which are tall and black like those of death. Jesus knocked and the doors shook, but they did not open. Before they do, the waters of the sea and the sands of the desert will be parted down to their very bottom.

And what would we gain? What is it we need?

Capital?

But capital is not the enemy; I would like to draw your attention to that. Capital, that is, the element of exchange and trade, industrial installations, warehouses, and machinery, is nothing but accumulated labor. Therefore, it will share the fate of labor. Rest assured that where wages are intolerably meagre, the interest on capital will also be so; where wages rise, interest rises. Open your eyes, go to the heights of civilization, to the great European and North American cities. There you will see that capital produces next to nothing, and that workers barely get what they strictly need in order to not immediately perish. In the countries that have not yet been plundered, interests are good, as are wages. Life is easy and thus dignified. The human condition is not disrespected by the impoverishment of the worker-beggar. But let us become civilized, let us progress; great luxury will soon appear at the top, poverty and crime at the bottom. The Dantean scenes of Chicago and London will soon be repeated; delirious vagabonds will crack their skulls against the walls of the palaces. We will have the presumptuousness of counting, as in New York, thirty suicides a day. Annual interest will continually fall until it reach 3, 2 percent, and the servants whose labor is most terrible and most necessary will be the very ones that are most tortured. They will die of starvation, of rot and anguish in filthy corners where no one reaches old age and where children are born old, or are born dead, where love becomes grotesque and vile, where woman, chosen vessel, smile of destiny, becomes an idiotic animal that, on engendering life, engenders nothing more than suffering. Why try a different way of distributing money? The pockets in which it rests will change, but the laws that govern it will not; we will have kneaded the dough of social pain without making it an iota smaller.

No, capital is not the enemy; it is not to capital that we must turn our eyes, nor to the charity of our fellow men, nor to science, that courtesan of gold and weapons, unfeeling mechanism at the disposal of all tyrannies. It is not interest or salaries that absorb the enormous amount of wealth that workers pour out into the world each day—enough wealth for a humanity ten times more numerous and refined—rather, it is *ground rent* that does so. Rent is the enormous, singular vampire. The landowner is the one that steals everything, putting labor, and everything represented by labor, on its last legs. This is because land is essential; without land there is nothing. The owner of the land is the one that imposes the law; he, and he alone, is the invincible despot. In the center of Paris—where, I tell you once more, capital is not worth much and it is quite feasible to die of hunger—you will find that a square meter of land costs a fortune. The same happens in all districts of high civilization. Why does capital prosper in the few civilized states of America, South Africa, Australia? Why are workers more comfortably off in those places? Simply because land is cheaper, because there is more land, because there is still land left. People speak with amazement of the *Yankee race*. What a race! Land and more land. How beautiful that famous race is when landowners begin to squeeze everything out of the land and those that work the land! That celebrated race must be studied in the sordid neighborhoods of New York. There is no difference, none, between the specters of New York and those of London, or those of Andalusia, or those of Sicily. They are always specters of hunger. And were not the initiators of the current extraordinary power of the United States largely Irish? Were they not the same slaves that, after fifteen hours of dreadful toil, barely received a handful of potatoes? Slaves? The Irish of 1840 would have asked, would have pleaded, to be slaves. A slave was worth a certain amount, but an Irishman, one of the eight million starving people subjected to the rapacity of the British landowners, was worth nothing. It cost less to tie him to the yoke than to give fodder to a horse. And—by God!—if eight million North Americans had been treated that way instead of eight million Irishmen, the result would have been the same.

Why be outraged at the mild-mannered capitalists? They are a species of walking checkbooks. Let us be outraged at the landowner. He is the usurper. He is the parasite. He is the trespasser. The land is for all men, and the wealth of each man should be in relation to the amount that he works. Natural riches—the water, the sun, the land—belong to everyone. May he who fertilizes the land take possession of it; this is how we take possession of woman. May man's enjoyment of the land be in proportion to his efforts. May the harvest be gathered by he who sowed the seed, watered it with the sweat of his brow, and watched over it with care. And what is all our power but a harvest? Everything emerges from the earth and we ourselves are earth. Vapor is given off by the seas, wafts through the atmosphere, condenses in the spaces above the cold of the high mountains, and transformed into snow and spring and rivers, descends until it once again buries itself in the ocean and evaporates anew. In the same way, a marvelous circulation of life takes place between the land and us through plants. Nourished by the sap that plants produce from the substances of the earth, we give our bodies back to the earth so that, transformed once more, they might feed future generations. As children of the land, we feel that possessing it without working on it, that is, without caressing it and serving it—leaving it infertile, fenced off, in order to speculate with it and thus grow rich through idleness—is a sacrilegious and savage act that demoralizes the executioners more than the victims. Rest assured that all economic crises proclaimed by nations, which increase oppression and general dismay even further, have no other cause than these speculations, which are reprehensible in their very essence. Let us emancipate the land, with its hidden gems and metals, and jungles and forests and gardens, nourisher of everything that breathes, source of immortality. We who think of something that does not yet exist—but will exist—and who hope for realities that grow nearer, and who look to the coming dawn and sing of it even while it is still night, must defend the earth. To defend the earth is to defend the happiness of our children. Let us not tolerate a parasite—for whom a six-foot grave would be enough land—needing leagues and leagues to spread out the idleness of his life, which is more harmful than the idleness of the dead. Those that live without working are no brothers of ours; we are closer to the bees, the ants, and the bird that weaves its fragile nest. Those that live without working do not exist; they are not men, they are shadows. Let us not tolerate shadows imprisoning us. Let us not tolerate the Earth, on whose venerable face we have sculpted our great history, being possessed by those that do not deserve it. Let us fight so that every man, when he is born, might find his share of natural inheritance, the share of land to which he has a right. Let us fight so that the land belongs to he who works it, and so there is no wealth other than labor. You will tell me that this is common sense. But there is nothing more revolutionary, more anarchist, than common sense.

Common sense will bring about peace on Earth when no one consents to murder or be murdered for reasons he does not understand or that are of no importance to him. And common sense will bring about the seminal revolution: the conquest of the land. All blood and all thought that is expended to reach that promised land, which does not await us on the other side of the horizon, but rather under our feet, will be thought and blood well spent. And I am convinced that this conquest will take place in America, where workers are, and will be, stronger and freer. Here, the land will be returned to humanity. Here, when we enter the era of definitive light and orientation, we will make peace with the land, the holy land, the immortal mother that is doubly our mother, because after giving us life, it offers us rest.

Strikes

Second speech to the Paraguayan workers

I want to say a few words to you about strikes, about the nature and significance of this instrument of emancipation.

I have heard it said a thousand times, as you all have, that such and such a strike is just and that such and such other strike is unjust. I have never understood such a term: "unjust strike." All strikes are just, because all men and all collectives of men have the right to declare themselves on strike. The opposite of this would be slavery. It would be monstrous if those that work were obliged to work forever. It would be monstrous if the infernal labor of the poor had to be perpetual so that the strike of the rich could be perpetual. I know that this right to collective strikes, which entails the right of association, has long been denied. The French Revolution—which, like an impatient steed, flung from its back the monarchic and ecclesiastical privileges that oppressed us exclusively with the weight of dead things—fell by the wayside. It shook off the aristocratic and political yoke, but not the economic yoke, the cruelest yoke of all. It toppled the weight of crowns and miters, but could not topple the weight of gold, heavy metal that sinks down into the depths of consciences. We are still crushed under a slab of gold. The Constituent Assembly prohibited workers from forming unions and, under its laws, the celebrations we are holding today would be broken up with gunshots and saber slashes. We have slowly conquered the right of association and the right to strike in countries that are called civilized and, in reality, are no more than less barbaric than the others. We must not lose these rights, because they are precious; if we did not have them, it would be our duty to take them. Thus, there are no unjust strikes. There are only inept strikes.

An inept strike is one that makes workers move backwards instead of forwards. One that ends in defeat instead of ending in victory. One that makes the serfs put their scrawny necks back into the yoke so that they can continue to drag out their miserable existence. No strike should be declared unless it is organized in light of a long resistance. In your case, you are aided by the mild climate and the resources of the ground, but you are not exempt from the need for strong organization. It would be madness to deny what well-organized strikes have achieved. Every advance of the working class has its roots in a strike. For example, without the formidable strikes that threatened the big companies, the French miners would never have wrested the eight-hour workday from the government. The underlying strength of a union that declares a strike lies in the solidarity of other unions that will also declare themselves on strike if prompt justice is not done in relation to the first union's demands. A confederation with enough reserves to sustain a week-long general strike overcomes everything in its path. This is because you all do not need to do anything more than stop working for a moment for society to collapse. What can capital accomplish if labor does not continually oxygenate it? All the gold in the universe would not be enough to buy a scrap of bread the day that no baker wants to make bread, and gold is not needed to make bread; here we have the sacred earth, which will never tire of rewarding the efforts of our limbs with the gold of its ripe wheat. And this is the reward for so many thousands of years of servitude bathed in tears and blood; you and you alone are the arbiters of destiny. Your presence, oh humble hands that do everything, is the indispensable condition for life!

It is extraordinary that the legitimacy of strikes is still disputed. Strikes are an omnipotent but peaceful method; they are provisional in nature. Strikes end when the capitalist—and here by capitalist I also mean landowner—gives in to fairness and eases the lot of wage earners. Even if the distribution and form of wealth does not change—an undertaking that is to come—the capitalist must be persuaded that the worker is not his slave, but a partner, and a partner who is more respectable than he is. He must renounce the comfortable theory of a minimum wage and stop imagining that a human can be satisfied by poorly suppressing his hunger and thirst. Today, men aspire to be treated just a little better than dogs. And this is subversion, a crime! Ah! It is not the principles of order that powerful people defend, but their appetites and desires. They do not defend ideas, but rather their bellies. The worker has the right to audit the business where he works and to demand his share of the capitalist's profits. "But I can be ruined," says the capitalist, "and you can't. My share should be bigger." "What a great advantage that is for me!" the worker—manual worker or inventor—will reply. "What a great advantage it is for me that I can't be ruined! I can't be ruined because I am already ruined. You have ruined me. Everything you possess is mine. I have constructed your buildings, I have made your machines, I have plowed your lands, and have scratched out your gold from the entrails of rocks with my fingernails." Can it be blameworthy for workers to employ simple abstinence—strikes—to improve their sorrowful situation when diplomats and bankers use the practice of murder to settle their affairs? For war is the practice of murder. The aim of war is to carve out the prosperity of one nation at the expense of that of another. But in what nation of either hemisphere is there not an innumerable multitude of miserable, dispossessed, and exploited people? These exploited people make up an enormous, lamentable nation across the entire surface of the planet. The prosperity of this great nation is what is urgently needed, not the prosperity of individual nations. Your true compatriots and brothers are neither your employers nor your bosses, but the workers of London, Saint Petersburg, and New York.

Strikes are the greatest threat to capital. Strikes immediately devalue capital and reveal the emptiness of the farce that created it. Capital, which is nothing but labor accumulated so that subsequent labor can be used under more favorable conditions, is annihilated as soon as labor ceases. Capital without labor turns into rubble, into a ruin, into a shadow. It has been claimed that a universal strike would destroy the working masses before the capitalist core. It has been said that the rich would withstand the effects of a worldwide strike longer than the poor.

Wrong! The rich's wealth will not help them to hold out. When there is no one to pull their daily sustenance from the earth, the rich will have nothing to eat, no matter how rich they are. The world lives from hand to mouth. Humanity bakes its bread each night. When the strike is declared, existing stores will be useless. Who will prepare those scarce supplies to be eaten? Who will transport them to where they are needed? The soldiers? Do you think it will be possible for them to protect the supplies and to restart labor at the same time? Do you think that those that only know how to kill will know how to rear animals and produce? Do you think, at the very least, that they will not drop their rifles as soon as you drop your tools? No! The desolation will be instantaneous, and the human species—reduced to nothing more than what it is in itself, naked and stripped of all the weapons and emblems of its false civilization—will suddenly be returned to the august nature from which it emerged.

The final judgment from which future society will arise! At last, all men will be equal; they will all know pain, abandonment, supreme tiredness, the harshness of the sky and the even harder harshness of hearts. As in a shipwreck, where, suddenly, before the open abyss, each person displays their fundamental virtues and vices, so the strike will reveal the true value of what each person is and what each person has. Justice will be restored, because it is fair for us all to share among ourselves the suffering and weakness of our species in the face of the unknown. The stupid injustice of making all suffering fall on just one class of men will be remedied. And in this new life, the rich will see that their wealth has been of little use to them. The children of the rich will finally be hungry—hungry!—as the children of the poor have been since time immemorial. What will they give them to eat? Banknotes, jewels, the marble of their statues, and the cloth of their tapestries. They will bite their gold and, in tears, will discover that you cannot live off gold, that gold murders. The rich will get lost on their estates. The jungles and fields will hide the bones of their very owners, and the poor will be redeemed by their infinite number and their way of getting by on little and enduring all evils. They, those that have always suffered under the risk of succumbing and in the grip of despair, will withstand more than the rich. But this experience will not go on for long. Annulled capital will pass into the proletariat: the ex-capitalists will not hesitate to beg the workers to resurrect wealth, to restore labor, and to get the world up and running again. We will have brought an entire region of the future under our control.

This is the probable role of strikes in human destiny. Their effect is still short-range. You make use of strikes in small conflicts, in local problems, but do not forget that the transcendental mission is to reach a global stoppage. Everything that is still standing at that point will collapse. And society will transform definitively.

How much merit you must have to accomplish such an arduous program! How much courage, given that you live under the oppression of force, the force responsible for safeguarding the vaults of the greedy! How much fraternity, how much perseverance, to firmly unite and walk together into the dawn! You cannot defeat the strong without being strong yourselves, and without having a different type of strength. You must be strong by virtue of being good and just. You will not defeat iron with iron, because that triumph would be fleeting: you must achieve victory through reason. Your strength lies in the invisible wave of opinion that strikes kings dumb and paralyzes armies. You will owe victory to fate and not to the randomness of weapons. The old laws will dissolve before you, and despotisms will vanish like ghosts when the universal consciousness perceives that they are falsehood and that you are truth.

Fight, but you must not be driven by greed. This is a society where, for every member with a secure existence, there are thousands and thousands condemned to disease, degeneration, anguish, and premature death, and where it is these very hundreds of millions of gaunt serfs that work and produce. We all understand that this society is absurdly constituted, and that if it is not regenerated from the bottom up, it will be inevitably struck by bankruptcy and disaster. But the origin of all this is none other than cruelty and greed. In every age, greed and cruelty have led a tiny minority to concoct and usurp power, sacrificing the defenseless majority and turning history into a repugnant series of crimes. Greed and cruelty make every advance in industry, far from favoring the destitute classes, increase their torment. If you are also greedy and cruel, you will not bring anything new into the world. If you want to make gold disappear, do not imitate the rich; do not aspire to be rich. Do not love gold. To love gold is to hate men, and it is not hatred that must inspire you. Hatred is not fertile; it is not hatred that will conceive new generations, but compassion and justice.

You will reply that it is difficult to be patient when right here, in a country like Paraguay, which is almost virgin and has benevolent characteristics, your life is sometimes made unbearable. Outside the capital, where the crisis is now plunging workers into poverty, while those that do not work calmly spend their savings, the labor force is mercilessly exploited. The timber forests are worthy of slavers, and the yerba mate forests are the shame of Paraguay and one of the greatest shames of America. Undoubtedly, when you recall that a million of your peers, who are fathers, are wandering jobless in England, and that in the United States tens of thousands of immigrants, ousted by machines, are returning to the European hell; when you recall that your children are born condemned and that their feeble breath depends on your own, while just steps away children are born with a capital in the bank to their name, anger blinds you. Righteous anger, for if it is terrible for there to be rich men and poor men, it is unspeakable for there to be rich children and poor children. But you must be heroes in emancipation, given that you were heroes in slavery. It is great to love our children, but it is greater to love the children of our children, those we have not met, those of the radiant tomorrow. Let us raise our ideals to the sky. Let us fight not for greed, not for vengeance, but for irresistible faith in a more useful and beautiful humanity. Do not be disheartened; let us use our fleeting lives nobly. Though it is true that we will not see the most beautiful fruits of our work, flowers of promise are already blooming before our eyes. The planet's most illustrious thinkers, from Tolstoy to France, are on your side. In spite of the bayonets, you have already taken many positions from the enemy: material positions in the contracting of labor, and moral positions. Universal restlessness can be felt. The least perceptive of people anticipate serious events. People are afraid, people are waiting. A savior descends for the second time to this vale of tears. And among the coming rewards for your disciplined efforts, count on international peace. It is not the four short-sighted bureaucrats that hold session in The Hague who will establish peace, but rather strikes. The soldiers will follow you and declare themselves on strike. You will free them from the weight of their weapons, and you will exchange their tools of killing for the tools of unity and labor.

The Sexual Problem

Third speech to the Paraguayan workers[85]

You want to be strong and righteous: you want to abolish hatred and establish humanity on earth.

The mass of workers that today cover the continents—suffering all and making all—are not enough for this task. You are nothing but a wave of the bitter, overpowering sea that will cleanse things and consciousnesses. How long will you live? One second. Space is not enough: time is needed. It is not enough to fill the world with your painful flesh and your avid thoughts. It is necessary to fill the age.

You must be endlessly reborn. We have love in the face of death. Behind us are our children.

Our children: the dream that is realized, the promise that is fulfilled, the hope that stands on its feet.

What generation can dare call itself strong and righteous if it does not leave strong and righteous children?

To exist? Above all, to endure.

The sexual problem is the problem of children, the problem of the continuation of our efforts.

---

85. Francisco Gaona states that this speech was given in March 1908. However, the 2011 Germinal/Arandurã *Complete Works* of Rafael Barrett lists the date as June 24, 1908. It has not been possible to resolve this discrepancy. See Gaona, *Introducción*, vol. 1, 226–45; and Rafael Barrett, "El problema sexual," in *Obras Completas*, vol. 6, 114.

Look around you and you will see nothing but the tremendous plan of universal renewal.

The root sinks below rocks and the leaf respires to guarantee the future of the seeds. If trees broaden their foliage, they do so to multiply the chances of reproduction in line with the number of fruits. If flowers exhaust the purest pallet of the rainbow in their calyxes, it is to seduce insects and entrust them with the magical pollen that will engender the flowers of tomorrow. There are flickering wings, suspended for an instant in a ray of sunlight. They appear, they inseminate, and they vanish. They gave life almost as soon as they received it, for it is not existing that matters, but coming back into existence. It is not being that matters, but moving forward. And to die is to move forward through the shadows. Why do pairs of birds, which sometimes adore each other with the faithfulness of spouses, weave their nests with such care? It is because baby birds, on breaking through their egg with fright, are naked and defenseless; they need protection, and to protect is to love. All love, all loves, love that we feel toward the beings most foreign to us, toward inanimate objects, toward what is inaccessible, absent, dead, forgotten; even the love we feel toward the unknown and even toward the very thing that hates us, emerged from the nest, from the sacred weakness of our children that must be saved: small ships that will cross time, defeating death.

And note that the greater the dangers that threaten the nest, the more indispensable love is. When its physical strength is diminished, its moral strength must be increased. Heroic love emerges from extreme risk. Thousands and thousands of years ago, when genius already radiated from the brow of man—before we had completely detached ourselves from the mysterious animal limbos—the cold and beasts were great enemies of ours. We took refuge—half animal, half Prometheus—in caverns lit by the wild light of flames. Flames, the only thing we had wrested from nature up until that point, flames that make the glacial ghosts of chaos retreat, flames, image of our spirit. Our nest was made of fire and light. Home, more than a fortress, was a torch. Inside, illuminated by the flames that defended our children, we became robust and loving, and we began to conquer the universe.

We have not been content to outlast other species; we have expanded our natural dominions in such a way that the most utterly grandiose projects are possible in our imagination. We have journeyed through a slice of infinity. Fire? We have not only imprisoned it; we have domesticated it and broken it in; it is our docile, powerful, multiple, and inexhaustible servant. Beasts? We enjoy ourselves hunting them. Ice? We produce it, we eat it in summer, and we travel to the Pole for sport. Torrents? We make them stop to water our gardens. Tempest? A window holds it back. Lightning? We have subdued it into silence, we have enclosed it in a wire, we have forced it to watch sweetly over our nights of study or fantasy, and to carry our orders beneath the immensity of the waters. We no longer feel fear before gloom, but rather defiance. We have met the abyss with our gaze.

Oh! All this security, all this pride, all this victory is not for all, but for just a few people. A treacherous minority has dispossessed the rest; the treasures that communal energy wrenched from the unknown fell into the power of those who had nothing but greed and cruelty. Iron and gold and science were swiped away by those who built nothing, discovered nothing, foresaw nothing. They robbed the magnificent palace of civilization and became ever more unassailable through the misfortune of others, and almost all of humanity was expelled from the soaring walls built with its blood; it was left naked and abandoned at the eternal mercy of the elements. For that humanity, that is, for you, who possess nothing and created everything, the centuries have not gone by. You serfs of the Russian desert, pursued in rags to Greece by Janissary ferocity; gloomy inhabitants of the Breton caves; miners buried alive beneath all fatherlands; larvae of the undergrounds of Berlin, Vienna, and London; Jobs of the dunghills of Chicago; moribund peasants of Italy and Spain; slaves of the rubber and yerba mate forests of America; prisoners of all industries; bones ground by machines; pariahs of the slum-planet, hell upon which states are perched; pallid nation of suicide victims, with no revenge other than crime, you are still in the remote age of caves, worse than that still, for there are not always flames in your caves: your children freeze; desperation extinguishes the flames of your spirits. For there is something more terrible than conquering

Nature: conquering man. There is something more rebellious than rock, colder than ice floes, more merciless than beasts and tempests, and darker than all abysses: the heart of the avaricious individual.

You, innumerable ones, innumerable and accursed, you must reconstruct that which is human, for you are alone among things that are not human. You must triumph for your children. You must enter an alliance with women, intimate and supreme alliance, without which the alliance between men themselves is of no use. Men plan the future: women make it. Love them, and your children will find less hate on earth. Betray them, and your children will be betrayed. If you do not have compassion for them, there will be no compassion for your children. If you abandon them, you abandon the world to chance, and chance is cruel.

Pity for poor women! What is your poverty compared to theirs? For the capitalist, woman is merely a beast that is cheaper than man, and a child is a beast that is cheaper than woman. In the major cities, thousands of female workers live on sixty-five or seventy French centimes a day. When the cost of labor goes up, they manage not to perish on twenty centimes. Do you know how much they are paid to sew corsets in Germany, in the great Germany? One and a half centimes an hour. Many of these miserable women sew while lying down so as to not suffer so much from the lack of food. Their lot is not preferable to that of those young women who, in the narrow passages of the mines, half naked and on all fours like dogs, drag the coal carts. You will ask: But are there so many women that work? Ah! Just in France, in illustrious France, around seven million work.

What is horrifying is not that women's hunger is worse than that of men; what is horrifying is that a special scourge is added to female hunger: prostitution. It was logical that the weakest of the weak would be most cowardly tortured. The male who fights can be stripped of his health, mind, life, but not his sex. Women have everything stripped from them, and their sex in addition. Their sex is stripped from them using dishonor. We have reached this degree of horror, poisoning love at its origins, turning the holy amphora of happiness and life—woman, which is to say, mother—into an obscene thing, on which all spit with laughter. The sad and hoarse prostitute that passes by is the very specter of humanity. Prostitute, sister of ours, there are no longer tears in your eyes, there is no breeze in your hair, no youth on your mouth, no hope in your heart. They have stabbed out the fertility of your womb. You have lost everything, even your memory, even sorrow, and the desire to die. You perhaps believe yourself to be a walking corpse. But we, sister, we will have hope for you, and we will return to you all that they have taken from you, and we will bring you back to life.

Listen. Where women are neither respected nor loved, there is no fatherland, freedom, vigor, or movement. Why is this race a race of melancholy and resigned people? Why are all despotisms, all exploitations, all infamies of those at the top, carried out here with a type of calm fatality, without obstacles or protest? It is because here the most horrendous anguish and the hardest labor are reserved for women; because women have not been made the companions nor the equals of men, but their servants; because here there are mothers, but there are no fathers. And these half-men, as long as they do not fulfill their manhood in the home, are condemned to disaster.

So do not betray women, do not push them toward the abyss. Your hands, which have been strengthened through struggle, which have been ennobled by humble everyday labor, are not made to help others fall down but rather to help them get up. Love! That is all.... Love, and you will be divinely compassionate. He who loves is truthful, faithful, unshakeable. What need for a law? What need for sacrament? I am not talking about free love, because love was always free, and if it is not free, it is not love. It is not a question of setting love free, but rather possessing it. So love and you will pay no heed to formulas and ceremonies, and the gratuitous oaths before the altar and before the judge. Love is greater than all of that. Love, and that will be enough. Love, and you will establish the invincible family. Wait for love; do not waste the genetic capital of which you are custodians on barren whims. Wait, and the woman will come, the chosen one, the one who will give you the healthiest and most abundant fruit, the best children, the victors of tomorrow. The one woman will come, your woman. And when you possess her, you will feel that what is beating against your chest is the ardent statue of destiny.

Be fertile. Let the rich, let the powerful, after stealing from humanity, set out to steal from nature by limiting their offspring to an arranged number and turning love into a solitary vice. Let them develop this sign of irreparable decadence. It is as if a sickly instinct were warning the plutocrats of the uselessness of their sexual organs. It is as if they understood that they are condemned to disappear and that the wisest thing for them to do is to not go to the trouble of being born and for a few of them to use up what is left of their miserable history as quickly as possible. However, you are not the wreckage of the past, but rather the seed of what is to come. Shake your pollen generously into the wind. Be the army that has no end, neither in time nor in place. Be uncountable like the stars in the sky. Do not waver before the tribulations that await your children. If you conceive them in love, have no fear. Do not pay attention to those that attribute poverty to overpopulation. It is not population that makes the earth smaller, but selfishness. Love, and the land will widen boundlessly. In spite of sorrow and injustice, life is good. Underneath evil is good; and if good does not exist, we will make it exist, and we will save the world even if it does not want to be saved.

On Politics

There is a common piece of wishful thinking related to the different forms of government. People believe that tyranny is diminished by doing away with the tyrant and establishing freedom by decree. They assume that the shape of the vessel changes the nature of the liquid, and that a constitution and a parliament serve a purpose. They are astonished that it is just as impossible to exercise civil rights now, with the law recognizing and recommending them, as during the era of despotism concentrated in one man and consecrated by the public. This is because the establishment of a sense of personal dignity is not work for politicians. Justice is not born of the agreements of the lucky conspirators, but in homes. Progress does not begin with public practices, but with private ones. When hearts remain in one piece, written reforms come down to a grotesque detail.

In the physical realm, we have discovered the conservation of matter and the conservation of energy. We should add to this, from the social sphere, the conservation of the barbaric coefficient. Use the futile wind of cherished revolutions to stir up the surface of the sea of the fatherland; the average levels of drives and passions will not change in the slightest. Beings live and are transformed from the inside out. There are no adornments, no matter how deft and brilliant they may seem, that can produce a lasting future. Governments and administrative practices are not a cause, but a result. They appear to be in control because they sit at the top. But lightning conductors do not invent electricity, even if they are struck by a lightning bolt, nor do the halls of bureaucracy give rise to one ounce of collective power: supreme misunderstanding of those that go into politics to save their country.

A fertile politics exists: not doing politics. An effective way of gaining power: fleeing from power and working at home. A group of people that has not brought a new truth to science or a new emotional category to art or morality is impotent; from nothing, nothing is gained. To govern is to distribute and redistribute old things along the old canals. The only useful labor: to repair the canals, to build others, to enrich and purify the circulating liquid. Is this possible from the top down? Never. The wall of bureaucracy and official adulation is unbreakable: the sap comes from below, from the roots. Let us not busy ourselves with politics, let us plant our land and not knock on the golden doors. The life of the nation will be born in our brains and in our hands, and not on the dusty tables and moth-eaten files of offices monitoring budgets. We will forget politics; perhaps it will continue visibly, like a floating husk, but it will only go as far as to have the influence of a limited, frugal association. Politics will be a vast *club*, a semi-inoffensive Freemasonry; what it is in the United States, in England, in Belgium, in Switzerland, in habitable countries. By isolating it, by turning our backs on it, politics will wilt permanently, and we will take back the helm of our destinies. We are masters of altering the course of vital currents, of making them water and ripen our crops instead of the empty desert of Borgian[86] ambitions. Let us do that.

Democracy? A dividing-up of cruelty and intrigue; that is all it is. In recent days, I have seen our young voters, revolvers at their waists and cravats around their necks, counting the shots fired at them from between the trees. Politics. The good faith of those that have started to think and to fight is evident; however, their error is a fundamental one. Do you want to correct politics? Spurn it. Study in silence, build up your spirit and your nest. Forge, from your own refuge, whatever piece of armor you are responsible for, and the nation, with its vertebrae put back together, will be strong. A good doctor, a good engineer, a good musician: these are far more important than a good president of the Republic.

[*Los Sucesos*, March 4, 1907]

The Political Virus

I will, as ever, steer clear of mentioning specific names. I will go on as if I did not know what people have been saying very loudly and often. But my optimism will not go as far as believing that political poison is less virulent here than it is in other countries. So let us use a reasonable middle ground to describe the disease, that used by the Latin-European nations, which are as distant from Russian cancerousness as they are from the classical integrity of the Swiss and Scandinavians.

"Oh, to be a congressman!" a student from Asunción said to me at the time that Congress approved the recent agreement with the Central Railway.

"Why?"

"Just imagine! Even the one who received the least must have got thirty thousand pesos."

At first, I smiled; then it saddened me to see in an adolescent such faith in the corruptness of the representatives of his fatherland. And the

---

86. *Borgian*. Pertaining to the House of Borgia, a Valencian noble family that held great power during the Italian Renaissance.

vast majority of people, young and old, share his opinion. In private conversations, it becomes clear that there is a general conviction that power has always been held by a caliphate of thieves.

I do not see it that way, but I can understand such notoriety. The effects of Paraguayan political corruption are incomparably more disastrous than could be estimated by examining its similarities to cases elsewhere. If we take North America as a benchmark—where the disgrace of electoral, parliamentary, and judicial intrigue is in no way inferior to our own—we would expect Paraguay to have a level of prosperity in logical proportion to that of the United States. However much we might lower our calculations, taking into account the underlying geographical and social conditions, we would still always be entitled to a numerical result favoring our progress. This is because exaggerated immorality in government does not seem to obstruct thriving collective development in the United States. Nonetheless, we are hopelessly and limitlessly demoralized by the most harmless public scandals as if we were all complicit in them.

Courier, the famous polemicist, will give us the key to the matter. "I," he said, "never write books, but rather pamphlets and short pamphlets. There is a certain dose of poison in my quill. This dose is not noticeable when it is poured into a bathtub, but when it is served in a cup, it causes illness, and a spoonful of it kills."[87]

In laboratories, the toxicity of a substance tends to be assessed by the quantity per kilogram of animal weight that causes death when injected. The political virus, as Mr. Hermogenes[88] would put it, is also relative.

We have forgotten the main thing—the *quantum*—when comparing Paraguay with the United States. A preliminary calculation is needed to draw conclusions: in both nations we must observe the relationship

---

87. Paul-Louis Courier (1772–1825) was a French classicist and pamphleteer. Barrett paraphrases Courier's original text, capturing the overall meaning, but drifting far from the original wording and structure. This creative form of quotation is a common feature in Barrett's work; he may have often drawn these references from memory.
88. Hermogenes of Tarsus (second century A.D.) was a celebrated Greek rhetorician.

between those that live from politics and those that do not. The relationship between what is poisonous and what is healthy.

Without getting into statistics, it will be clear that over there, almost the entire population, indifferent to politics, devotes itself to private business. Whereas here, unfortunately, almost everyone dedicates themselves to politicking.

What does it matter to that continent if a band of pirates stirs things up and triumphs, if they are an insignificant minority? In a smaller field of action, the same band would be lethal; it would be equivalent to Courier's spoonful.

The middle class does not exist in Paraguay. A few humble merchants, mostly foreigners, a few doctors and a few builders do not constitute classes. You need glasses to find the industrialists. Moving up the ladder of finance, we immediately discover profiteers, who are closely related to the politicians. Going down the ladder of mediocre jobs and miserly shop counters, we soon reach the multitude that is herded along by the chiefs of the subservient police force.

There is no central core, powerful defender of independent habits. At the top, sometimes consecrated by two or three years of university (we have had colorful characters who finished their law degrees after being ministers), are those that plunder at will; a festering bureaucracy in which even the clerks scheme; a military large enough to stretch the octopus's thousand tentacles down to the low authorities in the countryside. And at the bottom, directly trampled on, are the idle and resigned masses, rendered incapable of working by the whip that constantly reminds them of their civic duties. There is very little undamaged tissue in such an organism.

The only treatment in the face of such a colossal, unremovable, and irreducible cyst is to induce the proliferation of normal cells. The tumor must be isolated to prevent it from completely devouring us. It must be stopped using an unbreachable barrier, an ever-stronger *cordon sanitaire* made up of *non-political* elements. In short, the present generation must be disinfected, and the coming generation must be educated to distance themselves from politics and to scorn power.

[*Rojo y Azul*, February 15, 1907]

The Authorities

It is easy to overthrow a government; difficult to transform governmental customs. Easy to chop off heads, difficult to stop them from resprouting. The life of a nation has many of the characteristics of plant life. Sometimes it is useless to prune it and even to mutilate it; disease rises up with the sap in the trunk. The disease is in the roots, underground. That is where the wound must be inflicted in order to provide a cure.

The roots of the nation, like those of trees, are underground. They are the dead. The dead are alive. Past generations nourish the present generations. Our calamities are offshoots of old calamities that could not be stopped or diverted or exhausted at their source. Our past is terror, and we continue to live in terror.

Terror governs, as it has governed before. It appears like an inevitability. Those at the bottom expect it. Those at the top find themselves deprived of practically all tools for orientation and order, except the whip. Because of the fateful law of least resistance, they tightly grasp the whip. The current excesses, which are continually becoming more oppressive, are added to the old, genuine causes of stupefaction and moral decadence. These abuses constitute, especially in the countryside, the only system of government.

The unspeakable treatment of which an English subject named Jacks has been a victim in the capital lends itself to sad reflections.[89] These events highlight the unconscious scorn for all defenseless things that exists in certain circles. There is such naturalness in the exercise of callous despotisms that the critic is left confused and stunned. Cruelty is not shown to be abnormal or excessive in nature, but rather to have the mild characteristics of custom. Thrashings are given peacefully through force of habit. If faced with the indignant protest of those who

---

89. It was not possible to find information on the Englishman Jacks mentioned by Barrett other than what appears here and in the article "Torture," which is also included in *Paraguayan Sorrow*. In "Torture," Barrett writes that Jacks was poor and implies that he was arrested for idling before being whipped.

at least have nerves under their flesh, the first reaction of the tormentors would perhaps be one of astonishment.

The authorities are truly not what they should be. They tend to be the source of disorder and danger. A mutiny is sometimes needed to restore order. But unfortunately, when we talk about authorities, we are not talking about those at the top. We are talking about that chain of minor, middling, mediocre, small, and negligible managers. A chain in which every link pulls and is pulled, in which each person is subordinate and superior, is tormented and torments. And as we go down this grim scale, cruelty multiplies. Recall the case of the sergeant whose martyrdom was reported by the same organization that has managed to reveal all the details of the Jacks case. It is those that suffer that make others suffer with most pleasure. It is those that are punished that punish with most viciousness. It is slaves that become the most fearsome slavers. The lowly minions that inflict indignities on miserable prisoners are those that, perhaps since birth, have stomached the unjust abomination of servitude, and have inhaled pain alongside air, and have been unable to separate a feeling of ignominious humiliation from the light of day. In a desperate spasm, they return the beatings they have received, the spit that they have wiped, in silence, from their inert faces.

If only there were a man, just one man, however powerful and high he might be, who were to blame! That can be ruled out. Unfortunately, the disease is collective. The social masses have been impregnated with the hereditary shadow cast over the country by an atrocious succession of tyrannies and catastrophes. Souls have been tinged with the fateful melancholy of resignation. It is not revolutions or coups d'état that will save us, but a slow evolution, for which all our patience, all our bravery, and all our tenderness will not suffice.

[*Rojo y Azul*, October 20, 1907]

Terrible Meanness

The other day I had the chance to walk around the area of Lambaré.[90] It was very early; the purest of mornings illuminated all the beauties of the serene, modest landscape, full of undulations and whimsicality, natural garden, forest that perhaps conceals the ingenious hand of a contented horticulturist.

And the landscape lied!

I came across groups of women on the broad red path, some on donkeys, and others on foot. They were carrying vegetables, fruits, and milk to the market of the capital.

Their serious, almost sad faces were the solemn note in that smiling picture of nature. The plants, insects, the very air and light were joyful, but humanity was not. The universe, radiant with youth, seemed newly made. Only the human aspects had already withered.

I stopped to rest at the home of Mrs. A . . . I shared my impressions from the road with her.

"Those women you saw are scared," she replied. "Especially the milk sellers."

"Why?"

"I tend to send milk from my cows to my relatives in Asunción. Well, at this time of day, my servant will be trembling. The poor thing confessed to me that she cannot even speak and that she wets herself in fright."

"But why?"

"Because of the inspection."

"What inspection?"

"What? Don't you know that a chemist (and she told me his name) appears from time to time with two guards at the entrance to the city, stops the campesina women, puts a tube in their milk, spills it all out onto the ground if he sees fit, and fines the unfortunates?"

---

90. Lambaré is a municipality just to the south of Asunción. Though largely rural in Barrett's day, today it is a city that forms part of the continuous built-up area of Greater Asunción.

"And does that happen often?"

"I imagine that it is when he needs money. Half of the fine goes to the chemist."

"But, madam, I assume that here, as in other places, some tricksters add water to their milk. The little tube in question does the job of uncovering that."

"Pay no heed to that," Mrs. A . . . responded, laughing. "I don't put water in the milk I send to my relatives and, nonetheless, they've thrown out my milk as well, and they've fined me. I specifically sent to a cousin who was in poor health what we call *hindmilk*, that is, the last part that comes out during milking, the tastiest and creamiest part. Well, it was thrown out and there was a fine. That's what they're there for, not for inspections. On mornings that they rob one woman, as a rule, they rob them all. Sometimes they keep the milk for themselves at the police station. Do you want the counterevidence? For a bit of fun and enjoyment, several sellers took small quantities of milk that contained half water. The tube was stuck in and there were no objections that day. I've done that test myself."

"What barbarity!"

"Since those unfortunate women tend to go to market with no riches but their load of milk, they usually have to pay the fine with the modest jewelry they use to adorn themselves and which they never recover. Of course, they never give them a receipt."

"And what if men went instead of women?"

"No. The men don't dare go near the capital because they are more scared than the women."

"Scared of what?"

"Of being stopped on the street without a pretext, or on the pretext that they are barefoot. Of being dragged to the police and fined. My farmhands don't dare visit Asunción, no matter how much interest they might have in going. And that's the way it is across all of Lambaré."

This is the fatherland, if a region where these things happen is still a fatherland.

Education and Politics

Let us leave it to the jurists to talk about the state as an abstraction. Those of us who seek truth in life and not on paper, those of us who have learned at our own cost that there are no rights other than those clawed tooth and nail from the human beast, know that the state is flesh and blood, and that the most pompous republican doctrines are put together in the vain bowels of a minister. There are people who thank the gods that the state takes charge of educating children. It is, however, a great tragedy. Politics is a mundane art, an act of gallantry between males. Nothing is further from the qualities of competence and, above all, morality, which are needed by a director of public education than the aptitudes for rapacity and intrigue that are indispensable for a solid political leader. It must be agreed that holding power disqualifies people from any technical and productive work.

These are old reflections revived in relation to a member of the cabinet, decapitator of unpleasant teachers. He transfers some of them, dismisses others. Why? Because they are not his friends and personal admirers. This norm is not at all new, and that is what is irritating: to think that, if we get to the bottom of things, the centuries go by without bringing us fundamental differences. Keep things in perspective as you go back in time, and you will find in the skull of a secretary from 1908 the same spirit that moved Dr. Francia,[91] a solid political leader if ever there was one. He was a patriot who, having no other cement to hand, used clotted blood to strengthen the crude armor of his country. Francia was equally irritated by those who were not special friends of his and dismissed them from existence, or he transferred them to a safe place from which they would not return.

To be a friend of those in power! There is only one possible form of friendship with the powerful: slavery. The tyrants of old sealed it

---

91. José Gaspar Rodríguez de Francia (1766–1840), a lawyer and politician, was dictator of Paraguay from 1814 to 1840 as the new country looked to safeguard its independence, which had been gained in 1811. He was renowned for his severity, becoming known as "The Supreme One."

with blood; the modern monopolists of almost all civilized nations seal it with gold. Some of them, the stupidly romantic ones, put a muzzle on thinking. They distort ideas, which are a thousand times more precious than gold and blood. We barely have any ideas in tortured Paraguay, but perhaps they take them prisoner as soon as they appear. There are guards at the doors of the lecture halls. We must be friends with the local official in order to be able to teach our children. And what will we teach them other than that they should also become the official's friends? What a delightful result for a nation! All for one and nothing for all. It is terrible that nostalgia for a deadly past shudders in the veins of this silent, poor people. It is terrible that we are still perturbed by threats against teachers and the plan to profane children's spirits with the spectacle of politics.

Torment

During my short journey through the provinces of the Republic, I observed how familiar people are with police bludgeoning. Everyday conversation alludes to the beating that was dealt out yesterday, or to the one that will be dealt out tomorrow. Back in the quiet town where I spend the summer, I am told that seven campesinos received twenty lashes apiece in the halls of the police headquarters. They made use of the stocks until midnight to rest after that violent massage.

Paraguay cannot boast of being the only country whose authorities practice torture. The Argentine countryside is noteworthy from this perspective. Europe is not far behind. The French cops use their fists to smash in the faces of those that do not argue sensibly; see the arrest of Racadot in *Les Déracinés* by Maurice Barrès. The Spanish Civil Guard have perfected torture devices. Montjuïc,[92] for as long

---

92. Barrett refers to Montjuïc Castle, built on Montjuïc hill in Barcelona. The castle was the setting of the imprisonment of hundreds of anarchists following a bombing in the city that left six dead. More than four hundred workers were arrested. The prisoners were horrifically tortured and five were executed. Others were exiled from Spain.

as it stands, will be the somber monument to the Inquisition of the nineteenth century. The army, however, provides the most impeccable examples of unpunishable brutality. Germany, fatherland of metaphysicians, degrades itself in the depths of the barracks, tormenting the rifle-wielding slaves. There must be few nations where open-air military training exercises do not end up as impromptu popular festivals, in which the audience is entertained by the slaps and kicks that petty officers *bizarrely* deal out to the recruits. Discipline before all else. To govern is to make people suffer.[93]

If governing meant simply complying with laws, what would distinguish one party from another? He who clambers up into power is not prepared to sacrifice himself to the abstract rules of justice; he is not prepared to give up the initiative that has served his ambition. His loves and his hates will grow stronger in proportion to the new strength at his disposal. He needs to command, to issue orders that he himself comes up with, not regulations; he yearns to assert himself, to demonstrate that he still exists, that he is not reason, but rather a man. As soon as he starts to govern, he understands the impossibility of increasing the good of the governed. Unable to make them happy, he is left with no other means of action than to make them suffer. The instrument of government is the saber. The cutting edge is used against enemies from without, the flat against enemies from within. The saber must not lie idle. The organ must not atrophy. When foreign war does not satisfy collective ferocity and thirst for despotic glory, it is worth having a quiet domestic war, a war between the police and incomeless detainees, the homeless, the poor, the unarmed starving. It is worthwhile continuing to inscribe the bloody legend of national heroism on strong backs.

And this simple understanding of the mechanism of government is not only the understanding of those at the top, but also of those at the bottom. If the boss finds it natural to whip the laborer, the laborer

---

93. Barrett seems to parody the famous phrase "To govern is to populate" of nineteenth-century Argentine political theorist Juan Bautista Alberdi. Alberdi proposed that "civilized" European immigration on an immense scale was needed to govern the vast areas of Argentina inhabited by Indigenous peoples.

finds it natural to be whipped. "That's why he's the boss," he mumbles. A deep instinct tells him that the Constitution and the legal code are masquerades, administrative pretexts to multiply careers and jobs. He knows it is not writing or ideas that rule the world, but the eternal basic instincts of our animality. Convinced that the blows he receives are essentially *human*, he accepts them in silence.

Perhaps we agree. Perhaps, given that it blossoms everywhere, the practice of torture is inherent to our nature. So why do we hide? Why do we shut ourselves away with our victims and gag them? There was an age when torture was not hidden, nor did it cause shame; when it was legal and was carried out before the public and before monarchs. Society was healthy and harmonious. Now we live in doubt and regret. We have added impotent remorse to our misfortunes.

[*Los Sucesos*, January 26, 1907]

Trophies

There are two types of war: wars of conquest and invasion, and wars of defense; war that attacks, and war that resists.

There are two types of violence: that of the bandit that breaks into a house to steal and kill, and that of the owner that repels the bandit.

The first is criminal, the second is necessary. The Spaniard who undertook guerrilla warfare in 1808 to save his home is human, while Napoleon is a highwayman of the great roads of Europe.[94]

The Paraguayans that vied for their land with those that invaded it, mothers that defended their children, children that defended their mothers, are worthy of respect and pity. Those that reduced this nation to a handful of gaunt women are not; they cannot be anything other than murderers.

In present times, we must declare international aggression to be despicable, more despicable than any other type of aggression, because

---

94. The Peninsular War (1808–1814) was a conflict that formed part of the Napoleonic Wars. Spain, Portugal, and the United Kingdom fought against the forces of the First French Empire on the Iberian Peninsula.

it makes victims of thousands of innocent beings who succumb without knowing why.

The war in Paraguay should not have been remembered in Argentina with anything other than embarrassment and regret. That war of extermination was a great disgrace.

But I am mistaken: *Argentina* does not deserve such harsh words. The poor Argentine people! We should love peoples and abhor governments. No: the Argentine soldiers did not hate those wandering skeletons, those specters of heroism that wandered through the ruins of their fatherland. Soldiers fight outside their country due to ignorance and fear. There was nothing but ignorance and fear in those that embarked to be sacrificed in Cuba and the Philippines;[95] there is nothing but ignorance and fear in those French slaves that today embark to execute Moors at the word of their commander.[96]

But shame indeed be on governments, on political leaders. Shame on the members of the Argentine chamber who proudly evoke the feats of savages and dare say that the war in Paraguay was undertaken "with nobility and humanitarianism," that it was "work of redemption and freedom." Humanitarianism in the annihilation of a race? They did not bring freedom here, but rather death. To whom did you grant freedom, o generous "brothers"? To a pile of corpses?

Sinister farce.

And yet, we should still be grateful for this diplomatic, incredibly skillful return of war trophies![97] We should still be grateful for the painful wounds of the past being opened, and for the ashes of the martyrs being stirred!

No; let us forget the barbarities of the past and look toward the future. Let us not believe in official love. Let us not believe in those

---

95. Barrett refers to the 1898 Spanish-American War.
96. The French conquest of Morocco began in 1907, leading to the eventual establishment of a French Protectorate in 1912. Numerous rebellions would continue into the 1920s.
97. In 1908, the Argentine Congress analyzed the possibility of returning the trophies taken from Paraguay during the War of the Triple Alliance and cancelling Paraguay's enormous war debt. The proposal was not approved.

who look to evoke love by speaking to us of wars and blood. Let us not believe in those who, behind sickly sweet phrases, might be preparing a new bloodbath. The unity of peoples will never be achieved from the top down. It is not the civil servants, the politicians, who will erase borders. It is not those that parade about and enjoy themselves, but rather those at the bottom—those that work, dream, and suffer—that will make human fraternity a reality.

[*El Diario*, May 26, 1908]

Torture

It seems that the Paraguayan police employ torture. In doing so, they imitate the most civilized countries and observe a venerable tradition. Since time immemorial, the strong have locked up the weak and broken their joints, or they have roasted them over a low flame, or have flayed them alive. The art of inflicting suffering is complicated and solemn. Octave Mirbeau[98] has devoted one of his best books to the study of Chinese torture; he has left us with an elegant synopsis of humanity over two hundred pages.

Asunción's security squadron[99] is a squadron of strongmen. I think it is called the *security* squadron because they are the only ones that are secure. The Englishman Jacks, on the other hand, is the archetype of the weak man. He has neither money nor weapons. If he drinks, he is idling; nobody can get drunk peacefully anymore unless they do so in the salons. If Mr. Jacks strolls about without doing anything, he is idling; today only the rich and senior officials are allowed to be idle. So, the strongmen locked up the weak man and they tortured him.

It is difficult to feel outrage against them. They are repeating the primitive act, the eternal act common to the weak and the strong, of kicking and biting and strangling and crushing their fellow man. Civilization, however, means that this act becomes less impulsive, and

---

98. Octave Mirbeau (1848–1917) was a French journalist, novelist, and playwright.
99. The Security Squadron was founded in 1901 as a mounted police unit. The squadron's task was to keep order during public protests.

cruelty becomes more scientific. The *question*, as the French called judicial torture, required numerous pieces of delicate equipment. From the small hardwood wedges intended to be driven between nail and flesh, and the strapped boot that slowly crushed the bones of the foot, and the tourniquets and cudgels, to the great game of causing burns with molten lead and boiling oil, and the skull pincers with screws, and the vertical coffins lined with long steel spikes. Justice entailed a veritable laboratory of pain. The Colombian stocks,[100] the saber, the *mborevi*,[101] are simple, low-cost devices. Montjuïc was better supplied. There was a special little machine there to emasculate those suspected of anarchism.

Torture has disappeared from the civil code. It is quite another thing for it to disappear from customs. It has been pointed out, however, that the public now no longer puts up with certain bloody spectacles that it did put up with two or three centuries ago. There is, for example, an undeniable tendency toward abolishing the death penalty. A contemporary psychologist attributes the phenomenon to people's feelings—perhaps due to racial decline—becoming too weak, delicate, irritable. Everything unsettles them, hurts them, seems excessive to them. Some people remain upright and austere; thus, the wise Balmes,[102] compelled by his cassock to defend hell, justifies its presence on earth through the famous doctrine of expiation: "He who infringes the moral law," he says, "deserves to suffer." The entire inquisitorial system is contained in this sentence. But the Balmeses,

---

100. A method of torture in which two rifles were strapped together around the victim's body to create rudimentary stocks.
101. Guarani, *mborevi*. Whip made from the tapir's thick, rough hide. Literally means "tapir."
102. Jaime Balmes (1810–1848) was a philosopher, theologian, and Catholic priest.

the Trepovs,[103] the Weylers,[104] are not as widespread as before. A relative and apparent kindness is spreading across the world. It would be naïve to attribute it to an increase in virtue, to a dawn of altruism. No: social ferocity is more methodical, secret, miserly, and cowardly. That is all there is to it. The conscripts that are slapped, the workers that are kicked, the starving servants that are insulted, the vagabonds that have stones thrown at them, the applicants that are dismissed amid roaring laughter, the prostitutes that are spat on by passers-by, the children that are martyred, and the prisoners that are whipped like Mr. Jacks: if they were to speak, to complain, for a single day, all across the surface of the globe, a wave of sacred anger would perhaps awaken a new Christ among us. Desperation is broken down into small pieces and hidden, but that does not decrease the atrocious total amount of it. Instead of autos-da-fé,[105] conducted in the light of day in city squares, we torture gagged wretches, without fully murdering them, in the vile darkness of a dungeon. Have we made much progress?

And what is our instrument of torture? The saber is also used by the Spanish Civil Guard. The whip is used in Russia. When the peasants of Konstantinogradsky, Poltava, and Kharkov[106] dared resist autocracy,

---

103. Dmitri Feodorovich Trepov (1855-1906) was Governor-General of St. Petersburg during the Russian Revolution of 1905. He used extremely harsh measures to suppress the uprising.
104. Valeriano Weyler (1838-1930) was a Spanish general who implemented Spain's Reconcentration Policy in Cuba in 1896, which sought to relocate the rural population to concentration camps to undermine support for the pro-independence rebel movement during the Cuban War of Independence. The policy led to an estimated 200,000 deaths in the inhuman conditions of the camps.
105. Portuguese, *auto-da-fé*. Literally "act of faith." A public spectacle of the Inquisition in which Church representatives read out charges and sentences against the accused. The accused were then expected to show public penitence before being punished by secular authorities.
106. Barrett refers to the 1902 peasant uprising in the Poltava and Kharkov provinces of the Russian Empire (now Ukraine). The uprising came in response to food shortages faced by peasants. Capitalist land concentration had led to a lack of land for the peasantry.

they were whipped to death. Prince Obolensky[107] had a jolly idea: he ordered that the whips be soaked in salt and vinegar beforehand. Will we adopt this idea?

The saber! The noble blade, guardian of military honor, turned into the tool of the executioner! What can we deduce from this? Have we made progress since that age when people used to proclaim, "Do not draw it without reason, do not sheaf it without honor" and in which Tirso de Molina[108] wrote: "The offended gentleman's tongue / Is to be his sword and not his quill"?[109]

Or is it the case that violence, with or without a sword at one's hip, is always bad? I am inclined to think it is. If we still find war necessary, it is because we are still damned. War itself is odious, especially modern warfare. We should not be surprised at the ease with which the saber turns into Obolensky's whip in times of peace. It continues with the mournful, bloody task to which it is condemned.

[*El Diario*, October 14, 1907]

The State and the Shadow

A Paraguayan named Benítez, who was returning to his country after twenty years of absence, was unable to enjoy a moment of freedom in it. The far-sighted state arrested him while he was still on board and flung him in jail. Why? Because Benítez was coming from the austere

---

107. Prince Ivan Mikhailovich Obolensky (1853–1910) was an Imperial Russian lieutenant general.
108. Gabriel Téllez (1579–1648) was a Spanish dramatist and monk known by the pseudonym of Tirso de Molina. He was one of the most important dramatists of the Spanish Golden Age.
109. Spanish: "*De lengua al agraviado caballero / Ha de servir la espada y no la pluma.*"

Argentine Republic, where the Law of Residence[110] had been applied to him. Benítez was a dangerous agitator! If his ideas had been judged guilty in that exemplary nation, what could be more fitting for the nation that is its official disciple than to judge them guilty, even before they were expressed? And since in Argentina it was just to banish the perpetrator without trial or defense, must it not be doubly just to lock him up in a dungeon for an indefinite amount of time here? They have now sent him prisoner to Bahía Negra,[111] as if it were necessary to distance him from the judges of the capital. And it is not necessary: we have judges, but we do not have justice.

Oh, dear Benítez! Perhaps you believed in the Constitution. I will not be so naïve. I will not draw arguments from our delightful fundamental charter. It would be extremely arrogant to demand that laws be obeyed in Paraguay when they have never been obeyed anywhere on Earth. I will not cite articles, nor will I repeat what certain romantics exclaim: that the Law of Residence is the disgrace of Latin America. Not disgrace, but ineptitude. Do governments by chance need a law when they want to get rid of or suppress citizens that cause bother? Has a torture law been needed by chance in Spain, in Russia, and in Turkey to torture prisoners?

No; let us not gesticulate against the vile reality in which we must live and that—oh!—we must love. Let us study it. Let us not perceive crimes in the world, but rather facts. Let us put our eye to the microscope and not fog up the lens with useless tears.

The case of Benítez is odd. Benítez terrifies the state. Benítez is a dangerous agitator. He is not a danger to humanity, but rather to the

---

110. The Law of Residence, passed in 1902, allowed the Argentine Executive to impede entry to or expel foreigners who were considered to put national security at risk or disturb public order. These measures could be implemented with no intervention from the judiciary. The law was used to suppress workers' movements, allowing for the expulsion of anarchists and socialists. The Law of Residence was finally repealed in 1958.
111. Bahía Negra is a tiny town in the far northeast of Paraguay, more than five hundred miles from Asunción. It is extremely isolated; even today it is predominantly reached by boat or plane.

state, which is to say, to the money of those that have it. Benítez is an enemy of gold. He thinks that it is poorly distributed; he endeavors to spread thoughts that he believes accurate, and he is glad to find people who join him and help him. Benítez is an anarchist, and the state, which is gold, is persecuting and crushing Benítez.

For this to happen in Argentina, where there is gold, makes sense, even if the terror of the state reaches the foolish point of declaring *ad hoc* laws that consign the new republic to the dirty Middle Ages. In the end, someone like Benítez is not alone in Buenos Aires; he is linked to a powerful sect created by official terror itself.[112] That clumsy official terror that believes it can conquer through cruelty and raises clenched, greedy hands to the sky, where they will be struck by lightning. The most ferocious attacks will take place on the banks of the River Plate.

If the excess of fear is ridiculous in Argentina, what is it in Asunción? Who does the good Benítez threaten here? There is no gold here. The fright of the state at the appearance of Benítez is laughable. So much angst, so much severity, so much zeal! And all to protect whom?

There is nothing special about violating the Constitution; however, violating it through such a comical spectacle is not something that happens every day.

Before the Argentine state, Benítez was a man. In Paraguay, he is a shadow. A harmless wandering shadow, perhaps enamored of the land where he grew up and to which he was returning with hopes of peace. And the shadow filled the state with fear. Poor Benítez! Expelled from the Republic of Buenos Aires, he might have found hospitality in any nation. But he had the idea of disembarking in his fatherland, and that has been his ruin.

[*El Diario*, March 23, 1908]

---

112. Barrett refers to the strong anarchist movement that existed in Buenos Aires. Anarchists in the Argentine capital had utilized violence over the preceding years, including two failed attempts to kill Argentine presidents, the most recent of which had taken place the month before Barrett wrote this article.

Failure of Violence

Sergeants are killing group commanders in the Security Squadron.[113] The series of attacks across the regions hammers this home. The country has never seen such a wave of events.

Nothing is as easy, or as wrong, as labeling it "crime" and applying the rules of the Civil Code. We are beginning to understand that the word "crime" is meaningless and that what really matters is not punishment—or even forgiveness—but explaining, remedying, and anticipating.

The acts of violence of which the authorities are currently victim are the inevitable result of the violence that they have employed. Violence begets violence. Tenacious life responds to evil with evil. Men are not saints who offer their right cheek after receiving a slap on the left one. And if they do allow themselves to be slapped and spat upon, look at their shaking hands and foresee them holding the knife that, one day, in the shadows, will take revenge.

It is well known that torture is used in certain official departments. It would be very convenient to argue that people are barbaric, and that civilization will be beaten into them. But we cannot allow the venting of official cruelty to be authorized under such a pretext. Civilization does not consist of having lots of exports, nor of walking quickly, nor of having good spelling. It consists of the mildness of customs, of love and tolerance, of the natural elevation of feelings and ideas. Paraguayans are calm and modest, perhaps too much so. They are fond of peace and melancholy. They are poor, they have suffered greatly. They do not deserve—no!—to be treated this way, to be beaten, looked down on, and insulted.

For it is not only violence itself that inflicts damage, but also the spirit in which the violence is inflicted. There was a time when violence was natural in human relations. It was a normal way of getting along and behaving. People lived at war and from war. Their skin was

---

113. Two sergeants of the Security Squadron killed a commander of the unit in April 1908.

thicker, their flesh tougher. They spoke, and even loved, through beatings. Do not believe that, under that rough surface, the vital currents of self-denial and tenderness were missing. The parents that most punish their children are not always the ones that love them least. Violence tended to be bound to generosity and, instead of hate, bred respect. It was the instrument of great ideas and heroic undertakings. Today, our conception of the world has changed profoundly. Current violence, especially police violence, answers to the meanest, most decrepit, clumsiest, and most despicable elements of our instincts.

That is why those that wish for the well-being of our little corner of the world do not protest against violence itself so much as against the insolent contempt that is held for defenseless and dispossessed people. Contempt for the barefooted campesinos herded to police stations; the miserable, brutalized women who find no pity even if they are carrying their naked children in their arms.

For this reason, however much we bemoan "crime," we prefer it to shameful resignation.

After the Bloodbath

We have done a spot of politics: sixty dead, one hundred and fifty injured.

What crime did these unfortunates commit to be punished in this way? None. As they were poor, they were soldiers, and their defenseless blood could be of use. It has been of great use for the new ministers.

Enjoy your triumph in peace.

There have been other benefits. We have verified the excellent state of our society. From behind their windows, distinguished gentlemen fired at kids and old men that passed on the street, at the stretchers that carried victims, at women who ran crying in search of their children.

We have done a spot of politics. Do not ask me what I think of politics. I do not understand such a high and refined art. Ask the mothers of those murdered children and they will tell you the truth.[114]

The Revolution

A barracks uprising has thrown one party from power and installed another. This operation required one hundred and fifty injured and sixty dead. The city's best buildings have been peppered by the guns. The public has endured the resulting stoppage of business. Insecurity and disrepute have increased during this agonizing period of crisis; something that seemed impossible. Add to this the degrading spectacle of the two-day massacre.

Paraguay is following in the footsteps of the worst South American republics. It has had five presidents over the last four years. Strength is only to be found in the bayonets, and they govern the country. Politics is done through gunfire. It is claimed that the fallen government was somewhat monstrous, cruel, unbearable. Unquestionably. We know of no government that is not, especially when it is being replaced. The strange thing is that this has not been said in Parliament, nor have the people gathered to declare it or even to lawfully select better representatives. The new government is irreproachable. We believe so too. It is made up of young men. The sad thing is that power ages people.

In any case, it turns out that it is not possible for us to get a decent minister unless we murder each other first. We have soldiers to defend the fatherland and, above all, to destroy it from time to time. We suffer

---

114. "After the Bloodbath" and the following article, "The Revolution," were written in response to Coronel Albino Jara's military coup, which began on July 4, 1908, overthrowing the government of Benigno Ferreira. Barrett went to the aid of the injured on the streets of Asunción during the violent uprising.

from the famous malady of Spanish *pronunciamientos*.[115] A regiment *makes a pronouncement*, revolts: that is public life. The rest of the nation remains silent. Either war or tyranny. Peace is of no use to us. In other words: we are unworthy of peace.

It will be objected that many private citizens took up arms, and that public opinion has looked on the revolutionary victory with pleasure. It is true that human hope is incurable, and that sick people find relief in changing position. Several workers who had had their backs tickled by the police tried to hunt down the chief or at least a superintendent. They were the sincerest group. However, of the one hundred injured people tended to by Public Aid, only two were private citizens. Those that fought were soldiers: that is a fact. Private citizens, in ever-greater numbers as the triumph became more certain, showed up to ask for a rifle. This is because there are also civilian jobs to be had, and times are tough.

Oh! We do not mean to say that the revolution has only captivated selfish people. In the great steel and gold businesses they recite the noble words "Fatherland," "Freedom," "Civilization" at the top of their lungs, and there are always a few people that take those words seriously. Here is an outline of the state of public opinion. When the first shots were fired, the conjectures of the masses gave a picture of the political climate. One minute the movement was attributed to one of the various opposition parties and, the next, to internal intrigues within the government. Nothing resembling a clearly defined position. Curiosity, astonishment, passivity. The campesinos remained impassive in their rural shacks. The conscripted wretches died on one side and the other with the same impassiveness. The victims are always the same; the victors are always the same. There is only one type of combat: those at the top against those at the bottom. Up until now, the outcome has

---

115. Spanish, *pronunciamiento*, a type of coup d'état especially associated with Spain, Portugal, and Latin America. It is much more performative than other coups, with military leaders making their rebellious intentions known in an attempt to force a change of government without bloodshed. Literally means "proclamation."

continued to be obstinately identical. Those at the bottom are smashed to pieces. When will the game change?

Sixty dead, one hundred and fifty injured. There is no shortage of people who have been punished, but do not look among them for any ministers, any officials of the overthrown government. They are safe and sound. The doors of the legations were opened to them, while the dispossessed were executed on the streets. Other "treacherous" and "wicked" personalities are in their homes. Others are on trips, in conferences with foreign presidents. All of them in one piece, wealthy, and happy. What are they doing? It is claimed that they are already conspiring. Is there any party that does not do so?

Fifteen audacious men took control of the state. What a poisonous lesson! Their success shows that the country is at the mercy of any group that dares. We found out that armed troops had been crossing the borders at the same time, and that two raids were on the verge of coinciding. This was revealed by chance. We had no idea that, in different places, there were plans to carve out our happiness with cannon shot. The public is never asked what it thinks about these issues. What influence can the public have? It does nothing but work, and, *up until now*, that does not threaten anyone.

Let us not speak of the days following the formation of the new cabinet. Let us not speak of the processions of starving people, of the job-snatchers that congratulated the brand-new ministers, shaking their hands with the same zeal as if they were banknotes. The parties line up in the waiting rooms. There would be no parties if there were as many jobs as inhabitants of the republic. There is not enough bureaucracy to go around for everyone, and so there are sudden explosions of patriotism and civic virtue among those that are rejected. Then there are more plots, and so we go on, under the freest constitution in the world.

The revolution will be beneficial if it brings honest people into power who might remain honest while they are there. Perhaps this phenomenon will be put to the test. Let us have faith. But there is another aspect to the matter. The method of ascending to the Golden Palace was too cruel; we prefer the despicable conduct of normal times. The innocent blood that has been spilled is not, however, entirely useless; it will contribute to private citizens averting their eyes from the political leprosy with greater disgust.

[*Germinal*, August 2, 1908]

Under the Reign of Terror

I have come in from the countryside, where terror reigns.[116] The campesinos, poor, scared beasts, seek refuge in the forests as soon as there are suspicions that the government plans to pay attention to their local area. And the barefooted women, half naked, sad little mothers with their gaunt children on their backs, walk along the dusty, unending trails; they walk, white ghosts of hunger, to take the persecuted male something to gnaw on.

Terror reigns in the capital. Here, the mothers, the sorrowful females, knock on the doors of the prisons, trembling when they hear the funereal response: "They've already taken him away." And everywhere the threat of spies, the discreet advice: "Keep quiet, don't say a thing, don't speak, don't put yourself in danger."

It is because terror reigns within the government, and there is nothing as cruel as fear when fear holds the weapons. The government's terror, just like the terror that Dr. Francia and the Lópezes felt, sees a conspirator in every free citizen and uncovers plots that Dr. Audibert,[117] the

---

116. Just hours after distributing "Under the Reign of Terror" in central Asunción in the format of a pamphlet, Barrett was imprisoned as part of fierce repression by the new government. The article was reprinted the following day in *Germinal*, the short-lived magazine that had been created by Barrett when the doors of the Paraguayan press were closed to him after Albino Jara's uprising. Following his arrest, he would eventually be deported.
117. Alejandro Audibert (1858–1920) was a Paraguayan jurist, journalist, and educator. He was Barrett's brother-in-law and one of the minds behind the creation of Paraguay's biggest public university, the National University of Asunción.

medical doctor Romero Pereira,[118] and José Bertotto[119] have all joined at the same time. Oh! If we were to listen to the government, the whole country would be against it, unable to stand it after three months. No, there is no such unanimity, there is not, rest assured, public opinion. There is nothing but terror.

But behold, I am not terrified. I will speak.

Do not bemoan a foreigner speaking. I am not a foreigner among you. Truth and justice, whatever mouth might defend them, are not foreign anywhere in the world. And if they were so here, how deserving of infinite pity you would be!

The notion of justice must be restored. The nameless outrage that this government is committing against the inhabitants of Paraguay must be protested. It would be a despicable precedent in your history if not a single voice were raised to declare, with the serene omnipotence of the truth, the nature of the outrage of which we are victims.

The issue is not whether there was a plot.

It is not the mistreatment that the prisoners are made to endure.

It is not the grotesquely colossal number of people that have been accused. I accept that the government is terrified of Bertotto, that generous boy to whom so many Paraguayans owe their lives.

It is not the multiple violations of national laws, violations that Audibert demonstrated in his *in voce* statement before a deeply moved courtroom.

---

118. Cayo Romero Pereira (1886–1982) was a Paraguayan physician and important member of the Colorado Party. He would go on to fight in the Paraguayan Civil War of 1911 that would lead to the death of Albino Jara and the ousting of his government.
119. José Guillermo Bertotto (1886–1978) was an Argentine socialist journalist. He became a close friend of Barrett in 1908 and supported him in founding *Germinal*. Bertotto was initially in charge of administrative work related to the weekly paper, but became interim editor due to Barrett's worsening health. Bertotto also gave speeches before the Paraguayan workers' movement. He was arrested on September 24, 1908, after the publication of articles in *Germinal* criticizing the regime. He was tortured and forced to eat a page from the publication soaked in salt water. He was released two months later and would write several testimonies about Barrett in the years after the Spaniard's death.

The issue is to be found in the deepest, most sacred element of modern civilization: in the right that we all have, when we are accused, to know exactly what it is we are accused of, who is accusing us, what the charges against us are, what the evidence that is alleged against us is. In a word, the right to defense, a defense in public, to the four winds, in the light of day.

In the Brunetti trial,[120] we were astonished to discover that none of the accused have knowledge of the facts on which the persecution they suffer is based. The executive branch sends unfortunates into the desert—guilty or not: what does it matter?—unfortunates convicted without sentencing, without the slightest defensive formality, before a judge who, as unbelievable as it may seem, is incapable of coming up with the solution of submitting his resignation.

Are we dreaming?

What? You do not even observe formalities? Please, let there be false witnesses, legal deceptions, shady affairs with stamped documents, any means of disputing realities, of freeing us from this nightmare, from this disgraceful spectacle, the secret within the terror, the inquisition that kidnaps people in the shadows.

Is this a republic? *Is this* a human society? Until we have the right to defend ourselves in the light of day, to gaze face to face at what is being wrought against us, we will not be a nation, but a horde.

We still have time to save ourselves from moral death. Let those who were dragged off to the forts return. Lock up half the population if you want. But start a trial with appearances of equity. Let all be known! Let all defend themselves!

If this does not happen, we will not only be entitled to imagine that the demented government, eager for darkness, fabricator of slander, has been lying for two weeks, but we will also be entitled to deem Paraguay deceased. In a place where justice is not demanded and not done, what is needed is a gravedigger.

---

120. It is likely that Barrett is referring to the celebrated judge Tomás Vicente Brunetti (1874–1944), though the exact details of the trial in question are not clear.

Ah! Terror; terror among the people, in the cities, at the heights of power... it is the terror of dying men...

Paraguay of mine, where my son was born, where my fraternal dreams of new ideas, of freedom, of art and science were born. I believed them possible in this small desolate garden, and I still believe—yes! Do not die! Do not succumb! Bring about full, radiant justice in your innermost being, in one fell swoop, for an hour, for a minute, and you will rise again like Lazarus.

[Pamphlet distributed October 3, 1908, then published in *Germinal*, October 4, 1908]

The Truth of the Yerba Mate Forests

Slavery and the State

It is essential that the world know, once and for all, what is happening in the yerba mate forests. It is essential that when we want to cite a modern example of all that human greed is capable of conceiving and undertaking, we do not only speak of the Congo,[121] but of Paraguay.

Paraguay is being depopulated; it is being castrated and exterminated on the seven or eight thousand leagues[122] that have been handed

---

121. The terrible exploitation of workers extracting rubber from the forests of the Belgian-ruled Congo Free State, today Democratic Republic of the Congo, had gained strong international attention following campaigns to expose the abuses.
122. Barrett refers here to square leagues, a unit of area that varies between countries. In Paraguay, one square league is equivalent to 4,635 acres. Seven or eight thousand leagues are equivalent to 32,445,000 or 37,080,000 acres. Indeed, just thirty-two foreign companies came to control around 40 million acres of Paraguayan land—approximately forty percent of the country's total area—as governments sold off enormous extensions of public land in the decades after the war. See Arantxa Guereña and Luis Rojas Villagra, *Yvy Jára: Los dueños de la tierra en Paraguay* (Asunción: Oxfam, 2016), 11.

over to the Industrial Paraguaya Company,[123] to the Matte Larangeira,[124] and to the tenants and owners of the great estates of Alto Paraná.[125] The production of yerba mate rests on slavery, torture, and murder.

The facts that I am going to present in this series of articles, which is intended for reproduction in the civilized countries of America and Europe, stem from eyewitnesses, and have been cross-checked and used to confirm one another. I have not selected the most horrendous examples, but rather the things that are most common: not the exception, but the rule. And I will say to any who might doubt or deny: "Come with me to the yerba mate forests, and you will see the truth with your own eyes."

I do not expect justice from the state. The state hurried to reinstate slavery in Paraguay after the war. This is because, back then, it possessed yerba mate forests.[126] Here are the key parts of the decree of January 1, 1871:

> The President of the Republic.
> Being aware that processors of yerba mate and of other branches of the nation's industries continually suffer losses caused by workers who abandon their establishments with unpaid accounts . . .

---

123. The Industrial Paraguaya, subsequently referred to by Barrett as "the Industrial," was a British-Argentine company that held the second-largest extension of land in Paraguay: 5,281,878 acres. It bought these lands in 1883 and 1885 for the extraction of yerba mate and timber. Its central office was in London, with an administrative office in Asunción.
124. The Matte Larangeira, subsequently referred to by Barrett as "the Matte," was a Brazilian yerba mate company founded after the War of the Triple Alliance. The Brazilian businessman Thomaz Larangeira (1891–1975) was granted an imperial land grant following his role as a supplier to the Brazilian armed forces during the war. Larangeira was also part of the commission to establish the new international borders after the war. At its peak, the company held 4,701,921 acres in Paraguay.
125. The Alto Paraná is a region in the east of Paraguay that stretches to the Paraná River. An administrative department named Alto Paraná has existed since 1945; today, its capital, Ciudad del Este, is the country's second-largest city.
126. Barrett refers to the yerba mate forests on state-owned land that was later sold off to foreign companies.

DECREES

Art. 1. ...
Art. 2. In all cases where a laborer needs to temporarily take leave from his work, he must obtain ... consent in the form of a certificate signed by the establishment's owner or foreman.
Art. 3. Any laborer who leaves his work without this requisite will be taken back to the establishment as a prisoner, if the employer so requests, with the costs of transport and any other expenses arising from this situation being met by the laborer.

—Rivarola[127]
—Juan B. Gill[128]

The mechanism of slavery is as follows: the worker is never contracted without advancing him a certain amount of money, which the unfortunate man spends immediately or leaves with his family. A contract is signed before a judge in which the size of the advance is stated, stipulating that the owner will be reimbursed through work. Once driven into the jungle, the worker becomes a prisoner for the twelve or fifteen years, at most, that he will be able to bear the toil and hardships that await him. He is a slave that has sold himself. Nothing will save him. The advance has been calculated in relation to the salaries and the prices of provisions and clothing in the yerba mate forest so that the worker, even if he works himself into the ground, will always be in debt to the owners. If he tries to flee, they hunt him down. If they do not manage to bring him back alive, they kill him.

This was how it was done in Rivarola's time. This is how it is done today.

---

127. Cirilo Antonio Rivarola (1832–1878) was president from 1870 to 1871, part of the period of intense political turbulence in the immediate aftermath of the war. He had been part of a provisional Paraguayan triumvirate government installed by the Brazilian occupation forces in 1869. He was assassinated in 1878.

128. Juan Bautista Gill (1840–1877), who fought in the Paraguayan armed forces during the War of the Triple Alliance, was finance minister at the time this decree was produced in 1871. He would go on to be president from 1874 until his assassination in 1877.

It is well known that the state lost its yerba mate forests. Paraguayan territory was divided up among the friends of the government and then the Industrial went about taking almost everything. The state reached the extreme of giving one hundred and fifty leagues to an influential figure. That was an interesting period of selling and renting of land and buying of surveyors and judges. Nonetheless, for the moment, we are not interested in the political traditions of this nation, but in the question of slavery in the yerba mate forests.

The regulations of August 20, 1885, state:

> Art. 11. For any contract between the yerba mate producer and his workers to be enforceable, it must be signed before the respective local authority, etc.

Not a word to specify which contracts are legal and which are not. The judge continues to give the go-ahead to slavery.

In 1901, thirty years on, Rivarola's decree was specifically repealed. But the new decree was a novel, slyer authorization of slavery in Paraguay, given that the state no longer possessed yerba mate forests. The laborer is forbidden to leave his work, under penalty of paying damages and costs to the owners. However, the worker is always in debt to the owner; it is not possible for him to pay, and he is lawfully captured.

The state had, and has, its inspectors, who generally become rich quickly. The inspectors go to the yerba mate forests to:

> 1. Survey the entire jurisdiction of their section. 2. Inspect the production of yerba mate. 3. Ensure that companies do not destroy yerba mate plants. 4. Demand that every tenant show his license for rented housing, etcetera.

No order to verify if slavery is being practiced in the yerba mate forests, or if workers are being tortured and shot.

This legislative analysis is a little naïve, because even if slavery were not supported by law, it would be practiced anyway. The slave is as defenseless in the jungle as at the bottom of the sea.

In 1877, Mr. R. C. said that the Constitution stopped at the Jejuy River.[129] Supposing that a worker were to extract a scrap of independence from his diseased brain and, from his aching body, the energy needed to cross immense deserts in search of a judge, he would find a judge bought off by the Industrial, the Matte, or the large estate owners of Alto Paraná. Local authorities are paid off each month with a bonus, as the accountant of the Industrial Paraguaya has confirmed to me.

So both the judge and the local official have their palms greased. They tend to simultaneously be government officials and contractors of the yerba mate companies. In this fashion, Mr. B. A., a relative of the current president of the republic, is local official of San Estanislao[130] and a contractor of the Industrial. Mr. M., also a relative of the president, is judge in the fiefdom of Messrs. Casado[131] and an employee of theirs. The Casados exploit the quebracho tree forests through slavery. The murder of five quebracho workers who attempted to flee in a rowboat is still remembered.

There is nothing to be hoped for from a state that restores slavery, profits from it, and retails justice. I hope I am mistaken.

And now let us turn to the factual details.

[*El Diario*, June 15, 1908][132]

The Cattle Drive

Between fifteen and twenty thousand slaves of all sexes and ages are currently being exterminated in the yerba mate forests of Paraguay,

---

129. The Jejuy is a tributary of the Paraguay River that runs from east to west around eighty-five miles north of Asunción.
130. San Estanislao, a town eighty-five miles northeast of Asunción.
131. The Carlos Casado Company, a British-Argentine group, held more than sixteen million acres in the Paraguayan Chaco, making it the largest landowner in Paraguay at the time. The company extracted tannin—used for tanning leather—from the quebracho trees that grow in the Chaco.
132. The date of publication is recorded as June 13, 1908, in the Germinal-Arandurã edition of Barrett's complete works. However, access to an original archive copy of *El Diario* has shown it was published on June 15, 1908.

Argentina, and Brazil. The three republics are under identical ignominy. They are slaver mothers of their children.

But the slave soon becomes a corpse or a ghost. The fresh pulp must be continually renewed so that there is no lack of juice on site. Paraguay has always been the great provider of the flesh that sweats gold. This is because the poor are already half-slaves here. Flesh shaken by the latest whipping from the local official and the latest kicks in the army barracks. What is there in you, dark, sad flesh? The shadow of tyranny and the war? The race's misfortune? Sick children that vice—woman or alcohol—consoles for an instant in the sinister night in which you have been shipwrecked. Who will take pity on you? My God! So wretched that they are not even shocked by their own agony! No; that flesh is sacred; it is the flesh that has suffered most on earth. We will save it too.

Meanwhile, that flesh lies upon the block, offered up for the yerba mate agent's blow. There is no need to wait in Paraguay—as in India—for hunger or plague to knock down the price of the human mule. The Industrial's *racoleur*[133] examines his prey, measures it, and samples it, calculating the vigor of its muscles and how long it will withstand. He deceives it—an easy task—he seduces it. He paints a picture of hell using the colors of El Dorado. He adjusts the advance, sometimes payable in goods monopolized by the company, thus deceiving the worker even before contracting him. Finally, the deal is sealed. The gravedigger has seduced his client.

And everything is done with the formalities of going to prison. The judge is an advisor for slavery. See the printed forms of the Industrial and the Matte Larangeira. In Posadas and Villa Encarnación, important slave markets, there are anthropometric identification offices at the service of the businessmen, as if the jungle were not enough to crush all hope of escape.[134]

But the victim is rich and free for a few hours yet! Tomorrow the

---

133. French, *racoleur*, a recruiting officer.
134. Encarnación, previously known as Villa Encarnación, is a city in the south of Paraguay on the banks of the Paraná River. The Argentine population of Posadas sits directly on the other side of the river.

forced labor, the infinite fatigue, fever, torment, the desperation that ends only with death. Today fortune, pleasures, freedom. Today, live, live for the first and last time! And the sick child—who will be enclosed in the green immensity of the forest, where he will forever be the most harassed of beasts—shares out his treasure among the native-featured girls that pass by. He buys bottles of perfume by the dozen and throws them away before they are empty, he purchases a whole shop in order to scatter it to the four winds, he shouts, laughs, dances—oh, funereal frenzy!—he embraces prostitutes as wretched as he is, he gets drunk on a supreme desire for oblivion, he goes mad. Disgusting alcohol at ten pesos a liter, a woman gnawed by syphilis; this is the world's final smile to those condemned to the yerba mate forests.

That smile: how you exploit it, you bandits! The advance, paid for with ten, twelve, fifteen years of horror, after which the survivors are nothing more than decrepit beggars: what a remarkable invention! The advance is the glory of the procurers of millionaire greed. That is how they herd the martyrs of the Bolivian and Brazilian rubber forests, of the sugar mills of Peru. That is how they herd the girls from central Europe prostituted in Buenos Aires: the advance. The debt is the chain that they drag from brothel to brothel, just as the worker drags it from one of the yerba mate companies' contractors to another. The advance! A youth from Caacupé is contracted by the Matte for approximately 150 pesos a month. They offer him the advance; he refuses it. They take the unfortunate lad eighty leagues[135] from Concepción,[136] where they tell him that his food will have to be deducted from his salary if he does not accept the advance. The youth realizes that his work is not enough to pay for his miserable slop and, by some miracle, manages to return to his hometown. The advance! The Industrial alleges that its workers on the Paraná *owe* it one million pesos. Subtract the amount that the company

---

135. A Paraguayan league is equivalent to 2.7 miles. Eighty leagues is equivalent to 216 miles. As mentioned, Barrett also uses the term "league" to refer to square leagues, a unit of area.
136. Concepción, a city in the north of Paraguay's Eastern Region, 130 miles north of Asunción.

has robbed from these people since it imprisoned them, and you will get the brute price of slaves. A good slave today costs approximately what it did previously: from three to five hundred pesos.

The advance was taken and squandered. *Lasciate ogni speranza!*[137] Now, the cattle drive. The river: they pile them onboard with kicks and lashes. They are the Industrial's livestock. Hundreds of human beings in a space of fifty meters. Filthy pigswill, scurvy, black diarrhea; and they put them to work on the way! Squalid adolescents unload the boat; they scramble up the riverbank on all fours with eighty kilos on their backs. They must start getting used to it.

The wilderness: the troop, the herd of workers, with their women and their little ones if family is permitted. On foot, and the yerba mate forest is fifty, a hundred leagues away. The foremen are on horseback, revolvers at their hips. They call them drovers, or herders. The contractors that pass business among themselves write: "for such and such number of head." This is the Industrial's livestock.

And livestock is scarce. Young Paraguayans must be pursued in Villa Concepción and Villarrica. The departments where there are yerba mate forests—Ygatimí, San Estanislao—have become cemeteries. Thirty years of production has wiped out Paraguayan virility from the south Tebicuary to the Paraná.[138] Tacurú-pucú[139] has been depopulated eight times by the Industrial. Almost all the laborers that worked in Alto Paraná from 1890 to 1900 have died. Of three hundred men taken from Villarrica to the Tormenta yerba mate fields[140] in Brazil in 1900, no more than twenty returned. Now they are grabbing people in the Argentine provinces of Misiones, Corrientes, and Entre Ríos.[141]

In Paraguay, only children remain, and they take them away too.

---

137. Italian, *Lasciate ogni speranza!*: "Abandon all hope!"
138. The area between these two rivers represents an enormous swathe of eastern Paraguay, much of which is the region in which yerba mate extraction took place.
139. Tacurú-pucú, a small settlement in the far east of Paraguay.
140. It appears that Barrett is referring to the region of the Tormenta River, which is 90 miles to the east of Paraguay in the Brazilian state of Paraná.
141. Provinces in the north of Argentina. Both Corrientes and Misiones share a border with Paraguay.

Seventy percent of those herded to Alto Paraná are minors. From 1903 to date (1908), more than two thousand of them have gone from Villa Encarnación and Posadas; 1,700 were Paraguayan. There are about seven hundred left, of which barely thirty are healthy. Naturally, no one opposes such infamies. This is the harsh truth: we must defend our children from the usurious claws that are dismembering the country.

[*El Diario*, June 17, 1908]

The Yoke in the Jungle

Workers are not always herded using private contracts. Sometimes the *racoleurs* prepare reports of conscription or revolution and offer the simple campesino a "refuge" in the yerba mate forests. Such opportunities to acquire human livestock for free are made easier if the businessman, seeing eye to eye with the country's high authorities, has the security forces at his disposal. This is not just to guarantee that he can carry out fraud and smuggling, but to organize *razzias*[142] to herd those who want to go to the yerba mate forests, and hunting parties to make those that want to leave pay. Recently, the Matte Larangeira made a pact of this nature with Bentos Xavier,[143] to whom it advanced funds to topple an unaccommodating governor in Mato Grosso.

Whether by one system or another, the worker has fallen into the jungle. He has one chance in a thousand of making it out. Previously, work was paused from the end of August until December. The personnel were given "leave," adding the link of a new advance to the old chain. But the Matte abolished that semi-freedom of two or three

---

142. *Razzia*, a surprise attack to capture slaves and other spoils.
143. Bento Xavier (recorded as Bentos Xavier by Barrett) (1862–1915) was a leader of the movement for the separation of Mato Grosso do Sul from the Brazilian state of Mato Grosso. He fought as part of the defeated Federalist army of the Federalist Revolution (1893–1895) concentrated in his home state of Rio Grande do Sul. In November 1908, just months after the publication of the texts of *The Truth of the Yerba Mate Forests*, Barrett, during the brief period of his exile spent in Brazil, would find himself in the middle of an uprising led by Xavier in what is now the state of Mato Grosso do Sul.

months. It was a useless expense; the original advance is more than enough! The Industrial mimics the Matte; last year it did not pause the harvest. It can be stated quite literally that the worker will not return from the jungle until he has sweated out all his blood and they fire him because he is used up, not transformed into an old man, but into the shadow of an old man. That is, if they do not shoot him as a "deserter" or find him dead one morning and throw his corpse into the river.

The jungle! Slavers dressed in frock coats that stroll through the streets of Asunción, Buenos Aires, or Rio extract enormous fortunes from it, but it is not reached by any gust of spirituality, echo of culture, consolation from the society left behind. In the five thousand leagues of Alto Paraná, there is only one judge, bought off by the Industrial, and one schoolteacher, the one in Tacurú-pucú. You can be sure that they do not subsidize the teacher! Over those five thousand leagues there is no pharmacist or doctor. There would be if doctors' medicine were whips or rifles! Two types of extreme degeneration: the slave, poor frightened beast, and the contractor, ferocious beast, procurer of urban greed. This is all that humanity has dumped in the jungle. What does it matter! These two components are enough to constitute our lawful civilization: they provide the gold.

The jungle! The ancient layer of humus, bathed in the acrid transpiration of the earth; the inextricable, immobile monster, made up of millions of plants tied together in one infinite knot; the humid solitude, where death lies in wait and where horror drips as it does in caverns ... The jungle! The serpentine branch and the languid paw and the silent devouring of the invisible insects ... You who wane in a dungeon, do not envy the prisoner in the jungle. You still have the possibility of curling up in a corner to await the end. He does not, because his bed is made of poisonous thorns. Innumerable minuscule jaws, bred by a relentless fermentation, will dissect him alive if he stops moving. A single wall separates you from freedom. He is separated from freedom by immense distance, the walls of a never-ending labyrinth. Half-naked, defenseless, the yerba mate worker is a perpetual vagabond in his own prison. He must walk without rest, and the very path is a struggle; he must slash his way forward, and the track he opens with his machete closes itself up behind him like a wake in the sea!

This is how he labors, sniffing about the forest along his mole tunnels that "stretch out" from one narrow trail to another, holes in the bottom of a sack through which he searches for and extracts yerba mate. He snaps off, loads, and hauls the branches to the "bonfire." He arduously drags himself along under the weight that crushes him. This is what the brute toil of the yerba mate forests comes down to: that of a mule that sniffs about for its way back. The remote "site" is called a "mine," and the worker a "miner." The Paraguayan Court of Appeals has issued its opinion that the yerba mate field is a "mine." This terrible classification, more than anything else, is eloquent. Yes; there are "mines" in the open air, in the light of day. Man vanishes, buried under the greed of man.

By day, the miner breaks off branches and lugs them. By night—because one suffers day and night in the yerba mate forest!—he reaches the "bonfire," he dries the branches, that is, he toasts them on the flames, scorching his hands; he removes the leaves from the branches, destroying his fingers; he tramples the leaves into an enormous bundle, using strips of leather to fasten the bulk that he will carry on his back to the balance station, where it will be weighed...

Do you know how much leaf the Matte Larangeira and the Industrial Paraguaya demand from the miner each day? A minimum of eight arrobas![144] Eight arrobas carried on his shoulders, brought from one league away, one and a half leagues away, along the narrow trail. When the miner lets his bundle drop, he usually collapses on the ground. No one goes to the unfortunate man. The foremen show him respect at that moment. A nameless desperation takes control of him, and he would be capable of murder. It is a pity that he never does; he never executes his executioners.

Now, the *barbakua*,[145] the rudimentary oven in which the leaves

---

144. Ninety-two kilograms (202.8 pounds).
145. Guarani, *barbakua*. An oven used to toast yerba mate leaves. Hot air is channeled from a fire onto the leaves, which are spread out on a large wooden frame.

are baked. Up at the top, above the glaring mouth, the perched *uru*,[146] breathing in fire, watches over the blaze. How many times he has fallen down unconscious and been brought back around with kicks! Perhaps the cruelest work is hauling firewood to the *barbakua*; seventy or eighty kilos of thick trunks, under which naked backs bleed during the Calvary of a long walk through the jungle. Yes, naked flesh groans in the yerba mate forest; shirts are expensive there!

Add up the army of monthly workers, *mborovire* beaters,[147] cart drivers, choppers, oxherds, expeditionary workers, who are deprived of the most necessary things, forced to cross unending deserts and wastelands, bargemen, who are paid for a one-month trip and return after three or four months of battling upstream, hindered by droughts with their chests inflamed by the punt pole. Add it all up, and you will have the accursed throng of the yerba mate forests, panting for fourteen, sixteen hours a day, for whom there is no Sunday, nor any holiday other than Good Friday, remembrance of the martyrdom of Jesus, father of those who suffer ...

And these people, what do they eat? How are they treated? What wages are they paid and what profits do they produce for the contractors and the company?

To answer that is to reveal a litany of crimes. Let us get to it.

[*El Diario*, June 20, 1908]

Degeneration

Look closely beneath the vegetation of the jungle: you will find a walking bundle. Look beneath the bundle: you will find a stooped creature from whom the characteristics of his species are being erased. What you see is no longer a man; he is still a yerba mate worker. Perhaps there

---

146. Guarani, *uru*. Worker in charge of the *barbakua*. Is also the name of a species of wood quail found in Paraguay.
147. Guarani, *mborovire*. Name given to yerba mate leaf after it has been toasted and separated from the branches, traditionally by beating them with sticks. The leaf is subsequently milled.

is rebellion and tears in him. Miners have been seen crying with the enormous bundle on their backs. Others, powerless to commit suicide, dream of escape. To think that many are barely teenagers.

Their wages are illusory. Criminals can earn money in some prisons. They cannot. They must buy what they eat and the rags they wear from the company. I will reveal the prices in another article. They are so exorbitant that the worker, even if he works himself to death, has no chance of paying his debt. Each year, slavery and misery become more irremediably cemented as a single curse. Ninety percent of the workers of Alto Paraná are exploited with no pay other than food. Their fate is identical to that of the slaves of two centuries ago.

And what food it is! Generally, it is limited to *jopara*,[148] a mixture of maize, beans, *charque*,[149] and suet. *Jopara* in the morning and in the evening, all week, all month, all year. Such mean and monotonous food would itself be enough to profoundly damage the most robust organism. But furthermore—above all in Alto Paraná, where the horrors I narrate reach unheard-of levels—the food is half rotten. The *charque* produced in the Paraguayan south contains soil and maggots. The corn and beans are of the worst quality and, transported over long distances, end up decaying. These are the goods reserved especially for the lowly workers of the yerba mate forests and smuggled from one republic to the next by the honorable bandits of high finance. This is what is eaten in the "mine"; no civilized farmer's wife would agree to fatten her hogs on such pigswill.

The yerba mate worker's bedroom is a small hut covered in *pindo*[150] branches, shared among many people. To live there is to live exposed to the elements; they sleep on the ground, on dead plants, as animals do. The rain soaks everything. The deadly mist of the jungle penetrates to the bone.

---

148. Guarani, *jopara*. Literally means "mixture." As well as being the name of the food described by Barrett, "Jopara" is also the name given to the mixing of Guarani and Spanish languages that is characteristic of the speech of many Paraguayans.
149. Spanish, *charque*. Dried meat.
150. Guarani, *pindo*. A queen palm. *Arecastrum romanozoffianum*.

Added to hunger and fatigue is disease. This mob of alcoholics and syphilitics continually tremble with fever: the *shakes* of the tropics. Under the mule's load that is tossed on top of them, one in three ends up consumptive.

Oh! And the smaller delights? The *jarara*,[151] an extremely fast and deadly viper; the centipedes and scorpions that fall from the ceiling; the *tũ'i*,[152] an imperceptible flea that burns the epidermis; the *jatevu pytã*,[153] a colorful tick that produces incurable wounds; the *úra*[154] of the yerba mate forests, a big and hairy fly whose eggs, deposited on clothing, develop in sweat and produce enormous parasitic worms under the skin that devour muscle; the terrible legion of mosquitoes—from the *ñati'ũ kavaju*[155] to the *mbarigui*[156] and the microscopic *mbigui*[157]—which rise up in clouds from puddles and provoke fits of madness in the wretches deprived of even the light balm of sleep . . . You can understand that mosquito nets are too expensive for the slave of the yerba mate forests; it is the *financier* slaver of the capital who uses them.

---

151. Guarani, *jarara*. Commonly known as "jararaca" (*Bothrops jararaca*) in English. An extremely venomous pit viper.
152. Guarani, *tũ'i*. Barrett uses the term "*kuĩ*," though this appears to be a misspelling of "*tũ'i*," the diminutive form of "*tũ*," the jigger flea. The jigger flea (*Tunga penetrans*) is a parasitic flea that embeds itself in the skin, causing itching and discomfort.
153. Guarani, *jatevu pytã*. Literally means "red tick": "*jatevu*" (tick) and "*pytã*" (red). It is not clear what species Barrett is referring to. In the original text, Barrett uses the term "*jate'i pytã*"; however, this appears to be an error as the *jate'i* is a species of stingless bee (*Tetragonisca angustula*). As with other errors in Barrett's use of Guarani, we do not know how good his command of the language was.
154. Guarani, *úra*. *Dermatobia hominis*, the human botfly. "*Úra*" is also the name commonly given in Paraguay to the large moth *Ascalapha odorata*; there is a widespread mistaken belief that the moth lays its eggs under human skin in the fashion of the human botfly.
155. Guarani, *ñati'ũ kavaju*. Literally "horse mosquito": "*ñati'ũ*" (mosquito) and "*kavaju*" (horse). A mosquito of the genus *Psorophora* that is dark colored and has ravenous feeding habits.
156. Guarani, *mbarigui*. Small, biting black flies of the family *Simuliidae*.
157. Guarani, *mbigui*. A tiny red chigger mite. The bite of its larva is incredibly irritating.

What will the yerba mate worker use to try to ease his pains? Women. . . ? They are not allowed in the northern zones of the Industrial. In the southern zones they are. On the one hand, it suits the company to have fresh madwomen to whom it can sell the stinking paste that is *jopara*. On the other hand, it irritates it for the worker to get *distracted*. In some places, supplying females is a business; in others it is not. Chickens are always banned. Pretext: they cause disruption when moving the *barbakuas*. Real reason: to avoid at all costs the slaves having any property.

Ninety percent of the mine's women are professional prostitutes. Despite the hunger, the fatigue, the diseases, and the prostitution itself, these miserable women give birth, as beasts give birth in their dens. Children that are naked, gaunt, wrinkled before they learn to stand up, emaciated by dysentery: they swarm in the mud, larvae of the hell to which they have been condemned while still alive. Ten percent reach manhood. The most horrifying degeneration ravages the workers, their women, and their little ones. The yerba mate forest exterminates a generation in fifteen years. At forty years of age, man has been turned into a pitiful waste product of the greed of others. He has worked his ragged fingers to the bone in the forest. Decrepit, stupefied to the extreme of not remembering who his parents were; he is what they call an *"old worker."* His face was a pallid mask, then it took on the color of the earth, and finally that of ashes. He is a walking corpse. He is a former employee of the Industrial.

His son does not need to go to the yerba mate forests to gain the stigmas of degeneration. His progeny is promptly wiped out. The worker has not only had his bone marrow sucked out: he has been castrated.

But the "old worker" is a rarity. Workers tend to die in the mine without getting "old." One day the foreman finds his usual victim lying down. He is determined to get him up with a beating, but it does not do the trick. The worker is abandoned. His fellows get to their tasks and the dying man is left alone. He is in the jungle. He is the employee of the Industrial, diabolically reverted to a life of savagery through slavery. Scream, wretch! No one will hear you. There is no help for you. You will expire without a hand to squeeze yours, without a witness. Alone, alone, alone! Prisoners receive medical attention, and they are offered a glass of wine and a priest before they go up the scaffold. You are not—oh!—a criminal; you are no more than a worker. You will expire in the solitude of the jungle like a wounded rat.

Since the war, thirty or forty thousand Paraguayans have been "*harvested*" and annihilated in this way in the yerba mate forests of the three nations. As for those who currently suffer under the yoke—many of whom are now children, as I have explained—one piece of information will suffice to provide an image of the state they are in. They are far inferior to Indians in intelligence, energy, sense of dignity, and any other factor that might be examined. This is what the yerba mate companies have made of the white race.

Let us now turn to the monstrous part: torture and murder.

[EL DIARIO, JUNE 23, 1908]

Torture and Murder

"There is no God here but me," the foreman tells the fresh worker for the first and last time. And if his whip were not enough to prove it, his assistant's revolver would be. There is no talking in the yerba mate forest, only beatings.

With the police torturing prisoners in the heart of the capital for "love of their art," do you think it is possible that the slave will not be tortured in the jungle, where there are no witnesses other than idiot nature, and where the national authorities act as executioners at the service, as they are, of the most vile and insatiable greed?

Walk, haul, sweat, and bleed, accursed flesh! What does it matter if you fall down exhausted and die like an old beast on the banks of a bog? You are cheap and can be found everywhere. Woe is you if you rebel, if you draw yourself upright in a spasm of protest! Woe betide the donkey that forgets for a second that it is a donkey!

Then, on top of hunger, fatigue, fever, fatal dismay, will come the whip, will come torture with its complicated and sinister equipment. You know about the political inquisition and the religious inquisition.

Now acquaint yourself with the most despicable inquisition, the inquisition of gold.

Why mention the shackles and the stocks? They are classics in Paraguay, and I do not know why they are not the emblem of justice, instead of that inept matron with her cardboard sword and fake scales. The famous stocks of the M. S. company can be seen in Yaguatirica. *Lasso stocks* are a cheaper version of the instrument. It is also common for workers to be *stretched,* that is, for them to be tied down with their four limbs splayed out. Or they are hung from a tree by their feet. *Staking* is interesting: it consists of tying the victim by their ankles and wrists to four stakes using rawhide, in the sun. The leather shrinks and cuts into the muscle; the body is dislocated. Workers have even been *staked* on top of *takuru* (white termite mounds) that has been set on fire.

Do not tremble, pen of mine! Thrust home up to the hilt! The vile people that I execute do not have blood in their veins, but pus, and the surgeon gets covered in filth.

It is rare for a worker to try to escape. It requires an amount of energy that the degenerated men of the yerba mate forest are far from having. When it does happen, the contractors assemble groups from the *companies* of soldiers, and they hunt down the fugitive. The contractors inform each other. The rule is: "Bring him back dead or alive."

Ah! The joyful manhunt in the jungle! Messengers taking orders to neighboring guard posts! "Last night two of mine escaped. If they come out around here, shoot them" (verbatim). Last year, in the Argentine province of Misiones, seven workers were murdered, one of whom was a child. In Punta Porá,[158] when the police station declares a worker to be a runaway, "runaway" means "throat slit." Two months ago, D. C., an employer and contractor of the Matte Larangeira, bought a worker's lover for six hundred pesos and had the displeasure of finding

---

158. Punta Porá is a settlement in northeast Paraguay founded as a base for yerba mate extraction. Today it is the city of Pedro Juan Caballero, which sits directly alongside a Brazilian city that is still called Ponta Porã, the name in Portuguese for Punta Porá.

out that the woman had fled with her old lover and his brother. D. C. pursued them with men armed with Winchesters; one of the workers died instantly; the other was finished off with a knife. They tend to open fire without giving a verbal warning. The companies do not only slaughter workers, but other citizens that they take a disliking to. The Industrial Paraguaya, well-known in Tacuru-pucú for its atrocities, recently expelled the families from the town in order to seize control of the rum shops. Mr. E. R. expressed his opposition and the Industrial had the police kill him at his bedroom door.

All these crimes go unpunished. No judge takes them up, and if one were to do so, nothing would change. He is bought off!

It is frightening to think of the murders hidden by the jungle. The trails are dotted with crosses, half of which mark the spot where a child succumbed. Many of these anonymous crosses recall a hunt that ended in an execution.

And despite the thousand-to-one chance that the *"deserter"* (this is the term that has been enshrined by usage) has of not perishing, the dream of the martyr of the yerba mate forests is to escape, to reach the border or the fields, the free region that gleams from fifty, one hundred, one hundred and fifty leagues away . . . Leagues of dense forest, of swamps, leagues that must be crossed naked, weak, and trembling, like a rat trailed by dogs. . . . The slave does not sleep; he stirs his poor bones on the squalid foliage that he uses as a bed and stirs the mad hopes in his distressed brain. The silence of the night entices him. The enormous power of the gold that he himself has torn from the earth stops him. The Company has recaptured "deserters" that, following four or five years of absence, believed themselves to be saved. The Company is stronger than anything. Why go to his death? It is better to lose strength little by little, to lose the sap of life drop by drop, to renounce ever seeing the place where he was born again . . . The following day, the slave will get down to work and will offer up the reglementary eight arrobas to the businessman.

Oh! To look to flee from the yerba mate forest you must be a hero or not in your right mind.

In this way, the opulent swine, who spends enormous amounts

in our salons, exterminates Paraguayans by the thousand under the yoke or, if they seek freedom, shoots them like jackals in the desert. Generations of slaves do not last long, but the slavers keep themselves looking young. It is those at the top that I accuse. They are the true murderers, not the contractors or the foremen. The gang leaders are the ones responsible, because they are the ones that run the least risk and that profit most from the crime.

And that is what still remains for me to do: to describe in detail the spoils of slavery and show who shares in them and how.

[*El Diario*, June 25, 1908]

The Spoils

Let us take the Industrial Paraguaya as our typical example.

It started out with 400,000 pesos.

Who does not know about the machinations of the Industrial to take control of the land? Yerba mate forests turned into fields and fields turned into yerba mate forests; forests and rivers disappearing from the map and emerging one hundred leagues away from where they should have been; the auctions and sales, not of plots of land, but of surveyors and judges. In front of me is a map of the department of Villa Concepción, a strange document that shows the swindling of twelve leagues of yerba mate forests through alterations to the surveys of pre-dating properties. This was done in order to claim compensation for a new twelve-league yerba mate forest that they tried to bag without paying a cent. And the fraud was pulled off, as were a thousand like it. But the terrible thing is that the state, which failed to defend its territory, and today does not even know that the Company smuggles millions and millions of arrobas into Argentina, was, and is, unable to protect the innocent flesh of its citizens. And every year the Industrial carries away the number of victims that it needs to implement one of the most abject examples of exploitation in the modern world.

Here is a table of the average wages currently paid by the Industrial in Paraguayan currency. The figures are approximately the same in the other companies. At present, the yerba mate companies form an invincible *trust* and fix the prices they want. There is no competition to alleviate the fate of the slaves.

Miners: per arroba	0.60
Barbakua: per arroba	0.20
Beaters and machinists: per month	45.00
Foremen: per month	120.00
Drovers: per month	70.00
Oxherds: per month	60.00
Bargemen: per trip (1 to 3 months)	90.00
Assorted monthly workers:	30.00

These unfortunates must almost always buy the disgusting food that they eat, and always the rags that they wear, from the company. And at what prices!

Poor quality meat with bones in it costs the same as boneless meat in Asunción. A pound of suet costs one and a half pesos. A pound of fourth-rate flour, two pesos. Corn has gone up to two pesos a pound. Clothes are a rip-off. A meter of the worst-quality flannel, fifteen pesos; it is worth two. Pants made of the worst-quality canvas, twenty pesos; they are worth four. The worst-quality shirt, fifteen pesos; it is worth three. The worst-quality hat, sixty pesos; it is worth twelve. A poncho (aspiration of Paraguayans), two hundred pesos; it is worth sixty. A box of matches, one peso.

Let us take the best-case scenario: that of a "tough" miner who hauls out three hundred arrobas a month. He will earn one hundred and eighty pesos. Take away what he spends on poorly feeding himself and covering his modesty, and what does he have left? Thirty or forty pesos at most. It will take him years and even more years to pay off the advance of one thousand to two thousand pesos with which he was enchained. The fate of the other workers is incomparably worse. Many limit themselves to consuming just water, beans, and salt in the hope of one day saving themselves. Vain hope!

Note that salaries have not gone up much over the last fifteen years, while gold has reached 1,500. Of course! The Industrial pockets its earnings in gold and covers its expenses in paper money.[159] It suits it and the other export businesses for the price of gold to go up. They have come to an agreement with the usurers: the price of gold goes up, and it will go up to whatever price pleases this group of bandits that nobody has the courage to put in jail.

A simple calculation: if we consider the number of bags that the bag fastener dispatches every day and those that are transported an average distance of thirty leagues by cart or barge, alongside the common value per unit, we arrive at a maximum price of 2.50 pesos per arroba of yerba ready for export.

And this cost price is still nominal. The Company pays wages in goods, stealing at 300 percent. (Smuggled goods in Alto Paraná.) These transactions are not trivial in the eyes of the Industrial, which evicted the inhabitants of Tacuru-pucú from their homes in order to become the sole seller of rum. Now it distills rum, sells it at ten pesos per liter, and resells it to the workers through prostitutes that charge three pesos for an inch of alcohol. The worker gets a shirt on credit, pawns it, and drinks it up in exchange for a few minutes of oblivion. The Industrial is behind the counters of every business!

There is more. The Industrial makes use of two different arrobas: one that is equivalent to eleven and a half kilos for the worker, and another ten-kilo one for itself. If the miner takes eight arrobas and nineteen pounds to the *barbakua*, he is not paid for the pounds. Woe betide him if he does not arrive with the eight arrobas!

You were familiar with the employer-slaver, the employer-torturer, the employer-murderer. This is the employer-thief. This is where he shows the depths of his soul.

---

159. Barrett refers to the two units of currency that existed in parallel in Paraguay at the time. The *peso oro sellado* (stamped gold peso), used for accountancy and contracts, and the *peso fuerte* (strong peso) or *peso papel* (paper peso), that circulated in the form of notes. From 1906 to 1908, the exchange rate between the two units had risen significantly in favor of the *peso oro sellado*. Over the same period, the cost of living in *peso papel* rose by over 80 percent while the cost of living in *peso oro sellado* fell by almost 30 percent. See Juan Carlos Herken, "La Política económica durante la Era Liberal," *Cuadernos Históricos*, No. 9 (1989), 95.

So let us take the cost price of an arroba as two pesos.

The Company sells it for thirty.

Insert the enormous wedge of successive contractors between the figure of two and the figure of thirty, and there you have it! The worker is at the bottom.

The first contractor buys for two and sells for four, the next buys for four and sells for seven . . . The Company buys for seven and sells for thirty. This is how the spoils of slavery are divided up. It is not surprising, then, that the contractors get rich and the Industrial picks up five million each year and extracts up to 44 percent profit.

The directors of the Industrial are shrewd financiers. They have plundered the earth and exterminated the race.

They have not built a single road.

What for? Forty-four percent profit! There is nothing more to say.

I accuse the administrators of the Industrial Paraguaya and the other yerba mate companies of being pillagers, torturers of slaves, and murderers. I curse their bloodstained money.

And I let it be known to them that they will not disgrace this unfortunate country for much longer.

[*El Diario*, June 27, 1908]

Notes

INTRODUCTION

1. For accounts of the actions of Barrett and Bertotto during the uprising see José Guillermo Bertotto, "Rafael Barrett: Su vida en el Paraguay," in Rafael Barrett, *Artículos diversos* (San José: Alsina, 1913), 15–16; Francisca López Maíz, "Introducción" in Rafael Barrett, *Cartas Íntimas* (Asunción: Arandurã, 2022), 41–42; Letter from Santiago Talía reproduced in Francisco Gaona, *Introducción a la historia gremial y social del Paraguay*, vol. 1 (Asunción: Arandú, 1967), 213–14.
2. Bertotto, "Rafael Barrett: Su vida en el Paraguay," 15–16.
3. Rafael Barrett, "On the Ranch," article included in this book.
4. Francisco Corral, *El pensamiento cautivo de Rafael Barrett: Crisis de fin de siglo, juventud del 98 y anarquismo* (Madrid: Siglo XXI, 1994), 1, 121.
5. Augusto Roa Bastos, "Rafael Barrett: Descubridor de la realidad social del Paraguay," in Rafael Barrett, *El dolor paraguayo* (Caracas: Biblioteca Ayacucho, 1978), ix.
6. Bertotto, "Rafael Barrett: Su vida en el Paraguay," 5.
7. Texts were published with claims that Barrett had been born in places as diverse as Catalonia, Andalusia, Morocco, and Argentina. See Corral, *Pensamiento cautivo*, 3.
8. Although Barrett's family had links to the Dukes of Alba through the Álvarez de Toledo line, the last common ancestor lived in the sixteenth century. The family name also links Barrett to the family of Christopher Columbus and the conquistador Fernando Álvarez de Toledo. See Vladimiro Muñoz, *Barrett* (Asunción/Montevideo: Ediciones Germinal,1995), 8.
9. George Barrett's birth certificate shows he was born in Coventry, England,

to an Irish father who was a British military officer, and English mother. He published at least two books under the name Jorge Barrett y Clarke: *La Zona Fiscal* (Madrid: Segundo Martínez, 1871); and *Las sociedades cooperativas de crédito y los cupones de la hacienda española* (publication details unknown).

10. López Maíz, "Introducción," 37–38.
11. Barrett would consistently make use of his British nationality, although it appears he never lived in the United Kingdom. He was registered at the British consulate in Asunción, and the consul would intervene to secure his release when he was imprisoned in 1908. However, Barrett displayed a strong dislike for the British imperialist state and the English bourgeoisie and aristocracy; he often spoke of the English in quite disparaging terms.
12. Bernardo Rodríguez y Largo, *Resumen acerca del estado del Instituto de San Isidro de Madrid en el curso de 1889 a 1890* (Madrid: Sucesores de Rivadeneyra, 1891), 23. Barrett won prizes in Latin, Spanish, French, arithmetic and algebra, and Spanish history while studying at the Cardenal Cisneros and San Isidro schools in central Madrid. This broad array of interests and talents would be reflected in the topics he would cover in his texts.
13. Rafael Barrett, "El postulado de Euclides," *Revista Contemporánea*, vol.106 (1897); and Rafael Barrett, "Sobre el espesor y la rigidez de la corteza Terrestre," *Revista Contemporánea*, vol.109 (1898).
14. *La Correspondencia de España*, June 18, 1900.
15. Through his work as a playwright, poet, and novelist, Valle-Inclán would become one of the most important figures in twentieth-century Spanish literature. During a trip to South America in 1910, he traveled to Asunción to visit his friend Barrett. However, Barrett had left Paraguay just weeks before to seek treatment for his tuberculosis in Europe. See notes from López Maíz in Rafael Barrett, "LXXII," in *Cartas Íntimas*, 144.
16. Corral, *El pensamiento cautivo*, 84–100.
17. Ramiro de Maeztu, "Rafael Barrett en Madrid," in Rafael Barrett, *Lo que son los yerbales paraguayos* (Montevideo: Claudio García, 1926), 9–10.
18. Notes from Francisca López Maíz in Rafael Barrett, "XLVII," in *Cartas Íntimas*, 109.
19. *El Imparcial*, April 4, 1902.
20. Corral mentions that Barrett's descendants speak of him losing his inheritance through gambling. See Francisco Corral Sánchez-Cabezudo, "Vida y pensamiento de Rafael Barrett" (PhD diss., Universidad Compultense de Madrid, 1991), 55. Barrett was recorded in 1901 as a guest at a luxurious hotel in the exclusive French resort town of Biarritz, famous for its casinos. See *La Gazette Illustrée de Biarritz*, September 6, 1901.
21. Maeztu, "Rafael Barrett," 10.

22. See *El Imparcial*, February 19, 1902, and *El Globo*, February 20, 1902.
23. *El Liberal*, November 28, 1902.
24. López Maíz, "Introducción," 38.
25. Muñoz writes that a "Sr. Barrett, R." appears on the list of passengers of a transatlantic steamer that passed through Montevideo before reaching Buenos Aires on November 3, 1903. Barrett would have boarded in Cherbourg, France, in early October. See Rafael Barrett, *Marginalia*, ed. Vladimiro Muñoz (Asunción/Montevideo: Ediciones Germinal, 1991), 54–55. However, Barrett's first article in the Buenos Aires press, "Aguafuertes," was published in August 1903. As Muñoz suggests, the article might have been sent to Buenos Aires from Europe. Or had Barrett in fact traveled to Buenos Aires earlier in the year in 1903? When contacted, the Argentine Museum of Immigration responded that Barrett's name did not appear in their digital records of immigrants arriving in Argentina. Museo de la Inmigración, email message to author, July 10, 2023.
26. Rafael Barrett, "¡Carnaval!," in *Obras Completas*, vol. 1 (Asunción: Germinal and Arandurã, 2011), 30.
27. Alicia Vidaurreta, "Spanish Immigration to Argentina, 1870–1930," *Jahrbuch für Geschichte von Staat, Wirtschaft und Gesellschaft Lateinamerikas*, vol. 19 (1982): 294.
28. Chuck Morse, "Anarchism, Argentina," in *The International Encyclopedia of Revolution and Protest: 1500 to the Present*, ed. Immanuel Ness, vol. 1 (Malden, MA: Wiley-Blackwell, 2009), 101–2.
29. Rafael Barrett, "La Ley de Residencia," in *Obras Completas*, vol. 1, 40–45; and Rafael Barrett, "Los prudentes de la Liga Republicana," in *Obras Completas*, vol. 1, 32.
30. Rafael Barrett, "De pintura," in *Obras Completas*, vol. 1, 72.
31. López Maíz, "Introducción," 38.
32. Roa Bastos, "Rafael Barrett," xvii.
33. Margarita Durán Estragó, "Conquista y colonización (1537–1680)," in *Nueva historia del Paraguay*, ed. Ignacio Telesca (Buenos Aires: Sudamericana, 2020), 75–77.
34. Jennifer L. French, "Yerba," in *Latin American Literature in Transition 1870–1930*, ed. Fernando Degiovanni and Javier Uriarte (Cambridge: Cambridge University Press, 2022), 90.
35. Ignacio Telesca, "La colonia desde 1680 a 1780," in *Nueva historia del Paraguay*, ed. Ignacio Telesca (Buenos Aires: Sudamericana, 2020), 100.
36. Jerry W. Cooney, "Paraguayan Independence and Doctor Francia," *The Americas*, vol. 28, No. 4 (1972): 408.
37. Henryk Szlajfer, "Against Dependent Capitalist Development in Nineteenth-Century Latin America: The Case of Haiti and Paraguay," *Latin American Perspectives*, vol. 13, No. 1 (1986): 62.

38. Small-scale family farmers.
39. Szlajfer, "Against Dependent Capitalist Development," 62.
40. Cathy Kaiser, "Carlos Antonio López and the Birth of Paraguayan Diplomacy," *Jahrbuch für Geschichte von Staat, Wirtschaft und Gesellschaft Lateinamerikas* 19 (1982): 238–39, 250.
41. The figure of Francisco Solano López has long been a subject of enormous controversy in Paraguay. To this day, two competing Manichean views of him vie for dominance in the national imaginary. On one side, López is presented as the archvillain of Paraguayan history, the man who condemned his country to a war of annihilation. On the other, the official view, López is seen as the country's maximum hero, who defended his homeland to the last. Barrett was right to predict that "the López affair continues and will continue to be the crossroads at which underlying opinions in Paraguay meet, tremble, and clash." "En torno al libro del doctor Báez," in *Obras Completas*, vol. 2, 176.
42. Alex Weisiger, *Logics of War: Explanations for Limited and Unlimited Conflicts* (Ithaca, NY: Cornell University Press, 2013), 88.
43. Jan M. G. Kleinpenning, "Strong Reservations about 'New Insights into the Demographics of the Paraguayan War,'" *Latin American Research Review* 37 (2002): 137–42. Kleinpenning uses the best available data to make an estimate of Paraguayan deaths during the war. In 1864, the country had between 388,511 and 456,979 inhabitants; in 1873 the population had fallen to 221,079, a reduction of from 43.1 to 51.6 percent on prewar estimates.
44. Harris Gaylord Warren, *Paraguay and the Triple Alliance: The Postwar Decade, 1869–1878* (Austin: University of Texas Press, 1978), 138–39.
45. Arantxa Guereña and Luis Rojas Villagra, *Yvy Jára: Los dueños de la tierra en Paraguay* (Asunción: Oxfam, 2016), 11.
46. Carlos Pastore, *La lucha por la tierra en el Paraguay* (Montevideo: Antequera, 1972), 216.
47. Sergio Guerra Vilaboy, *Paraguay: De la independencia a la dominación imperialista 1811–1870* (Havana: Editorial de Ciencias Sociales, 1984), 178.
48. Paul H. Lewis, "Paraguay from the War of the Triple Alliance to the Chaco War, 1870–1932," in *The Cambridge History of Latin America*, ed. Leslie Bethell (Cambridge: Cambridge University Press, 1986), 481–82. The Liberal Party was known as Democratic Center from its founding in 1887 until 1894. The Colorado Party ("*colorado*" means "red") was also founded in 1887.
49. Juan Carlos Herken Krauer, "Diplomacia británica en el Río de la Plata: el «caso Rafael Barrett» (1908–1910)," *Cahiers du monde hispanique et luso-brésilien*, No. 41 (1983): 43.

NOTES TO PAGES 17-19 | 199

50. Eduardo Galeano, *Memoria del fuego, vol. 3: El siglo del viento* (Madrid: Siglo XXI, 1990), 25.
51. Boceta had been secretary of music at the Ateneo de Madrid in 1902. According to Barrett's friend Herib Campos Cervera, Boceta would soon return to Europe as part of an unsuccessful scheme hatched alongside Barrett to export *ñanduti*, a Paraguayan lace. See Herib Campos Cervera, "Rafael Barrett," available at https://www.portalguarani.com/355_herib_padre__campos_cervera_/19911_rafael_barrett__prosa_de_herib_campos_cervera.html.
52. Rafael Barrett, "La revolución de 1904," in *Obras completas*, vol. 1, 45.
53. Rafael Barrett, "Cartas a Campos Cervera I," in *Obras completas*, vol. 6, 233.
54. Campos Cervera, "Rafael Barrett."
55. Francisca López Maíz, known as Panchita, was from a family of the Asunción bourgeoisie. Her father was Spanish and her mother Paraguayan. She was seventeen when she married Barrett; her age was increased on the wedding certificate to bypass the need for parental permission. It appears that there was strong opposition from her family to the relationship. See notes by Francisca López Maíz in Rafael Barrett, "VII," in *Cartas Íntimas*, 46.
56. José Rodríguez Alcalá, "Rafael Barrett en el Paraguay," *La Nación*, January 1944, cited in Francisco Gaona, *Introducción a la historia gremial y social del Paraguay*, vol. 1 (Asunción: Arandú, 1967), 209.
57. Ibid.
58. Rafael Barrett, "A propósito de una frase," in *Obras Completas*, vol. 1, 142-44.
59. Miguel Ángel Fernández, "Rafael Barrett: escritor y pensador revolucionario," section 1.1, https://www.portalguarani.com/411_miguel_angel_fernandez/14884_rafael_barrett__escritor_y_pensador_revolucionario__obra_de_miguel_angel_fernandez__ano_2011.html.
60. Peter Lambert and Ricardo Medina, "Contested Discourse, Contested Power: Nationalism and the Left in Paraguay," *Bulletin of Latin American Research*, vol. 26, no. 3 (2007): 342-43.
61. Carlos Castells, "Política e historia: Rafael Barrett y una tercera mirada en las polémicas sobre el pasado y el presente en el Paraguay del novecientos," *Folia Histórica del Nordeste* 33 (2018): 71.
62. Rafael Barrett, "La huelga," in *Obras Completas*, vol. 2, 15-16.
63. Rafael Barrett, "El oro," in *Obras Completas*, vol. 2, 43-44.
64. Rafael Barrett, "Los colmillos de la raza blanca," in *Obras Completas*, vol. 1, 200-1.
65. Notes by López Maíz in Rafael Barrett, "XI," in *Cartas Íntimas*, 45-46.
66. Rafael Barrett, "X," in *Cartas Íntimas*, 49.
67. Rafael Barrett, "En torno al libro del doctor Báez," in *Obras Completas*, vol. 2, 177.

68. Rafael Barrett, "On the Ranch," included in this book.
69. Campos Cervera, "Rafael Barrett." Campos Cervera writes that while he, Barrett, and Boceta were employed at the Statistics Office, they were paid their salaries despite not doing any work. Campos Cervera, who was head of department, states that he quit his position out of shame. Following Campos Cervera's departure, Barrett briefly became head of department. He soon left the post, perhaps for the same reason as his friend.
70. Francisco Gaona, *Introducción a la historia gremial y social del Paraguay*, vol. 2, (Asunción: R. P. Ediciones, 1987), 19.
71. Rafael Barrett, "On Politics," included in this book.
72. Campos Cervera, "Rafael Barrett."
73. Rafael Barrett, "On the Ranch," included in this book.
74. Corral, *Pensamiento cautivo*, 40.
75. Robert J. Alexander, *A History of Organized Labor in Uruguay and Paraguay* (Westport, CT: Praeger, 2005), 96–97.
76. Rafael Barrett, "Deudas," in *Obras Completas*, vol. 2, 58.
77. Rafael Barrett, "Glosa (III)," in *Obras Completas*, vol. 1, 140.
78. Rafael Barrett, "Vagancia," in *Obras Completas*, vol. 2, 56–57.
79. Gaona, *Introducción*, vol. 1, 220.
80. Ibid., 226.
81. *El Diario*, March 23, 1908, cited in Gaona, *Introducción*, vol. 1, 233.
82. Corral, "Vida y pensamiento," 219–25.
83. Bertotto, "Rafael Barrett: Su vida en el Paraguay," 11.
84. The original Spanish title of *The Truth of the Yerba Mate Forests*, *Lo que son los yerbales*, is more literally translated as "What the Yerba Mate Forests Are."
85. Luis A. Galeano, "Extranjerización reciente y actual del territorio paraguayo," in *Con la soja al cuello 2017: Informe sobre agronegocios en Paraguay*, ed. Marielle Palau (Asunción: Base Investigaciones Sociales, 2017), 58.
86. Julia J. S. Sarreal, *Yerba Mate: The Drink That Shaped a Nation* (Oakland: University of California Press, 2022), 191.
87. Julián Bouvier, a journalist, farmer, and teacher, is a largely forgotten figure in Paraguayan history. The Frenchman, a committed socialist, spent over two decades chronicling social issues across the south of the country, writing for numerous Paraguayan, Brazilian, and Argentine publications. Months before Barrett's attack on the yerba mate companies, Bouvier had denounced the conditions of slavery in the yerba mate forests, concentrating on the enormous enclave owned by Frenchman Domingo Barthe across southern Paraguay and northern Argentina. Bouvier stated that he had spent seven years working in the yerba industry, giving him great knowledge of the subject. In contrast, it is not clear if or when Barrett had direct experience of the yerba mate forests. Barrett refers to Bouvier's work in an article

(Rafael Barrett, "La cuestión social" in *Obras Completas*, vol. 6, 59) and the two are reported to have met while Barrett was in hiding in Yabebyry in 1909. See Sarreal, *Yerba Mate*, 189–218; Julio Sotelo, "Julián S. Bouvier, fuente de los escritos de Rafael Barrett," *La Prensa del Sur*, November 10, 2017; and Julio Sotelo, "Rafael Barrett conoció el 'dolor paraguayo' a través de los escritos de Julián S. Bouvier," *La Prensa del Sur*, November 17, 2017.

88. Javier Gortari, " 'Maldita' yerba mate: Explotación de la mano de obra en las minas yerbateras del Paraguay colonial," *Transatlantic Studies Network*, vol. 3 (2017): 40–41.
89. Report from Governor Baltasar García Ros to the King, cited in Ignacio Telesca, "La colonia desde 1680 a 1780," in *Nueva historia del Paraguay*, ed. Ignacio Telesca (Buenos Aires: Sudamericana, 2020), 101.
90. Nidia R. Areces, "De la independencia a la Guerra de la Triple Alianza (1811–1870)," in *Nueva historia del Paraguay*, ed. Ignacio Telesca (Buenos Aires: Sudamericana, 2020), 201.
91. Guaranization of Spanish word *mensual* (monthly). This term was used to refer to the workers as, in theory, they were paid on a monthly basis.
92. Alejandro Quin, "Guerra, biopolítica e inadaptación: los yerbales paraguayos de Rafael Barrett," *Latin American Literary Review*, vol. 46, no. 92 (2019): 17.
93. Petr Táborský, "La representación de la problemática infantil paraguaya en la obra de Rafael Barrett" (Master's dissertation, Palacký University Olomouc, 2019), 50–55.
94. Ana María Vara, "El anti-imperialismo de Rafael Barrett, entre la crónica y los cuentos," conference paper, VI Jornadas de la Historia de las Izquierdas "José Ingenieros y sus mundos," CEDINC, UNSAM, Buenos Aires, November 2011, 32.
95. Eduardo Galeano, *Open Veins of Latin America: Five Centuries of the Pillage of a Continent* (New York: Monthly Review Press, 1996).
96. Rafael Barrett, "La verdadera política," in *Obras Completas*, vol. 1, 50.
97. Flyer by Rafael Barrett reproduced in Alvaro Yunque, *Barrett: Su vida y su obra* (Buenos Aires: Claridad, 1929), 25.
98. Bertotto, "Rafael Barrett: Su vida en el Paraguay," 14–15.
99. *El Diario*, June 29, 1908.
100. Rafael Barrett, "Contesto," in *Obras Completas*, vol. 3, 74.
101. Barrett and Jara had become enemies following the death of Barrett's friend Carlos García in a duel in 1906. Barrett publicly criticized Jara, who had been one of García's seconders, for allowing the visually impaired journalist to participate in the bout. See Rafael Barrett, "La tragedia de hoy," in *Obras Completas*, vol. 1, 127–28.
102. Herken Krauer, "Diplomacia británica," 14.
103. Rafael Barrett, "The Revolution," essay included in this book.

104. José Guillermo Bertotto, "Rafael Barrett," *El Manifiesto*, Buenos Aires, December 1, 1912.
105. López Maíz, "Introducción," 41.
106. The paper's name is taken from the seventh month of the French Revolutionary Calendar that was implemented in 1793; Germinal was the first month of spring. Émile Zola's 1885 novel of the same name had produced a deep impact in Spain, and a group of writers, including Barrett's friend Ramón del Valle-Inclán, had founded a short-lived progressive magazine titled *Germinal* in Madrid in 1897. See Gregorio Morán, *Asombro y búsqueda de Rafael Barrett* (Barcelona: Anagrama, 2007), 169–72.
107. See López Maíz, "Introducción," 40, and Bertotto, "Rafael Barrett: Su vida en el Paraguay," 21.
108. Gaona, *Introducción*, vol. 1, 245.
109. Rafael Barrett, "Nuestro programa," in *Obras Completas*, vol. 3, 87–88.
110. Bertotto, "Rafael Barrett: Su vida en el Paraguay," 11.
111. Rafael Barrett, "Under the Reign of Terror," essay included in this book.
112. Bertotto was in prison much longer than Barrett. On November 24, he was eventually expelled from Paraguay to his native Argentina, where he would go into hiding. In a letter to Bertotto's father, Barrett implies that the Argentine authorities had not pressured for Bertotto's release because of an issue regarding military service. Bertotto had first moved to Uruguay—where he had been imprisoned for his activism—and then to Paraguay to evade obligatory military service in Argentina. He would go on to publish several books, including one on Barrett, and be elected as a member of Argentina's lower house. See Rafael Barrett, "Carta al padre de José Guillermo Bertotto," in *Obras Completas*, vol. 6, 238; and Muñoz, *Barrett*, 45.
113. Gaona, *Introducción*, vol. 1, 215–16.
114. Luis Hierro Gambardella, "Prólogo de la primera edición," in Rafael Barrett, *Cartas Íntimas* (Asunción: Arandurã, 2022), 16.
115. Rafael Barrett, "XXXV," in *Cartas Íntimas*, 84.
116. The Laguna Porã ranch belonged to Dr. Alejandro Audibert, Barrett's brother-in-law. Barrett had already spent time there with López Maíz and Alex in 1907.
117. Rafael Barrett, "Cartas a Peyrot IX," in *Obras Completas*, vol. 6, 227.
118. Rafael Barrett, "XLVIII," in *Cartas Íntimas*, 110.
119. Rafael Barrett, "Cartas a Peyrot XIII," in *Obras Completas*, vol. 6, 230.
120. Rafael Barrett, "Cartas a Vila III," in *Obras Completas*, vol. 6, 237.
121. Rafael Barrett, "El terror argentino," in *Obras Completas*, vol. 5, 15–29.
122. Rafael Barrett, "No mintáis," in *Obras Completas*, vol. 4, 110.
123. Rafael Barrett, "Cartas de un viajero," in *Obras Completas*, vol. 5, 78.
124. Rafael Barrett, "LXIII," in *Cartas Íntimas*, 129.
125. Corral, "Vida y pensamiento," 109.

126. Susan Barrett, the youngest sibling of Barrett's father, George, was born in Newcastle upon Tyne, England. It appears she moved to live with her brother in Spain after being the lone companion of her elderly father until he was in his eighties. When Barrett left Spain, she remained with his brother Fernando, who died of a strain of tuberculosis in 1907.
127. Muñoz, *Barrett*, 70.
128. Rafael Barrett, "Cartas a Peyrot XIII," in *Obras Completas*, vol. 6, 231.
129. Rafael Barrett, "LXXIV," in *Cartas Íntimas*, 147. Rafael's grandson Alberto writes that the letter was bloodstained. See Alberto Barrett, *Autobiografía clandestina* (Asunción: Arandurã, 2017), 5.
130. Gaona, *Introducción*, vol. 2, 49–50.
131. Gaona, *Introducción*, vol. 1, 217.
132. Manuel Domínguez, *Rafael Barret* (Asunción: La Colmena, 1913), unpaginated.
133. *El Dependiente*, Havana, August 29, 1911.
134. Rafael Barrett, *El dolor paraguayo* (Montevideo: O. M. Bertani, 1911), 227. Orsini Bertani, an important publisher of radical texts in Uruguay, had already published Barrett's first book *Present Moralities* [*Moralidades actuales* (Montevideo: O. M. Bertani, 1910)]; and *The Truth of the Yerba Mate Forests* [*Lo que son los yerbales* (Montevideo: O. M. Bertani, 1910)]. He would go on to release numerous posthumous collections of his work, including *Paraguayan Sorrow*. In his correspondence, Barrett shows great esteem for Bertani; however, López Maíz states that neither Barrett nor she ever received any payment for his books. See notes by López Maíz in Rafael Barrett, "LIX," in *Cartas Íntimas*, 123.
135. Carla D. Benisz, "Panta y Maria Gonçalves: Patriarcado en cien años de literatura paraguaya," conference paper, XI Taller: Paraguay desde las Ciencias Sociales, Universidad Nacional de Pilar, Pilar, June 2018, unpaginated.
136. Rafael Barrett, "The Sexual Problem," included in this book.
137. Rafael Barrett, "Cartas de un viajero (III)," in *Obras Completas*, vol. 5, 105–6.
138. Rafael Barrett, "Juries," included in this book.
139. Rafael Barrett, "¡Toma y lee!" in *Obras Completas*, vol. 4, 146.
140. Rafael Barrett, "Juries," included in this book.
141. Rafael Barrett, "Trophies," included in this book.
142. The police chief Elías García banned the *poguasu* (thick) cigars that were popular among Paraguayan women and the use of ponchos by men. See Bernardo Gutiérrez, "Entérese," *ABC*, July 31, 2010, https://www.abc.com.py/edicion-impresa/suplementos/abc-revista/enterese-139612.html.
143. Paraguayan Guarani is a language descended from the languages of the Indigenous Guarani peoples of the region that is today Paraguay. It continues to be the country's most spoken language and is the only native language

in the Americas to be spoken by the majority of a national population, including by non-Indigenous sectors.
144. Manuel Domínguez, "El idioma guaraní," *El Pueblo*, November 19, 1894, reproduced in Gustavo Acosta, *Posguerra contra la Triple Alianza: Aspectos sociales (1869-1904)* (Asunción: Servilibro, 2019), 50-51.
145. Rafael Barrett, "Trophies," included in this book.
146. Corral, *Pensamiento cautivo*, 152, 154, 298.
147. Rocío Virgina Gómez, "El discurso anarquista sobre la educación estatal: La mirada original de Rafael Barrett," conference paper, V jornadas nacionales espacio, memoria e identidad, Universidad Nacional de Rosario, Rosario, October 8-10, 2008, unpaginated.
148. Rafael Barrett, "Sad Children," included in this book.
149. Rafael Barrett, "Primary Education," included in this book.
150. Rafael Barrett, "The Political Virus," included in this book.
151. Rafael Barrett, "El progreso," in *Obras Completas*, vol. 6, 80-102.
152. Francisco Corral, "Rafael Barrett ante la condición humana," unpaginated, https://portalguarani.com/674_francisco_corral/15155_rafael_barrett_ante_la_condicion_humana_francisco_corral_.html.
153. Leandro Delgado, "Modernidad y anarquía: sobre lo colectivo en las crónicas de Rafael Barrett," *Tekoporá. Revista Latinoamericana De Humanidades Ambientales Y Estudios Territoriales*, vol. 3, no. 1 (2021): 219.
154. Rafael Barrett, "Hatred of Trees," included in this book.
155. Rafael Barrett, "Land," included in this book.
156. Daniel Runnels, "El fracaso como praxis política en Manuel González Prada y Rafael Barrett," *Vorágine*, vol. 2, No. 4 (2021): 127.
157. Campos Cervera, "Rafael Barrett."
158. Morán, *Asombro y búsqueda*, 155-56.
159. Rafael Barrett, "La lucha social," in *Obras Completas*, vol. 4, 173.
160. Rafael Barrett, "Mi anarquismo," in *Obras Completas*, vol. 3, 198.
161. While emphatically rejecting the Catholic Church, Barrett showed enormous admiration for the ethical principles of Jesus and the early Christians.
162. Corral, *Pensamiento cautivo*, 105, 309.
163. Interview with Martín Albornoz, in Juan Ferro, Facundo Juárez, and Facundo Rolandi, "Rafael Barrett, la exigencia de lo real" (Undergraduate thesis, Universidad Nacional de La Plata, 2018), 83.
164. Carlos Castells and Mario Castells, "'La huelga es la peor amenaza para el capital': Rafael Barrett en el Paraguay de la república liberal," conference paper, XII Jornadas Interescuelas/Departamentos de Historia, National University of Comahue, Comahue, 2009, unpaginated.
165. Rafael Barrett, "El esfuerzo," in *Obras Completas*, vol. 5, 147-48.
166. Rafael Barrett, "Filosofía del altruismo," in *Obras Completas*, vol. 6, 35.
167. Rafael Barrett, "Epifonemas," in *Obras Completas*, vol. 6, 245.

168. Rafael Barrett, "Mi anarquismo," 200.
169. Rafael Barrett, "La cuestión social," in *Obras Completas*, vol. 6, 54.
170. Ibid., 56.
171. Rafael Barrett, "Entendámonos," in *Obras Completas*, vol. 2, 127.
172. Alberto Lasplaces, "Rafael Barrett," in Rafael Barrett, *Diálogos, conversaciones y otros escritos* (Montevideo: Claudio García, 1918), vi.
173. Rafael Barrett, "El progreso," in *Obras Completas*, vol. 6, 82.
174. Rafael Barrett, "Marruecos," in *Obras Completas*, vol. 2, 108–10.
175. Rafael Barrett, "El antipatriotismo," in *Obras Completas*, vol. 2, 139.
176. Rafael Barrett, "El terror argentino," in *Obras Completas*, vol. 5, 26–27.
177. Rafael Barrett, "Degeneration," included in this book.
178. Rafael Barrett, "Cartas de un viajero (III)," in *Obras Completas*, vol. 5, 103–4.
179. Miguel Ángel Fernández, "Prólogo," in Rafael Barrett, *Cartas Íntimas* (Asunción: Arandurã, 2022), 9.
180. Obdulio Barthe, "Dos palabras sobre Barrett," *Impulso*, December 1928, 8–9. Obdulio Barthe, who would go on to become a legendary leader of the Paraguayan Communist Party, was a nephew of Domingo Barthe, the French businessman denounced by journalist Julián Bouvier for the conditions of slavery in the yerba forests of his enormous enclave in southern Paraguay and northern Argentina. After the failure of the Taking of Encarnación, Obdulio would lead a group of rebels in commandeering boats from his late uncle's company to make an escape to Brazil. During this journey to the border, they stopped at ports of the Barthe Company to burn administrative archives related to yerba mate production. See Milda Rivarola, *Obreros, utopías & revoluciones* (Asunción: CDE, 1993), 268.
181. *El Hombre*, Montevideo, January 5, 1918.
182. José Guillermo Bertotto to Félix Álvarez Ferreras, Buenos Aires, November 20, 1976, cited in Virginia Martínez, *La vida es tempestad: Historia de la familia Barrett: Literatura, Resistencia y revolución* (Asunción: Arandurã, 2018), 83.
183. The process of scouring the archives for Barrett's texts was carried out over several years by Miguel Ángel Fernández with assistance from Graciela Molinas. To this day, the original newspapers containing his writings, perhaps even unrecorded texts, lay crumbling—many too fragile to be touched—in the archives of the National Library of Paraguay, endlessly awaiting funding for digitalization to preserve their pages.
184. Martínez, *La vida es tempestad*, 83–84.
185. Roa Bastos, "Rafael Barrett," xxx.
186. Rafael Barrett, *Cartas Íntimas* (Montevideo: Biblioteca Artigas, 1967).
187. For a complete exploration of the life of Alex Barrett, see Martínez, *La vida es tempestad*.

188. Alexander, *History of Organized Labor*, 105.
189. Ricardo Scavone Yegros, "Guerra internacional y confrontaciones políticas (1920-1954)," in *Nueva historia del Paraguay*, ed. Ignacio Telesca (Buenos Aires: Sudamericana, 2020), 265.
190. The 2008 report of the Paraguayan Commission of Truth and Justice found that the regime of Alfredo Stroessner tortured almost nineteen thousand people, conducted fifty-nine extrajudicial executions, and disappeared 336 people. Almost no official actions have been conducted to seek justice for the victims of these crimes. See Comisión de Verdad y Justicia del Paraguay, "Informe final de la Comisión de Verdad y Justicia del Paraguay" (Asunción: Comisión de Verdad y Justicia del Paraguay, 2008), 29. For information on sexual abuse of young girls by Stroessner and members of his regime see José Elizeche, "Calle de silencio," YouTube video, posted by Jose Antonio Elizeche, November 30, 2017, https://youtu.be/te0K-UfphEg.
191. See Andrés Colmán Gutiérrez, *Mengele en Paraguay* (Asunción: Servilibro, 2018).
192. María Antonia Sánchez and Luis Roniger, "El destierro paraguayo: aspectos transnacionales y generacionales," *Revista Mexicana de Ciencias Políticas y Sociales*, 52/208 (2010): 141.
193. Lambert and Medina, "Contested Discourse," 347-48.
194. Rafael Barrett Viedma, email message to author, March 26, 2024. See Rafael Barrett Viedma, *Mis andares en el Partido Comunista Paraguayo y alrededores* (Asunción: Arandurã, 2021).
195. See Alberto Barrett, *Autobiografía clandestina*.
196. See Alfredo Boccia Paz, *La novela de los Barrett* (Asunción: Servilibro, 2019).
197. Mario Benedetti, "Muerte de Soledad Barrett," available at https://www.antiwarsongs.org/canzone.php?lang=en&id=44539.
198. Roa Bastos, "Rafael Barrett," ix.
199. Transparency International, *Corruption Perceptions Index 2022* (Berlin: Transparency International, 2023), 3.
200. Lambert and Medina, "Contested Discourse," 347-48.
201. Perrine Toledano and Nicolas Maennling, *Leveraging Paraguay's Hydropower for Sustainable Economic Development* (New York: Columbia Center on Sustainable Investment, 2013), 59.
202. Alexander, *History of Organized Labor*, 92.
203. For information on the development of agribusiness in Paraguay and its impact on campesino and Indigenous communities see Lis García and Sarah Zevaco, *Resistencias campesinas: Características y desafíos* (Asunción: Base Investigaciones Sociales, 2021).
204. Earthsight, *Grand Theft Chaco* (London: Earthsight, 2020), 11.
205. Ibid., 10.

206. Luis Rojas Villagra, "Lo que son los sojales: Homenaje a Rafael Barrett," *Última Hora*, June 21, 2008.
207. Victoria Tauli-Corpuz, *Report of the Special Rapporteur on the Rights of Indigenous Peoples, Regarding the Situation of INDIGENOUS peoples in Paraguay* (New York: United Nations, 2015).
208. Guereña and Rojas Villagra, *Yvy Jára*, 13.
209. World Bank Group, *Paraguay—Policy notes 2018* (Washington, D.C.: World Bank Group, 2018), 7.
210. For information on the participation of key figures from the Stroessner dictatorship in drug trafficking see *Paraguay, droga y banana*, directed by Juan Manuel Salinas Aguirre (Asunción: Juan Manuel Salinas Aguirre, 2016), https://www.primevideo.com/detail/Paraguay-Droga-y-Banana/0MAWSOKQS6D04TADS3GPNQ5Z66.
211. Paraguay is ranked fourth for overall criminality out of 193 countries. It ranks first for the indicators of "cannabis trade" and "foreign actors," and second for "arms trafficking." See https://www.ocindex.net/.
212. "21 de febrero, Día Internacional de la Lengua Materna," *Instituto Nacional de Estadística*, February 21, 2023, https://www.ine.gov.py/news/news-contenido.php?cod-news=1484.
213. Speech, available at https://iela.ufsc.br/discurso-de-fernando-lugo-presidente-do-paraguai/.
214. See Julio Benegas Vidallet, *La masacre de Curuguaty: Golpe sicario en el Paraguay* (Asunción: Julio Benegas Vidallet, 2013). Eleven campesinos and six police officers were killed at the Marina Cué land occupation in the district of Curuguaty in June 2012. Campesino families had occupied land that had been designated for distribution to campesinos through agrarian reform. However, a neighboring agricultural firm, Campos Morombí, claimed ownership of the area. The company, owned by the powerful Riquelme family of the Colorado Party, pushed for the families to be evicted. The "Curuguaty Massacre" took place as hundreds of heavily armed officers entered the land occupation to carry out the eviction. Twelve campesinos were imprisoned for the police deaths; however, the deaths of campesinos were not investigated.
215. See Chris Dalby, "Paraguay's Former President Horacio Cartes Losing Aura of Impunity," *InSight Crime*, October 24, 2022, https://www.insightcrime.org/news/paraguays-former-president-horacio-cartes-losing-aura-of-impunity/.
216. "Cartes propone a empresarios del Brasil 'usar y abusar del Paraguay,'" *ABC*, February 18, 2014, https://www.abc.com.py/edicion-impresa/politica/cartes-propone-a-empresarios-del-brasil-usar-y-abusar-del-paraguay-1216497.html.
217. A November 2023 law gave the executive branch increased powers to make huge budgetary changes without approval from Congress. See "Peña

promulga ley de emisión de bonos por US$ 600 millones y poderes para 'gobernar por decreto,'" *ABC*, November 21, 2023, https://www.abc.com. py/politica/2023/11/21/pena-promulga-ley-de-emision-de-bonos-por-us-600-millones-y-poderes-para-gobernar-por-decreto/.

218. Colorado legislators made use of a majority in the Senate to arbitrarily expel Senator Kattya González in February 2024. González, who was among the senators with the highest number of votes in the 2023 elections, had made increasingly vocal criticisms of the government. The expulsion sparked protests and was questioned by a large number of civil society organizations and foreign diplomats. See "Paraguay senate expels one of few opposition members, sparking protests," *The Guardian*, February 14, 2024, https://www.theguardian.com/world/2024/feb/14/paraguay-opposition-expelled-senate.

219. Benisz, "Panta y Maria Gonçalves."

220. María Estela Asilvera, "Con las letras, más allá del libro y el aula: el proyecto 'Lectura en la ruta histórico-literaria-turístico-cultural Rafael Barrett,'" *UNES: Universidad, Escuela y Sociedad*, vol. 14 (2023).

221. For novels based on Barrett's life see Alcibiades González Delvalle, *El dolor de Barrett* (Asunción: Servilibro, 2019); and Andrés Colmán Gutiérrez, *Dos hombres junto al río* (Asunción: Servilibro, 2022).

222. Rafael Barrett Viedma, email message to author, March 26, 2024. The website of the Fundación Rafael Barrett is www.rafaelbarrett.org.

223. See *Freedom*, November 1910; *Justice*, May 20, 1911.

224. Alexander K. MacDonald, *Picturesque Paraguay: Sport, Pioneering, Travel—A Land of Promise, Stock-Raising, Plantation Industries, Forest Products, Commercial Possibilities* (London: Charles H. Kelly, 1911), 384.

225. There is very little information available about the Rafael Barrett Press. The publishing house released a series of satirical, erotically charged titles, some of which are related to Japanese culture, for example, Aikiku, *Kaguya Hime* (London: Rafael Barrett Press, 1980). Ian Kaliszewski, who appears to have been the founder of the publishing house, had links to Bolivia, perhaps explaining his familiarity with Barrett.

226. Rafael Barrett, *Cosa sono gli Yerbales* (Turin: II Libero Acordo, 1979).

227. Rafael Barrett, *O que são os ervais* (Desterro, Florianópolis: Cultura e Barbárie, 2012).

228. William Costa, "Leaves of Change: Paraguay's small-scale farmers see a new future in yerba mate tea," *The Guardian*, August 2, 2021, https://www.theguardian.com/global-development/2021/aug/02/leaves-of-change-paraguays-small-scale-farmers-see-a-new-future-in-yerba-mate-tea.

229. Many thanks to Mirna Robles and Sofía Espíndola Oviedo for their help with Guarani usage.

230. Rafael Barrett, "Cartas a Campos Cervera I," 234.